PRAISE FOR *THE PRICE YOU PAY FOR COLLEGE*

Named One of the Best Books of the Year by NPR

"Masterly . . . represents an extraordinary achievement: It is comprehensive and detailed without being tedious, practical without being banal, impeccably well-judged and unusually rigorous."
—Daniel Markovits, professor, Yale Law School, *New York Times Book Review*

"Ron Lieber is a gift."
—Scott Galloway, professor of marketing, New York University

"A book that is packed with data and yet manages to be presented in such a beautiful narrative that is warm, engaging, compassionate, and informative. Ron will hold you by the hand, by the heart, and by the head."
—Julie Lythcott-Haims, author of *How to Raise an Adult*

"I love thinking of books like this as conversation grenades. Like you throw them in a room and conversations break out. And this is one of those books that can be sat on the dining room table and the conversations happening around the dining room table will be sponsored by you for having dropped this book off."
—Carl Richards, author of *The Behavior Gap*

"Unbelievably excellent reporting. . . . Eye-opening and hugely, hugely useful and important."
—Lisa Damour, PhD, author of *Under Pressure* and host of the podcast *Ask Lisa*

"Pardon my French, but this shit is messed up."
—John Warner, *Inside Higher Ed*

"OMG is it good. A delight for fans of narrative and data geeks alike. Anyone contemplating college for themselves or their kids (or grandkids) NEEDS this book."
—Jessica Lahey, author of *The Gift of Failure*

"He answered a lot of questions and, honestly, a lot of the answers were not what I anticipated. I really thought this was great."
—Ben Carlson, cohost of the podcast *Animal Spirits*

"Shrewd yet rueful, brilliantly practical yet wise. From its brilliant title forward, it explores what a shameful mess we have made of higher ed."
—Dan Chiasson, professor of English, Wellesley College

Also by Ron Lieber

The Opposite of Spoiled: Raising Kids Who Are
Grounded, Generous, and Smart About Money

Best Entry- Level Jobs: Paying Your Dues Without
Losing Your Mind (with Tom Meltzer)

Upstart Start- Ups! How 34 Young Entrepreneurs Overcame Youth,
Inexperience, and Lack of Money to Create Thriving Businesses

Taking Time Off: Inspiring Stories of Students Who
Enjoyed Successful Breaks from College and How
You Can Plan Your Own (with Colin Hall)

THE PRICE
YOU PAY
FOR
COLLEGE

An Entirely New Road Map
for the Biggest Financial Decision
Your Family Will Ever Make

RON LIEBER

HARPER

NEW YORK • LONDON • TORONTO • SYDNEY

To Violet, who is worth every penny . . .

HARPER

A hardcover edition of this book was published in 2021 by HarperCollins Publishers.

HarperCollins books may be purchased for educational, business, or sales promotional use. For information, please email the Special Markets Department at SPsales@harpercollins.com.

FIRST HARPER PAPERBACKS EDITION PUBLISHED 2022.

Designed by Bonni Leon-Berman

Library of Congress Cataloging-in-Publication Data has been applied for.

ISBN 978-0-06-286731-5 (pbk.)

22 23 24 25 26   LSC   10 9 8 7 6 5 4 3 2 1

CONTENTS

Introduction 1

PART I: THE PRICE AND COST OF COLLEGE AND THE SYSTEMS BEHIND IT

Chapter 1: Who Pays What and Why the Price Is So High..................... 15

Chapter 2: FAFSA and Its Confounding Calculations
Will Probably Make You Furious; Blame the Federal
Government's Great Expectations... 23

Chapter 3: How (and Why) Merit Aid Became Mainstream 35

Chapter 4: The Billion-Dollar Consultants Who Are Wooing You 43

Chapter 5: But Wait, Isn't Tuition a Bubble, and All of Higher
Education Is Going to Come Apart at the Seams? 58

PART II: THE UNHELPFUL FEELINGS YOU MAY FEEL

Chapter 6: Fear 71

Chapter 7: Guilt... 76

Chapter 8: The Pull of Snobbery and Elitism 85

PART III: VALUE: THINGS WORTH PAYING FOR

Chapter 9: Classrooms Where Experienced Instructors Have
Time to Teach (and Actually Want To)... 97

Chapter 10: Schools Where Students Learn (Because Many of
Them Don't) 110

Chapter 11: Undergraduate Mental Health Centers That Are
Not in Crisis..116

Chapter 12: Peers Worth Friending (or Marrying) 126

Chapter 13: The Special Power of Historically Women's Colleges......... 136

Chapter 14: Diversity in All Its Forms... 140

Chapter 15: How and When Small School Size Matters........................149

Chapter 16: Amenities (but Is a Lazy River a Plus?)............................ 160

Chapter 17: Genuinely Reinvented Career Counseling Offices 168

Chapter 18: Places That Create Better Odds When Applying
to Grad School 177

Chapter 19: Better Salaries When You Finish—*if* You Finish...............181
Chapter 20: How the College of Wooster Puts It All Together............... 187

PART IV: MONEY-SAVING HACKS THAT WILL TEMPT YOU

Chapter 21: Community College Will Save You Money, but
What Might You Lose?... 199
Chapter 22: Honors Colleges and Programs Can Make Bigger
Schools Smaller —if You Stick with the Program 207
Chapter 23: Attending College Abroad Is Often Cheaper, but You Won't
Get What You Don't Pay For 214
Chapter 24: Athletic Scholarships for the Few (and Probably
Not in Full or at Your First-Choice School) 221
Chapter 25: Gap Years: Great, Sometimes Pricey, Might Help
You Get a Better Job Someday 225
Chapter 26: Army, Navy, Air Force, Marines, Coast Guard:
Decent Money, Big Responsibility................................. 230
Chapter 27: Skipping College Is Probably Not a Great Idea.................. 233

**PART V: THE PLANS: SAVING, TALKING, TOURING,
BARGAINING, AND BORROWING**

Chapter 28: How to Make the Big Financial Plan................................. 243
Chapter 29: How to Have the College Money Talk with Your Child...... 252
Chapter 30: All Your Questions About Saving for College
and 529 Plans... 260
Chapter 31: How to Shop for College (and Where to Find the
Juicy Merit Aid Data)..274
Chapter 32: When (and How) to Hire an Independent College
Counselor or Financial Planner...................................... 288
Chapter 33: How to Appeal Your Financial Aid Award 294
Chapter 34: All the Student Loan Basics in One Tidy Place 303
Chapter 35: One More Feeling: Hope.......................................313

Acknowledgments *319*
Notes *325*
Bibliography *343*
Index *347*

INTRODUCTION

Not long ago, just a handful of years before a frightening virus caused nearly everyone to question almost everything, we reached a startling threshold in the financial life of American families that went mostly unnoticed: All of a sudden, sending an eighteen-year-old away to a state university for four years cost over $100,000 in many parts of the country. Many families of first-year students who head off to any of several dozen of the most selective private colleges these days will spend over $325,000 before they graduate. So not only is the price of college often a six-figure expense per child, the *difference* in price between public and private colleges is itself a six-figure number.

Multiply these figures by two or three kids, all of whom may be a decade or more away from matriculating, and an overall picture comes into focus: For many families, the total bill for college could well add up to more than what they paid for their homes. Add in the potential impact of those four years on the trajectory of any adolescent's life—and the fact that so many of our own hopes and dreams for our children are mixed up in the college choice—and the magnitude of the decision looms even larger. This is the most complex and emotionally fraught financial decision that many families will ever make.

The numbers are staggering, and they have reached these heights at the same time that other fast-growing personal finance line items have come into sharper focus. Retirement is now mostly the responsibility of workers, not employers. The out-of-pocket costs of health insurance continue to rise for families who earn more than average. Housing prices in many urban and suburban markets, especially the ones with good public schools, are near all-time highs. And in places where the cost of living is more reasonable, salaries tend to be lower, which makes saving for higher education that much harder.

Perhaps you set a goal on the day of the positive pregnancy test or adoption notice to pay that $325,000 private college bill in full. Saving that much from the day that child was born would have meant putting away $1,000 per month. For those of us with two or more kids (mine are now sixteen and seven), saving at that level is akin to making another mortgage payment. The large number of people who have saved something—but could not save the full $325,000 over twenty years or so—might turn to loans with up to a thirty-year repayment period to help pay the resulting tuition bills. They could end up spending a combined fifty years paying for college. That's longer than most people spend in the workforce and twenty years longer than most people spend paying off a mortgage.

The prospect of a half century of saving and paying is troubling enough, but the most daunting part of the process is this: There is often no way to know what you'll actually pay until the very end of a tumultuous application process. Only after you've paid application fees and the acceptances are out do the schools offer unpublished discounts and negotiate with families who file appeals, one by one, over the final bill. It all happens in secret. And if you've qualified for need-based financial aid, the aid application process generally begins anew each year of college for every student who has already matriculated.

Getting to the final, cumulative price tag requires a long journey, and the maps available to guide families are pretty crude. To even try to navigate it all requires an understanding of the way in which the definition of "financial aid" has become warped beyond all measure in less than a generation. The primary definition is the one that most of us know from when we were in college: You apply for aid, and if the federal government and your college determine that your family doesn't earn or have enough to pay full freight, you might get some scholarships and grants. Loans and perhaps a work-study job fill out the rest of that financial aid package.

But in the last two decades or so, another form of assistance has grown so quickly as to confuse things entirely. It is called merit aid, although using "merit" and "aid" in this context is misleading. Merit scholarships are actually, more often than not, a discounting system whereby colleges below the overall top thirty to forty or so in the *U.S. News & World Report* rankings slash prices in individually targeted offer letters in the hope of persuading students to enroll. This has nothing to do with financial need, just to be crystal clear. But the private colleges—and many of the public universities charging inflated prices to out-of-state students—know all too well that a $40,000 or $50,000 price gap per year between the cost to attend their institutions and the flagship state universities (in the applicants' home states) that they compete with will be too much for many families to bear. So at the end of the process, they cut the price for many students, especially good ones. Some of them come from the 1 percent.

This raises some obvious questions about equity, for what merit aid really does is "aid" the family that may be *able* to afford the sticker price but isn't sure that it's *willing* to pay $200,000 more for Oberlin or Connecticut College over the in-state rates at the University of Virginia or Michigan or Washington. Whereas the old-fashioned system of need-based aid exists to help families who have less, merit aid is as much about psychographics as it is about demographics. Flattery is part of the goal: A child has been judged "meritorious" enough to get the award! Wouldn't it be foolish to turn it down?

This should not, in fact, be a rhetorical question, and some parents do spend many months during their child's junior and senior years of high school wrestling with possible answers. Perhaps that's you, and you've already started ingesting anecdotal information in frantic late-night gulps through ad hoc online grapevines as anonymous commenters on College Confidential and its ilk toss around out-of-context numbers. Locally, fellow parents who went through the process last year will pontificate with Great Authority (but much less accuracy) about how or why this or that family could have gotten a "scholarship," given its supposedly flush financial situation.

Most college counselors and outside consultants, stretched just to define the right academic fit for each student and work over the ever-worsening admissions odds at many schools, can't possibly keep up with all of the various schools' financial machinations. Yet they're who anxious parents turn to (or turn on) when, come April, supposedly undeserving seniors get huge merit aid awards that other students never even knew about. The parents of the students who receive no merit aid—and there are many—wonder if they're suckers for signing up anywhere at full price. Meanwhile, befuddled families that include younger high school students hear vague rumors about this process and look to colleges' own websites for information about merit aid. When they do, they often find little or nothing that provides much clarity.

Now imagine you're a parent who does not speak English. Or you didn't go to college yourself. Or you're seventeen years old and, for one reason or another, you're navigating the system all by yourself in a high school that has one guidance counselor for every 430 students. (That's the average ratio in public schools nationwide, by the way.) Good luck sorting it all out in time to pick the schools where you have the best chance of getting the most financial help.

But this is only the half of it. Once you do figure out what you might have to pay, you have to make a decision about value. Economists are fond of declaring "Game over" on this front, given what we know about how much more college graduates earn on average than people who never attend college or drop out. So many families have already decided that college is mission critical, and once you confront the price you might have to pay, you then have to try to assign a value to each school. What is the degree from any particular college worth? When is the extra $50,000 or $100,000 or $150,000 or $200,000 for one school versus another worth it? What is the return on investment going to be? And how on earth is anyone supposed to figure it all out?

Answering these questions is too large a task for any one family, and data about any of this are scant. Experts feel for you, even as they call out your struggle. In a classic paper, "Subsidies, Hierarchy and Peers: The Awkward Economics of Higher Education," a Williams College professor described the "massive ignorance about what is being bought and sold." In this absence of knowledge or data, there is only the crossing of fingers. And with the crossing of fingers comes wishful thinking and a great deal of confused decision-making, which has only been compounded by the global pandemic and the resulting chaos in higher education.

To make sense of it all, you have to start with the elemental question that I've learned to ask about nearly every complicated area of personal decision-making that I've encountered as a journalist and a human being: What is the definition of success? Or, to put it another way, what is college—the residential undergraduate experience that so many traditional-aged students seek that is the primary focus of this book—for?

As of early 2020, after a few years of reporting, I had boiled the answer down to a small handful of elements that covered most of the families I had interviewed. Consider the goals for your own teenager as a pie chart with as many as three pieces. Perhaps you're old school about this, and to you the highest and best reason for people to go to college is to have their mind blown and their mind grown. In other words, it's all about the learning. Or maybe you believe that college is about a search for kinship—a group of people, both peers and older grown-ups, you meet along the way who will stand up for you at your wedding and carry your casket and be by your side for every other good or bad thing along the way. Finally, you may be the practical type, for whom college is a means to an end, and that end is a credential and a job, maybe one that will enable your child to move a rung higher on the socioeconomic ladder than where you are. Perhaps there is some additional, incremental gain in personal branding via the credential too, if the degree is from a school that doesn't let very many people past the admissions committee.

But then the coronavirus hit. Within a period of days, many college students went home and classes moved online. And within weeks, these three definitions of success got a real-world test that I could never have anticipated. Students and parents very quickly experienced something more like failure on at least two of the three counts. Before long, they sued for tuition refunds, and hundreds of thousands of students made a deliberate choice to sit out the fall of 2020 until things got better.

First came the learning, or lack thereof. Colleges pivoted fast and moved courses to Zoom and other online platforms, but many of the professors had never taught this way or used these tools. Anything hands-on—lab science, the arts—became incredibly challenging. The rest of it was merely suboptimal. "Most online instruction isn't as effective as the traditional kind," wrote Jonathan Zimmerman, a University of Pennsylvania professor and the author of a book on the history of college teaching, in a *Philadelphia Inquirer* op-ed. "Which is why elite schools have consistently resisted it." In May 2020, about 60 percent of professors and administrators surveyed by the *Chronicle of Higher Education* said that their online courses were worse than their in-person offerings had been. Many colleges devoted more energy in the summer of 2020 to securing tents and plexiglass (in what often proved to be fruitless attempts to restore in-person learning) than to training professors to use digital tools for remote learning.

The second element of success—the seeking and finding of like-minded individuals—wasn't conducive to Zoom room conversations either. Even at Spelman College in Atlanta, where undergraduates already have a fair bit in common, so much was lost so fast. "Overnight, our small liberal arts college, designed exclusively for the success of black women, which cherishes close relationships among its Spelman Sisters and between students and faculty, had become a bastion of distance and separation," wrote Mary Schmidt Campbell, its president, in a searing *New York Times* essay that April. The transition to online learning was "barely" bridgeable, the undergraduates told her. "Our students' grief and exasperation with those barriers soon turned to anger." And who can blame them, really? Think about the most indelible memories of your time as an undergraduate. Are any of them set in your childhood bedroom? Were you alone when even one of the events surrounding these recollections implanted themselves permanently in your brain?

All that was left after the forced eviction from campus and the two months of online instruction that followed was the credential. It eventually arrived at the homes of graduating seniors in the mail, if it came at all. And even that degree didn't seem as though it was worth what recent graduates had thought it would be six months before. During the weeks when commencement ceremonies were supposed to take place, the headlines told the story of a U.S economy that had shed millions of jobs in a near instant.

By the fall of 2020, families knew as never before what they were paying for when they decided what to pay for college. In many cases, in-person classes either weren't happening at all or were happening only for some courses, often for a fraction of the semester's sessions. Many campuses welcomed some or even all students back, but with warnings that parties were forbidden and many extracurricular activities would be impossible. Robert Kelchen, who was at the time an associate professor of higher education at Seton Hall University, likened it to some strange combination of a monastery and a medium-security prison. With few exceptions, colleges didn't cut the price. Instead, they kept tuition flat or even raised it by the normal handful of percentage points. And in higher numbers than ever before, students said to hell with it and decided to take at least one semester off or head someplace cheaper, rather than pay for an experience that had little resemblance to any other undergraduate term in the history of higher education.

I have no idea whether they did the right thing. Nor do I wish to judge people who come to college for the kinship and the credential alone—and then coast their way through large lecture classes for four years without making any effort to grow and blow their own minds with the learning that is available. This is not a book about the values that lead you to choose one or two of the definitions of undergraduate success over others, but it *is* a book about value. And if we learned anything from the first couple of years of college life in the age of corona, it's that all those people paying five figures of money each year ought to have a clear idea of what it is they think they are buying.

The Price You Pay for College will help you figure this out for yourself. It's the culmination of nearly two decades of full-time work on the money beat—and fifteen years of my wife and me wrestling with our own feelings about what we owe our daughters and where and whether parental financial obligation ought to end. I have never come across a consumer decision that inspires more confusion and emotion than this one.

But after years of reporting, I am also full of wonder—and jealousy, frankly, that my daughters will get to do this neat thing in some fantastic place. In the time I spent figuring out what this book was supposed to be and then reporting it, I visited dozens of colleges and universities and spoke to hundreds of faculty members, experts on higher education, and parents—and not a few faculty member experts on higher education who are also parents. There are so many schools that can do great things for the right student—scores of them—and lots of them cost nothing close to $300,000. When I visited their campuses before they all shut down for a time, it was hard not to feel optimism. I still feel it.

That said, I understand why the most selective and expensive schools are enticing, and I'm not here to tell you that they are never worth the price. I went to one—Amherst—albeit on a need-based financial aid package decades ago that paid half of the bill. It changed my life profoundly. One of my professors encouraged me to send an op-ed to the *New York Times*, which published it when I was a junior. And although my friends from my hometown of Chicago will always be my second family, the people I met in college have enriched my life beyond all measure. There is no algorithm that could have predicted or accounted for what I've gained by knowing them.

Amherst was incredible, but it was not easy. My parents struggled and sacrificed; to this day, I get emotional when I think about graduation day on the quad in 1993. I burst into tears when I saw my family after I got my diploma and hugged the financial aid director (that would be Joe Paul Case, or "Saint Joe," as he's known in our family) and the custodian from my freshman dorm. (Hi, George!) It was gratitude, yes. But there was also just sheer, utter relief that we had somehow pulled it off. I want, more than anything else, to make sure my daughters don't have to think quite so hard about money during their undergraduate years. You may feel the same way.

This book is for them—and for you. We lack the clarity we deserve and a sense of control over the college process, especially now that nearly every higher education institution is reeling. Moreover, I want us all to feel much more competent about this decision, given that it sure seems as though someone designed this entire multiyear gauntlet that we run to sow maximum confusion. I don't doubt the sincerity or the good intentions of the thoughtful people I've met who are the gatekeepers and overseers at these schools. But something isn't quite right in all of this, and with this book I hope to help us all begin to make it right.

A couple of things to that end: I do not have a formula that spits out the true value of any given undergraduate experience. As the financial planner Tim Maurer says—and it can't be said enough—personal finance is more personal than it is finance. Your family is different from mine, your child is different from you, your first child (if you have more than one) is different from your second, and so on. And, to quote another great money sage, Carl Richards, the author of the essential money guide *The Behavior Gap: Simple Ways to Stop Doing Dumb Things with Money*: money = feelings. If nothing else, I hope this book helps you be much more emotionally honest with yourself. How might your feelings about this powerful—and powerfully expensive—transition point in the life of your family affect your decision-making in all sorts of ways?

There is no way to answer such cosmic questions about success and ambition and the emotions behind them without a lot more information. In these pages I'm going to provide a fair bit of it and then help you learn to gather everything else you need for yourself. In Part One, I'll explain how we got here; how the pricing, financial aid, and discounting systems work today; and why. I'll also walk you through whether the coronavirus and its aftermath will fundamentally alter the residential undergraduate experience, one that has changed little for many decades aside from its price and the debt that often comes with it.

Part Two will address those feelings—and there are three big ones— that mark the college picking and paying process and can easily lead to bad decision-making. First, fear—fear of children tumbling down the social class ladder if the family makes the wrong college choice. Second, guilt—that parents haven't saved enough or don't earn enough and thus must go six figures into hock for a first-choice college. And finally, snobbery and elitism: Private is better than public, a name brand is better than a school 1,500 miles away that few people have heard of. I want you to be aware and be wary—and, most of all, be intensely honest with yourself. This isn't easy, but reckoning with the feelings that arise around the college process is a matter of absolute urgency.

Part Three will name a variety of aspects of the college experience that are worth a whole lot of money under the very best circumstances. For instance, real professors who stand a chance of becoming mentors are worth paying extra for, and your odds of finding them are higher at colleges with smaller classes. Mental health care—or the lack thereof—is perhaps the greatest underreported challenge on campuses nationwide. So how do you know whether any given school is above average at providing it? I've read the studies and done the homework in each of these areas and many others. Through interviews with dozens of presidents at large universities and small colleges and with scores of families who have already navigated the process and come out the other end, I've developed a list of questions that most families will want to ask to help them clarify what is important to them.

Part Four covers the potentially money-saving hacks that tempt families: community college, honors colleges at public universities, gap years, attending college outside the United States, skipping college altogether, enlisting in the military, getting an athletic scholarship. What works, and what should people watch out for?

Finally, Part Five will condense fifteen years of reporting and dozens of columns worth of my own writing and learning into my very best personal finance advice on saving, planning, researching (by finding the schools that are the most generous and the most transparent), touring, applying, negotiating, and borrowing for college.

I wrote this book with parents in mind. I'm one too, so you'll see the word "we" in these pages. When you see the word "you," I'm talking about you parents, who are footing much of the bill. But grandparents, welcome! Please help pay for all of this. You too will find lots to chew on in these pages if you're inclined to assist. And if you're in high school yourself, by all means keep reading. None of this stuff is meant to fall into the category of proprietary parental secrets, because that would be blatant institutional adultism. I hope your mother or father or mothers or fathers or mother and father or stepparents (that gets complicated with financial aid, alas) will be completely transparent with you throughout this process as tricky questions about money arise. I think they owe it to you, in fact. And if you're a teenager navigating this process by yourself for whatever reason, I believe in you. You are not, in fact, alone; many people have walked this same path, and there are counselors at your school or elsewhere who can help.

I do not have all the answers. I'm not even sure that I have all the best questions. But reading this book will help you develop your own lines of inquiry and more. The system of educating undergraduates is under strain. At some schools, things just may crack wide open. So it is precisely the right moment to poke and prod and ask the most fundamental of questions about exactly what it is that we want to extract from an undergraduate education.

I hope that whatever you do end up asking of the schools on your list yields satisfactory answers. You shouldn't pay full price—or any price, really—for any school that is unresponsive, and you deserve more data. In fact, you should demand it, especially after you have an offer of admission but before you say yes. And if there are no good answers to your questions, a school should say why and explain how it's going to try to generate the data to better answer any given question for future applicants. "The public has the right to ask these questions and demand more information and data," said Vince Cuseo, who was once a philosophy graduate student and is now the vice president of enrollment at Occidental College.

Does he resent when people do make those demands? "No, I do not. Colleges and universities have gotten away with 'We are who we are, we do a good job, and you should know that and believe that it is the case.' It's ludicrous. Maybe it's my philosophy background, but you should have evidence. I'm not in any way opposed to that."

My wish for you is what Cuseo seems to welcome: that you will gain a much healthier sense of entitlement—and not the kind of expectation of special or singular treatment that you may criticize your teenagers for from time to time. I'm talking about a basic kind of entitlement to more information that ought to be standard in any six-figure transaction that involves something so important. Parents have been paying so much for so long without knowing nearly enough about value, and too many people have been afraid to ask about it lest it affect their child's admission or financial aid odds. That ends here, with my questions and yours, starting today.

Here we go.

PART I

The Price and Cost of College and the Systems Behind It

CHAPTER 1

Who Pays What and Why the Price Is So High

So why does college come with such a big price tag, anyway?

It's not because of lavish dorms or climbing walls. And it's not because the schools themselves insist on too many deputy associate vice provosts. But to even begin searching for an answer, we need to start by taking a quick look at how the market for college works and what most people actually pay for a degree.

And before we do that, we need to have a word about words. In this chapter, when we talk about *costs*, we're talking about the expenses that colleges and universities face when educating students.

Price is something else; it's what you pay. It's what you see when you do an internet search for the "cost of attendance" at whatever school you're considering. It's what you might refer to as the retail price or list price or rack rate in other parts of your life.

But for many families approaching college, this number is only the beginning. If you're on need-based financial aid, you're paying a lower price based on what the federal government and the school think your family can afford. With merit aid, the school is lowering the price for up to two additional reasons: It may believe that your child can add something of particular value to its community and wishes to keep your family from accepting offers from other schools. And it may recognize that many or even most people are unwilling to pay the list price. In other words, it's giving you a straight-up four-year coupon to lower the price to one that it thinks you will be willing to accept.

At the 361 private colleges and universities that are part of the National Association of College and University Business Officers (NACUBO) annual discounting study, the average first-time, full-time, first-year student got a discount of 53.9 percent off the list price of tuition during the 2020–21 school year. What do they mean by "discount"? When schools talk to you and send financial aid communications, they often use words such as "grants" and "scholarships" interchangeably. They call the notes that they send "award" letters, and, with merit aid in particular, they want the candidate to feel good about having "earned" a scholarship or grant that represents free money that their families might otherwise have to pay (or pay back, in the case of loans). But behind the scenes, administrators often call them "discounts," since a lot of the "aid" in this instance doesn't come from a special endowment; it's simply a price cut per student that the schools dole out in piecemeal fashion.

Most people who work in higher education track this annual discounting study because they are aware of something that the rest of us mostly aren't: 89 percent of students at private colleges get a need-based or merit aid discount. Yes, you read that right: Only a small fraction of families actually pay full price. What do the 89 percent pay? Ruffalo Noel Levitz, a consulting firm that we'll learn more about in the merit aid chapter, runs a survey of 280 private colleges and universities each year and pegged this number at $23,952, including room and board. Again, you read that right: The actual revenue that private colleges take in per student, on average, is less than the list price (including room and board) at many public universities.

Who pays full price? Half or more of families at plenty of the colleges and universities that you read about the most. The more selective the school (especially the private ones), the lower the discount rate, according to the Ruffalo Noel Levitz data. The firm calculates the overall discount rate at 42.7 percent (different from NACUBO's 52.6 percent, since NACUBO leaves out room and board charges when calculating its discount rate). But at highly selective schools the discount rate is just 39.7 percent, even though those schools almost always have the highest list prices. Again, this is the market in action: If more people are willing to pay for any given school, not only is the list price higher but the school doesn't have to discount as much.

Public universities discount too, but because their list prices are much lower, the discount is smaller as well. In its survey, Ruffalo Noel Levitz cited data showing that for undergraduates attending public four-year schools, the average grant from their schools is $4,148.

The overall result of all of these price cuts is an even bigger surprise: On average, what families are actually spending hasn't gone up by completely unreasonable amounts over the past twenty years, even as the list prices have gone to the moon. That's because the discount rate has gone up steadily over time as well. Colleges hope that their tuition increases will outpace the discounts they have to offer, but it hasn't always worked that way in recent years.

The College Board tracks all of this data very carefully, and the full cost of attendance that families paid for tuition, room, board, and other expenses for full-time, in-state students at four-year public universities, averaged $19,230 during the 2021–22 school year. For private schools, it was $32,720. Neither has gone up that much, at least in inflation-adjusted terms, since 2006–7.

Once nonprofit colleges have the money—from us, from donors, from their endowments, from grants, or from the state appropriations that public universities receive—they spend it. There are no investors or owners around to capture excess profit. So what do they spend it on, and how does that influence what we all pay?

Let's start with what is *not* a big part of their budgets. According to the Organisation for Economic Co-operation and Development, American families and the government spend $30,000 per year on the average undergraduate, including money they borrow. That's almost twice the average spent in other developed countries. Still, $23,000 of it goes where we'd probably want it to go: The core operation of teaching students and paying instructors.

That leaves just $7,000—a mere 23 percent of the total—for all of the college costs that you may have read about, such as dorms with video game lounges and new gyms with Peloton bikes. (Big-time intercollegiate sports fall into their own category outside these numbers, since they often generate revenue and draw restricted donations.) The authors of the book *Why Does College Cost So Much?* refer to reports of gaudy amenities as "the dysfunctionality narrative." And it's not all that surprising that people would seize on the things they can see, such as campus amenities or a bunch of new associate deans who are quoted in the college newspaper.

A word about lazy rivers: I've been able to identify just a couple dozen of them on college campuses nationwide or in the plazas of off-campus housing developments. Most colleges do not have them, and many of the ones that exist aren't as nice as the ones at even the most middling resorts. Colleges are not building them willy-nilly and then raising tuition to pay for them.

Demos, a left-wing think tank, took a deep dive into the data in 2015 and came to the following conclusion: All of the nonacademic construction that people might be tempted to criticize as extravagant—dorms that resemble condos, dining halls that are better than local restaurants, gyms that faculty prefer to nearby health clubs—contributed just 6 percent to the rising prices at public universities in recent years. Jane Wellman, who spent years overseeing a microscopic examination of higher education budgets called the Delta Cost Project, summed up the amenities story nicely in 2015: "The symbolism of this is worse than the reality of it."

Is it so-called administrative bloat that's driving tuition higher? Too many associate deans and vice presidents? If you've heard about this supposed phenomenon in recent years, the rhetoric probably came from one of two places. First, there are the editorial page writers at places such as the *Wall Street Journal*. They live to mock the growing human resources infrastructure around diversity on campuses and the regulation-driven efforts at gender equity there. Then there are the college faculty organizations, which worry that the new administrative positions at campuses nationwide have resulted in fewer new tenured faculty jobs and more low-paid part-timers.

Let's take the *Wall Street Journal* critique first. To a certain extent, as voters and consumers, we choose the administrators we want. Voters elect the politicians who create the regulations that govern, say, gender equity in college sports and rules around the adjudication of sexual assault and access for people with physical disabilities or learning differences. When new rules come into existence or our elected officials enforce existing ones more carefully, colleges need administrators to help them stay on track. If we want fewer rules and fewer administrators, we can make those choices on election day. So far, we haven't made those choices though. In fact, we've done something more like the opposite.

As student populations have become more diverse, the number of students who are the first in their families to attend college has increased. Ditto the number of undergraduates attending college with diagnoses for moderate to severe mental health conditions that might have kept them home a decade or two ago. And most students arrive with a computer and a phone. All of these undergraduates and their parents expect that diversity administrators, mental health counselors, and information technology experts will be on call, and not in small numbers, either. "The most common complaint I received from students and faculty members is that we don't have enough administrators," said Brian Rosenberg, a former president of Macalester College, in an essay he wrote for administrators who worried that they might have "BS jobs."

A quick look at federal data shows that there aren't that many more full-time employees working at colleges than there used to be, when you express it as the number of people working there for every 1,000 full-time students. What's changed is their composition, according to the Delta Cost Project, which used the same federal data: The average number of faculty and instructional staff per administrator declined by about 40 percent at most types of colleges and universities between 1990 and 2012. This continuing trend is what upsets the faculty organizations. You'd be mad too if you were they, and we'll come back to their concerns that are most relevant to college shoppers in the chapter on teachers and teaching.

So to the extent that many of us are or will be paying more for our children's college education than our parents did for ours, what or who is actually responsible? At state schools, the economic downturn at the end of the first decade of the century squeezed state budgets in a variety of ways. One easy fix was for the states to give fewer subsidies to their public universities. That meant that most schools had to raise tuition for the in-state residents who often (but not always, as in the case of the University of Alabama and the University of Vermont) make up the majority of their undergraduates. Many state schools also tried to cover the lost state subsidies by marketing harder to international students and affluent students from out of state—and charging them even more. The Demos study I mentioned earlier determined that the decline in state appropriations accounted for nearly 80 percent of the price hike at public universities.

But the biggest cost of all—one that every undergraduate institution faces whether it is public or private—is labor. The majority of the money that goes to educating undergraduates is for salary and benefits for the people who teach and the staff who support them. These are figures that were nearly always on the tips of the tongues of the presidents I interviewed at the highest-priced schools. On a single day of reporting in Maine, I saw or heard the presidents of both Bates College and Bowdoin College cite a figure of 60-something percent of their overall budget that pays for salaries, retirement benefits, and health insurance.

Even administrators at well-resourced schools like those do not ever stop thinking about this.

Why do faculty and administrators cost so much? As you might imagine, academic economists love studying their own industry, and they've more or less figured all of this out. There are few areas of our lives where prices have risen as fast as higher education, but medical services is one. Medicine is a service industry where people want as much individualized attention as possible. The same thing is true for college, and students want many of the same things that patients do.

Faculty and administrator salaries are hardly outrageous, but they are above average. This seems fair, given that their pay rewards the fact that professors spend more time in formal education than do nearly any other working adults. Few people would spend so much time training for these jobs without the promise of some kind of economic return. And in undergraduate fields where professors could easily make more money in the private sector—say, computer science or many hard sciences or economics—tenured instructors may make even more than your average faculty member.

High wages for professors don't necessarily have to lead to ever-higher college prices for all of us. After all, there are ways for these schools to deliver four courses to each student per semester in a more efficient fashion. But for that to happen, schools would need to require faculty to teach more often, and professors don't like that. Good ones would leave for lighter course loads elsewhere, shun the schools that work faculty the hardest in the classroom, or leave the teaching profession altogether. Class sizes could get bigger instead, but who among us parents would willingly sign our kids up for lots more lectures and much less faculty contact or mentorship? Anyone up for way more online instruction, given how much so many of our kids enjoyed their experiences on Zoom?

A school could certainly test parental will; we'll probably see more of this kind of experimentation before long. But here's the thing: Few educators or administrators got into this line of work to provide a cut-rate, impersonal educational experience. They're competitive. They want to be the best at what they do—or better than their peer institutions at least. Few schools want to run the risk of creating a disgruntled faculty and having prospective students avoid their institutions altogether. And isn't this how we want them to think?

It's not a rhetorical question. It is, in fact, the very question that we all need to answer for every kid we push through the system, and we may not answer it the same way for each prospective student. In the meantime, costs rise because well-educated people expect good salaries. We can all cross our fingers and hope that states start subsidizing more of this cost once again, but that could require new or higher taxes at a time when most states are struggling to pay for crumbling infrastructure and rising Medicaid costs and deal with underfunded public sector pensions. At private colleges and universities, few endowments have enough money to subsidize even more of the annual cost to educate students. The federal government has shown little desire to raise the lending limits for undergraduate student loans or substantially increase the size of Pell Grants.

That leaves all of us to cover the costs. And everyone else in this crazy system is betting that we will—or at least hoping that we will.

CHAPTER 2

FAFSA and Its Confounding Calculations Will Probably Make You Furious; Blame the Federal Government's Great Expectations

After several years in the technology industry and a few more in the wine business, Ann Garcia found her way to financial planning. At that point her twins were young, but not so young that she and her husband were not already studying up on how to save and pay for college.

By the time they were ready to apply many years later, college planning had become a professional specialty. Garcia even maintained a blog called *The College Financial Lady*, which I first encountered years ago when I got fed up with all of the internet message boards telling people not to save for college at all. The logic—intensely flawed, as I suspected at the time and then set out to prove—was that you'd get better financial aid if you didn't have any money saved. She set the readers of my *New York Times* column straight right quick in a piece I wrote in 2015 that you can still find online: "Why It Makes Good Sense to Save for College Now."

Garcia promised to stay in touch as her twins' senior year approached, and when I caught up with her in 2018, everyone in the family was rolling up their sleeves at home in Portland, Oregon. Their situation was a fascinating mix of facts and possibilities. Ann's husband works in technology and she has her own business, so their annual income definitely fluctuated and was rarely predictable. They were going to have two kids in college at the same time, which can create more financial aid eligibility.

Meanwhile, the kids were very different. One was an academic superstar who had a shot at getting into the most selective colleges in the country, albeit many with annual list prices near or above $80,000 all in. Merit aid was likely at less selective schools, plus it looked like she would qualify for additional money from the National Hispanic Recognition Program.

The other twin was a fine test taker but hadn't worked quite as hard in the classroom as his sister. He was probably headed for the University of Oregon, although his test scores might qualify him for merit aid elsewhere. Ann and her husband were not inclined to pay more than the price of an in-state school, given his classroom effort to date, and he wasn't asking for more, either.

And so they began. Ann was practically chomping at the bit to finally get a real live federal financial aid identification number and fill out the FAFSA (Free Application for Federal Student Aid) form for her own family. "I'm enjoying the process a lot," said no one, perhaps ever, except for her.

The family had saved about $120,000 total, a healthy sum that would put them in good shape if both kids went to a state school, although that seemed unlikely. Even though Ann and her husband had a six-figure household income, they threw their lot in with the financial aid gods to see what would happen.

Financial aid is decidedly not just for low-income people—not nowadays, with some schools getting ready to charge over $325,000 for four years to entering first-year students. According to the Ruffalo Noel Levitz discount study I mentioned in the previous chapter, the average parental income of FAFSA filers in the colleges it surveyed was about

$110,000. If you have two or more children in school, you may get need-based financial aid if you earn more than $200,000. To read more how this might work, search online for a column I wrote called "What a $300,000 College Might Cost a $200,000 Family."

And as you probably know already, you can't get any need-based financial aid without filling out the FAFSA on October 1 or later of your child's senior year in high school. This chapter is not a comprehensive guide to filling it out. If you're looking for one, I like Kalman A. Chany's *Paying for College: Everything You Need to Maximize Financial Aid and Afford College.* But I do want to explain not only how the federal government defines your supposed ability to pay but also the feelings that number is likely to evoke.

First, a bit about what FAFSA is and is not. FAFSA isn't a person. FAFSA doesn't "say" anything. Instead, it's a way that helps the federal government determine what sort of aid you are eligible for. Close to 20 million students and their families fill it out each year, and you have to do it every year you're paying for college. If your income is low enough, you might qualify for Pell Grants—money you don't have to pay back. There is also something known as work-study—money that the government gives to your school to help pay you for work you do on campus. Then, there is the federal loan system; in some instances, the federal government will subsidize you by paying the interest on your loans during college and for six months after you leave school.

Once you fill out the FAFSA, the end result has traditionally been something called the Expected Family Contribution, or EFC. At the end of 2020, however, a new law introduced a new term, Student Aid Index, or SAI, that will replace the EFC in the coming years. The timeline is still a bit uncertain, though all of the changes are supposed to be in place for people starting their senior year of high school in 2023.

The EFC/SAI is essentially about rationing; the government has only so much money it's willing to devote to helping with college costs, and EFC/SAI is how it decides who gets what. Where this gets confusing is when colleges and universities use this figure as a starting point for handing out their own grants or scholarships. Remember, it's a starting point; it's not necessarily what any school will demand that you pay. Still, just so you can get clarity, this should be among your first questions if you think you'll need help paying for college: Does your school only use the EFC/SAI to determine what we can pay and what sort of help we might need?

If you've completed your own FAFSA already, you may be dumbfounded as to why it's so high. Let's break it down here. To get the EFC/SAI figure, the federal government wants to know all sorts of financial information about your family. Here, we'll look at the two big components: parental income and parental assets.

Income counts the most, by far. This is a bit of an oversimplification, but for most families the income calculation works like so: If you earn very little, your EFC/SAI will say that you can afford to pay nothing at all. Once you earn above basic subsistence levels, the formula makes some allowances for employment expenses and taxes and then sets the remaining money against a kind of model monthly household budget. Once the formula accounts for the money you need to devote to your budget, it then assumes that you can spend between 22 and 47 percent of whatever is left over on tuition. So it grabs that money and sets it aside to be part of the EFC/SAI.

Now, some quirks about that income calculation and its components. Many, actually. It makes no allowances for student debt that the parents may still have. There is no adjustment mechanism for people who live in places where the cost of housing is much higher than average. People who own their own businesses can use a variety of strategies to lower their incomes for certain periods to create more aid eligibility, and the system isn't sophisticated enough to track or audit all of them. If you're divorced, the formula counts only the income from the parent with primary custody, which means a wealthier parent who intends to contribute money isn't part of the calculation. And that's just for starters.

The FAFSA formula also considers your assets. There's some good news here: Home equity isn't part of this equation, so the EFC/SAI figure is not a reflection of an assumption that you will be downsizing your living space or borrowing against the value of your home. Retirement accounts are not part of the calculation, either. The asset list does include all checking and savings accounts, plus brokerage accounts where you might hold stocks or mutual funds that are not in a specific retirement account. And it also includes 529 plans, the college savings accounts where the Garcias had put away $120,000.

Here's the thing, though: The formula only assumes that parents will pay up to 5.64 percent of these assets each year for college. Why so low? Because the people who created the formula did not want to discourage saving. So you may be wondering: If the Garcias were only going to have to pay, say, $6,500 each year from their savings—a bit over 5 percent of their $120,000 each year, or $26,000 total over four years—what would happen to the rest of the money in their 529 account? Well, this is where the numbers get a little funky. The formula doesn't explicitly assume that people with higher incomes have been able to save all along in those 529 plans and can use all of the savings above and beyond that 5.64 percent to help cover the college bills. But the system sort of counts on it.

If your life hasn't quite worked out in the tidy way that the formula assumes, with six figures saved and years of stable income and no emergencies in your wake, well, join the club. When the EFC/SAI arrives in your inbox and you wonder whether the enormous figure is in fact an estimate for what you can afford over *all four* years and not just the one year that it actually dictates, you will not be alone. And the professionals have some sympathy for you. Jon Boeckenstedt, the unofficial dean of data-fluent enrollment management Twitter (seriously, he should be your first follow as you start thinking about what to pay for college), tossed off the following quip to me in a DePaul University conference room before he headed west for a big job at Oregon State. "Remember the Peacekeeper missile?" he said. "If there is a better example of something that has a label on it that is completely disassociated from reality, then the expected family contribution is probably it." Better, he continued, to just think of it as a formula that the government uses to control expenditures on higher education. "By almost any objective measure, the system is not fair. Trying to understand it against the framework of fairness is a fool's game. Disabuse yourself of the notion that it will make sense to you."

And here's the thing that makes so many people happy about the fact that the term is going to be retired after decades of causing offense: This phrase "expected family contribution" is absolutely stuffed with judgment and assumptions that invoke feelings that we ought to call out. Let's begin with these great expectations. Who is doing the expecting, anyway? At one point I made an appointment at the U.S. Department of Education in Washington, D.C., hoping to meet the keeper of the formula, the Expecter-in-chief and crusher of affordability dreams. In fact, there is no such person. Congress set the basics of the modern version of the formula in 1992, and it hasn't changed dramatically since then. And Congress, speaking for the federal government, declares the following: Not only will we not provide free college tuition, we will quite literally render judgment from on high before allowing you to receive any assistance with that tuition at all. The government is *expecting* you.

As for the "family" part of this, let's begin with the baseline assumption that goes unsaid but shouldn't: College tuition is not the responsibility of government, for the most part. Nor is it the responsibility of the student in most cases, either. No, "family" in this instance is the parent or parents. Any parent who declares that a child who can vote (at age 18) and go to war (at age 18) ought to provide their own money for college (at age 18) is welcome to that opinion. And they can toss off all they want about how the government should pay for it all, given how much the government gains in labor productivity when people get college degrees—not to mention the benefit of a more educated citizenry.

The federal government, however, does not see it that way. Its expectations are that undergraduate education is something that families should pay for if they can. "Family" here is a misnomer. What we're talking about is the expected *parental* contribution. Or more like the *demanded* one.

That use of the term "family" is apt in one respect, though, given that it adequately hints at the kinds of household conflicts it can cause. In her book *Indebted: How Families Make College Work at Any Cost*, the economic anthropologist Caitlin Zaloom describes the expectations here as "moral tensions." Sure, providing for your kid is "sacred," as she puts it. But there are other cultural forces at work here, too, like the financial expectation that we will all, increasingly, provide for our own retirement savings and health insurance premiums. The federal government may help a bit, but it probably won't be quite enough. If you can't meet Uncle Sam's expectations, you'll face some difficult choices in your household and the uncomfortable conversations that follow. Thus does the EFC became, in Zaloom's words, a piece of "moral technology [by means of which] the FAFSA form turns abstract ideas about how families should live into an instrument that families must apply to their lives."

Feeling the pressure yet? Well, then there's this: This number that the federal government presents you with is a contribution you're making. To what, you might ask? Is it a gift, like charity? If so, why isn't tuition fully tax-deductible? Perhaps it's meant to connote a kind of shared burden, with the government pitching in with a little something and then families contributing their fair share. But with contributions you don't really expect anything in return. At up to $325,000, though, paying for college sure starts to seem like an investment. And given the lack of good data about what happens to students while they're enrolled and once they graduate, we don't have much information about returns. So perhaps "wage" is the right term. How about "expected family speculation," given that Zaloom has it right again when she describes the entire enterprise of paying for college as a kind of "social speculation" on whether footing the bill will risk a family's overall financial well-being.

Financial aid professionals are well aware of your raised eyebrows and offer up some harsh words of their own. "The notion that if you make $200,000 that you will have saved X, I think, is clearly detached from the reality of most families," said Rick Bischoff, the vice president for enrollment management at Case Western Reserve University. "For upper-income families, the financial aid process doesn't work for many of them."

At the University of Southern California, where plenty of people are willing to pay full price, there are similar frustrations. "What I struggle with is two related things," said Katharine Harrington, USC's former vice president of admissions and planning. The first, she pointed out, is "how damn complex the financial aid application process is on the FAFSA side. I have an MBA. I was senior vice president at the second largest savings bank in the country. I couldn't figure out FAFSA the first time I tried, and that is not right." And then there is how much the system asks of each family. As a banker, she explained, she often made $25 million loan decisions with less information than what the FAFSA requires of a family that merely seeks half off or so on a child's college bill.

After decades where millions of aid applicants suffered under those requirements, the FAFSA form is about to change. The same new law that turns the EFC into the SAI will reduce the number of questions from 108 to 36. Now, it will be 2 pages instead of 36.

There are other big changes too. Over 2 million lower-income students will get bigger Pell Grants or qualify for one that they would not have been eligible for before. Higher income families, however, worry about a part of the bill that no longer gives them a lower EFC/SAI when there are two or more members of the household enrolled in college at once. It is possible (though not likely) that legislators will alter this unpopular change yet again. If they don't, it's hard to predict how schools will change their own distribution of aid to families in this spot. You'll want to ask about this at every school that interests you, since it's likely that different schools will do it differently.

Speaking of those differences, there is one more big one that you need to be aware of. Once you've got the EFC/SAI, a few hundred colleges and universities then go ahead and ask for even more information. They use something called the CSS Profile form to make decisions about distributing their own discounts. What we're talking about here are the grants or "scholarships" (other than Pell Grants) that will appear on a financial aid award letter, a dollar figure that the school will subtract from the overall list price and that you do not have to repay. Different schools have different ways of using the data they gather, and it can lead to their being more generous than the EFC/SAI formula. But one big differentiator from the FAFSA-EFC/SAI approach is that the CSS Profile form wants to know about the equity you have in your home. Many colleges will, in effect, tax that home equity. They treat it as an asset and expect you to hand over some of it each year. How you extract it is your business. If you can find a way to come up with the money without a home equity loan or line of credit or a mortgage refinance, great. If not, then you do the HELOC or refinance your mortgage and pull cash out.

The reasonableness or fairness of these financial aid policies is not a topic for this book. Transparency, however, is within our line of inquiry, and many schools do a terrible job of explaining how they handle home equity. If it's not on a school's website and it uses the CSS Profile formula, call and ask about its policy. All financial aid officers know the formula for their own institutions. If you have the nerve, go ahead and politely suggest that they post their policy prominently on their websites so people don't have to call and ask about it anymore.

Because Ann Garcia is a professional—a trained assassin in this area, really—she knew all of the above. She also knew about something called the net price calculator, which every school maintains somewhere on its website. You input your financial information (and sometimes a bit of information about your child's test scores and grades), and the calculator spits out an estimate of what it thinks the school would ask you to pay if your child is granted admission. In other words, you're supposed to try the calculator before you even apply in order to give yourself a sense of whether the school would be affordable if you were to get in. It's a nonbinding estimate, but the schools have an incentive to make it close to reality lest people howl in protest if their actual aid offers upon admission are lower than the estimates.

The Garcias got mixed news when they put themselves through the calculators. And, yes, you have to spend lots of time filling out each one separately. A few years ago, several schools helped quash a private effort to create a website that would allow people to fill out several calculators at once. Now some members of Congress are trying to pass legislation making a combined calculator mandatory. It will take years at a minimum, since there is never as big a political constituency for making personal finance simpler as one might think.

On one hand, the Garcias were going to be eligible for some need-based aid, due to having twins enrolled simultaneously. On the other, the most generous estimates for their daughter came from schools with the longest admissions odds, such as the Massachusetts Institute of Technology and the University of Chicago. Boston College would be easier to get into, but its calculator estimated a price that was much higher than what the other two were offering. As a result, she ended up not applying there. But would staying in state at the honors college at the University of Oregon make more sense?

The family wasn't sure. It had gone through a value exercise with Northwestern University when their daughter thought she might want to take a run at its vaunted undergraduate theater program. Once they figured out what a median union actor might earn per year upon graduation, they realized that it didn't even make sense to apply. "I just wanted her to compare investment return to investment return," Ann said.

When the admissions offers and letters arrived, Boston University gave her some merit aid, something its net price calculator had not predicted.

But its discount was not as big as the one at the University of Chicago, which had both the highest list price of any school that either Garcia child applied to and the second-lowest net price to the family of any school from which their daughter got an acceptance letter. Was it a quirky set of financial aid criteria that did the trick at Chicago? Or was the school trying to punch its way into better *U.S. News & World Report* rankings by increasing the all-important "yield" number by being so generous that few people could afford to say no to its financial aid offers? It's hard to say for sure, but the Garcia daughter said yes to Chicago.

There was a bigger surprise in store for the Garcias' son. While the twins were in their early teenage years, the family was on a trip to Tucson, Arizona, for a relative's birthday. They took a wrong turn and found themselves on the University of Arizona campus on the day of a football game. There were students partying all over the place, and their son was enthralled.

Okay, his parents told him. *You* figure out how this can get to the same price as the University of Oregon. And suddenly all the drive that he hadn't always displayed in the classroom was fully in evidence. His ACT score was so good that he qualified for a big discount that the university offers to out-of-state students with excellent marks. That made up some of the price difference. Then he found a cheap dorm and a low-priced meal plan and showed up for admitted students day to investigate further. There, he met with a resident adviser who told him that there was a shortage of males in the RA applicant pool, so the Garcia son resolved to do whatever he could to get that job for at least one year.

After all that, things penciled out to just $1,500 per year more than the University of Oregon in year one, a decent bet for a matriculating student suddenly alive with enthusiasm for meeting faculty and getting acquainted with the undergraduate business school. It didn't hurt that the University of Arizona nearly bombarded him with welcome notes and congratulations on his big scholarship, while Oregon took its own sweet time to even admit the young man. We'll learn more about all this in the merit aid chapter, but if you think that teenagers can't be swayed by higher education marketing, think again.

"As a seventeen-year-old, he was thinking that maybe he wasn't hearing [from Oregon] because he just wasn't going to get in, and he spent time thinking that maybe he should be picturing himself in Tucson," Ann said of her son. "That was the biggest surprise in the whole process. I thought we'd be making an analytical apples-to-apples comparison and not that things would be filtered through a seventeen-year-old thinking 'They want me, they want me.'"

The Garcia twins thrived academically, and their mother was relieved as much as anything else. She also did not regret saving for college in line with what she had predicted years earlier, when we spoke for my *New York Times* column. As a financial adviser, she fully understands that not everyone can afford to save. But she was lucky enough to be able to, and it didn't end up hurting the aid picture much. "Our EFC was higher as a result of having saved, but not higher enough to justify not having done so," she said. "A family with high income and no college savings doesn't usually come across as a family that places a priority on college."

Come across to whom? I've spent years trying to get financial aid officers to discuss whether they literally punish high-income families who apply for aid and have no savings. No one would quite say that they "award" such families lower grants than they might otherwise; after all, neither the FAFSA nor the CSS Profile takes in the two decades of earning history that financial aid officers would need to even begin to pass judgment on a family's capacity for having saved.

Still, they are human, for better or worse, and humans are often skeptical. If you think your EFC or CSS Profile might tell an incomplete story, be sure to send a letter explaining any extenuating circumstances that kept you from saving or forced you to break into your savings. It certainly can't hurt, since the people who read the applications are, after all, real people just like you.

CHAPTER 3

How (and Why) Merit Aid Became Mainstream

Perhaps you believe that your child's college application process will be something like your own. Maybe you attended a selective school in the United States, prepped hard for the SAT, and wrote a few essays.

Sure, things are more competitive than they used to be, what with so many more teenagers applying to a larger number of schools. Even so, the schools on the tip of most families' tongues haven't changed all that much, and there have been hardly any startups. You probably feel like you're in a pretty good position to offer guidance.

And maybe you are. But what has changed entirely is the price: Not only has the list price grown at a far higher rate than inflation, but a somewhat hidden system has emerged with the help of consultants operating behind the scenes to offer untold billions in discounts each year.

What we're talking about here is merit aid, although it may not deserve that name anymore. It is messy—difficult to define, hard to predict, and economically complex. It has become such a tricky enterprise, in fact, that colleges collectively spend something like $1 billion each year to hire those consultants to help them find students, figure out which ones should pay what and then spend a whole lot more to chase the applicants down. The end result is an exercise in rampant unpredictability, even though this is the biggest financial decision your family will ever make. You will pick a limited number of schools to apply to without necessarily knowing what they'll cost. In fact, any of them might offer you a $100,000 price break or more over four years. Or they might not offer a discount of a single cent.

This is confusing. So let's begin by explaining what merit aid—an imperfect term that I'm nevertheless using since it's a common one that we probably can't get rid of—actually is and what it is not. We already know that the FAFSA yields a dollar figure estimating what you might be able to pay. And we've learned that many private colleges run their own numbers using the CSS Profile. There they are trying to figure out what a family can afford to pay. The schools generally describe any money they give away based on those formulas as "need-based" aid.

Merit aid exists because colleges worry that if they don't give out even more discounts aside from the need-based ones, not enough students and families will choose to pay for their school. To solve for that, many give merit aid money to applicants they most want. And at some schools every student gets merit aid even if they are wealthy B students, which undercuts the notion of "merit" as most of us think about it.

As for the "aid" part, you probably came to this process thinking that financial aid of any sort would go to people who are somehow needy. But merit aid often goes to people who are wealthy, even in the 1 percent. Nevertheless, the schools that offer it believe that families "need" a discount to believe that a particular school offers a good enough value to commit.

You may hear schools and other applicants using different words and phrases to describe merit aid, and you may not know what they are actually talking about when they do. They may not know what they are talking about, either. At some colleges, people with financial need may get "grants" while the schools woo more affluent applicants with "academic scholarships." The financial aid office may decide how much money your family needs, while the admissions office decides (with the help of those consultants) how much merit aid you deserve (or what they think it will take to get you to commit). Moreover, you may find out about your own financial fate through what's known as a "financial aid award letter," which uses all of your merit aid to satisfy some of your demonstrated financial need. This too is confusing, and it's also purposeful, as we'll soon learn. As ever, it pays to ask lots of questions.

If this is starting to feel strange, uncomfortable, and inequitable, suffice it to say that the schools feel that, too. They don't enjoy much of anything about merit aid, but most of them can't stop offering it, either. To see why, it helps to understand why they started offering it in the first place.

The year-to-year challenges for a reasonably selective undergraduate institution haven't actually changed much over time. They all want to provide a quality education, and they don't want to lose more than their fair share of students to competing colleges. To maintain a school that can meet those goals, they need significant revenue, which means admitting the highest-quality students who can provide the money. But they also want to help students in need who can't afford to pay full price, both because they care about equity and because it's a bad look to run a school filled with rich kids.

And while most colleges do have endowments, they often are not large enough to produce enough income each year to help with more than part of the annual financial aid budget. These colleges, especially smaller ones that don't have a bunch of profitable graduate students roaming around or professors who bring in millions in government research funding, live and die by their tuition revenue. And if their projections are off by even 1 percent, it can make a real hash of a budget. This is true even at the smallest schools, with 2,000 undergraduates. If they are expecting an incoming class of 500 but only get 495 to say yes (having missed their number by 1 percent), then the negative math rolls out over the four years of college that the five people are spending elsewhere. Five people might represent a yearly infusion of $250,000, or $50,000 a year for each kid. So all of a sudden, *poof!* There goes a million bucks. That's a few salaries right there, just because competitors did something compelling to sway some students who the losing school had hoped would attend their institution instead.

But what do those competitors do, exactly? Not that long ago, even the most prestigious schools didn't really do much picking and choosing among applicants. In a book called *Crafting a Class: College Admissions and Financial Aid: 1955–1994*, which chronicles the evolution of admissions and financial aid at sixteen selective small liberal arts colleges in Ohio and Massachusetts over four decades, the authors cited the various feelings that the admissions staffs had expressed in the early part of their study. The gatekeepers referred to the newfound phenomenon of people applying to multiple colleges as a form of "harassment" of the institutions. This "plague" of people seeking "selfish security" created "an educator's blind man's bluff" where it was not clear how many people they ought to admit, since there was no longer any certainty about how many of them would enroll. Competition! Consumer choice!! The nerve!!!

In the decades following World War II, a variety of policy and demographic phenomena led to enormous growth in the number of people starting college. States responded, expanding existing universities and opening new branches. Many private colleges began admitting women for the first time. The flood of new choices and new students led to conditions that increasingly resembled an actual market, with all of the emerging price wars one would expect. In the 1950s, it merely appeared to be "a good sharp contest," according to Harvard's dean of admission at the time. By the 1980s, the dean at Wellesley noted the "outright buying or bribing of top candidates" and lamented the "real beginnings of cut-throat competition." Whatever genteel clubbiness had existed in this world previously was evolving into something else entirely, and the old-school deans did not like it one single bit.

Though it's hard to determine who invented merit aid or coined the phrase, Ohio was one of the places where intense competition broke out earliest. The combination of many private colleges and a thriving state university system presented the perfect conditions, and Ohio Wesleyan, a somewhat less selective private college, was one of the first to start discounting. It began in earnest in the early 1980s, figuring it could throw some money at the best students in its applicant pool, and once word spread that the quality of the student body was improving, better-than-average students—who might not ultimately need an incentive to join their fellow larger-brained peers—would apply. It didn't exactly work out that way, given that, by 1994, Ohio Wesleyan was handing out merit aid to 39 percent of its students.

Whenever one school among a set of competitors makes a strategic decision to discount aggressively, at least one of the others is likely to respond in kind. But with colleges this doesn't necessarily happen in real time. Schools have various ways of finding out where the students they admitted (but did not enroll) end up attending and why, whether it's by talking to high school counselors or polling admitted students who went elsewhere. By the time the next admissions season rolls around, admissions staff have decided whether to respond with their own additional merit aid. If that tactic works, then the discount dominoes may fall again in a different direction the following year at yet another school. Maybe the school that started it all responds to the second one in kind, or a third or fourth school gets into the game to keep its prized applicants from choosing cheaper options elsewhere.

Denison University found itself in the middle of all of this in Ohio, and it had another problem lurking in the background. It had developed a reputation for *Animal House* antics and a fraternity culture that was becoming detrimental to the institution. By 1980 the average SAT score of entering first-year students had fallen 220 points in just fifteen years. It determined that a merit aid campaign was necessary as well if it had any hope of attracting undergraduates who liked the classroom as much as the taproom. "They squandered their birthright and had to buy their way back," said David R. Anderson, president of St. Olaf College in Minnesota, who served as provost at Denison for seven years earlier in his career.

Denison started with just a bit of merit aid but then felt it had to increase it. Kenyon College, which had managed to stay above the fray, eventually folded and started throwing money around too. Oberlin was the last Ohio holdout, but it eventually gave in and now offers merit aid to all of its first-year students who show no actual financial need. They get over $21,000 each. Case Western Reserve University in Cleveland cuts the price by an average of just over $23,000 for 72 percent of the same demographic group.

In other parts of the country, schools tried to band together to stem the tide. In 1979, thirty schools in the Northeast issued a statement positively sniffing about the fact that any offer of admission should be merit award enough. As the president of Wheaton College in Massachusetts put it plainly not long after, "The message was that if you had to go to merit aid, it was a sign of weakness." Smith and Mount Holyoke tested merit aid anyway in 1983 and came in for a torrent of criticism from peers. They backed off, but Mount Holyoke introduced it again years later, and Smith eventually felt like it had to begin offering some—and even more after that. "We would look at applicants who were admitted to Smith and then Mount Holyoke or Bryn Mawr, and $10,000 was making a difference," said Smith's president, Kathleen McCartney. "I'm ambivalent about it. I hope we don't do more."

Strategic pivots are rare, but they do happen. Both Hamilton in New York and Franklin & Marshall have done away with merit aid in recent years. Around the same time, however, Connecticut College started using it in earnest, infuriating other schools in its athletic conference that do not deploy the same tools. Farther down the food chain, colleges went all in with an "Everybody gets a trophy!" strategy. Guilford College, a Quaker college in North Carolina, explicitly reminded college counselors in email blasts in 2018 that everyone in the previous year's accepted students pool had received a "merit scholarship."

Public universities did not sit idly by while all of this was happening. When state appropriations fell after the 2007–09 economic meltdown, many flagship state schools decided to raise their sticker prices for out-of-state students. Then they recruited them more aggressively, using direct mail campaigns akin to what a credit card company would use to find high-income prospects. The next step was to offer merit aid to a decent percentage of applicants who took the bait. The aid didn't necessarily lower the recipients' price to what an in-state student would pay, but it often amounted to a five-figure annual discount while still being a good deal for the school.

If you're wondering why so many of the kids in your region are going to the University of Alabama or Delaware or the honors college at Arizona State all of a sudden, merit aid is a big part of the reason. Here's how Roger Thompson, who used to oversee enrollment at Alabama, described his target high school students with high test scores. "There are some kids there that we'll buy," he told a reporter from the *Atlantic*. "The National Merit kids, they're going to get a full ride. But if you're sitting at a private high school in Florida, where they pay twenty grand to go, we don't even bring financial-aid material. What's the point? You don't even need to talk about cost."

The University of Alabama now spends over $158 million on merit aid each year for students with no financial need, up from under $10 million in 2006. That's $81 million more than it gives in grant aid to people who demonstrate financial need. Enrollment is up by more than half since then, and fewer than half of the undergraduates are from the state. When Dawn Rhodes, a *Chicago Tribune* reporter, took note of the brain drain of teenagers from Illinois to Alabama, she wrote a long story about it in 2018 for the newspaper. Within months, the state, one of the most fiscally troubled in the country, nevertheless coughed up $25 million in merit money to try to keep those students closer to home.

It only makes sense, given Alabama's success, that other schools are copying the strategy. Take it from the insiders themselves. "Price is the most malleable and powerful tool that most institutions have in their arsenal," wrote Jon McGee, who was vice president for planning and public affairs at the College of Saint Benedict and St. John's University in Minnesota when he wrote his book *Breakpoint: The Changing Market-*

place for Higher Education. "That colleges manipulate it as much as they do should not be at all surprising."

Bob Bontrager, who once helped oversee discounting for Oregon State, put it this way to the *Atlantic*: "It's a zero-sum game. There's a finite number of prospective students out there. Are you going to get them, or is your competitor going to get them? You face the pressure and say, 'That feels burdensome to me; I don't want to deal with that.' Or you say, 'That's a pretty interesting challenge; I'm going to go out there and try to eat their lunch. I'm going to try to kick their ass.'"

CHAPTER 4

The Billion-Dollar Consultants Who Are Wooing You

You want some of this merit aid, and that's understandable. But here's what you probably don't realize: There is a system that operates behind the scenes to distribute these discounts that itself requires about $1 billion of annual care and feeding. It works in part by manipulating you emotionally. And because you may not be expecting a sly, soft sell, you probably don't know to look out for it.

Let's fix that. If there is a single bit of emotional truth that undergirds the merit aid system, it's the one that Davin Sweeney uttered on *The Crush*, his podcast about college admissions: No families are longing to have college administrators single them out for their financial need. Instead, they want authority figures to focus on their record. Merit aid puts achievement before disadvantage.

Sweeney should know, since he got an insider's view of the merit aid toolbox as an admissions staffer at the University of Rochester. Now he's on the other side, working as a school-based college counselor. Many families come to him blind, with an only child or a firstborn son or daughter, and have no idea how the system works or why a school that they can already afford might target their child with a discount. But as we've learned, affordability is often not the point when colleges put a pile of merit aid onto the table. Parents are susceptible to offers of unsolicited gold stars for having raised fine children. Teenagers, meanwhile, might buy a hard sell, given that most people have been telling them all along that it is the *applicants* who must prostrate themselves these days. It is hard to resist a pat on the back and a discount, and the colleges know this. They've proved it, in fact.

If you spend any amount of time on college admissions and financial aid websites trying to figure out who the gatekeepers are and whom they report to, you'll often notice someone overseeing something called enrollment management. Perhaps this rings a bell. Maybe you know something about the airline industry, where American Airlines used mainframe computers to popularize what came to be known as yield management. The big idea was to use historical data to try to predict which seats on which flights would sell out by what date. Then the airline would price seats accordingly, changing fares constantly right up until takeoff in order to maximize revenue.

Enrollment management, which emerged in the 1980s but really came into its own a decade or so later, isn't all that different. Just think about an empty classroom seat or a dorm bed the same way you would an airline seat: Both are useless when a plane pushes back from the gate or a semester begins. Enrollment management calls for using data to figure out which students to recruit and how to woo them. To do this, schools draw in part on information that students supply when taking the PSAT. Test takers pay for the privilege of taking the test in most instances; then the test administrator performs the nifty trick of turning around and selling colleges access to the data so they can use it for marketing.

The merit aid strategizing extends to figuring out what to say to the students during the courtship and finding out whether they need incentives, such as application fee waivers. Once high school seniors apply, schools often use algorithms and software to predict what sort of discount to offer, if any, to get them to say yes. The wooing continues over the summer lest incoming students change their minds during what is known as the "summer melt" period. Finally, schools track the undergraduates themselves once they arrive, since any single one who drops out or transfers can represent lost revenue of well over $100,000.

This is where the $1 billion comes in. Given the stakes, most colleges have long since stopped trying to manipulate the data themselves. Instead, most of them spend piles of money on consultants who suck in the figures and put the numbers through proprietary algorithms. The software spits out custom-crafted, head-spinning offer grids that help dictate who gets what amount of merit aid. You've probably never heard of these companies (though I quoted one of them, Ruffalo Noel Levitz, earlier), and they and their clients are fine with that. When they market themselves to colleges, they refer to what they do as "financial aid optimization." That sounds rather nice, with its hints of smoothing things out and spreading the discounts around so all students get just what they need. But eventually the firms get around to using the word "leverage," as in using brute force, involving large amounts of money to maximum advantage.

The consultants help schools leverage information about your family to optimize your discount, if any, and the process can get quite granular. Each year, colleges decide where their priorities lie, and they mostly have similar goals. They hope to attract a larger pool of applicants who are more racially and geographically diverse than the previous year's pool and who have even better credentials. They would also like their net tuition revenue per student—the money they take in after all need-based and merit grant aid—to rise. And they want to lose even fewer students to their rivals.

To try to win—or not to lose ground, at least—the consultants help schools keep track of which students are coming to their websites, how much time they spend on which page, and how quickly they open emails. The schools tap into proprietary databases that the consultants maintain in order to track the quality of thousands of high schools and the sorts of colleges that their graduates have attended in the past. Then the consultants pull in as much data from each college as it has, including what sorts of students responded to earlier marketing campaigns and the numbers and demographics of all the people who applied, who got in, and who matriculated at what price point. Once the latest applicant pool is in place, the consultants provide algorithms that suggest what size discount, if any, to offer to whom.

Human beings can and do intervene. Some merit programs are limited or lucrative enough that real people run the entire process. In others, admissions officers grade each admitted student with a numerical score that translates into a merit aid offer. But overall, software does far more work than most applicants ever know. Because algorithms don't know what to do until humans program them, it might be helpful to consider a programming script that amounts to something like this: "Discount only as much as you have to in order to get someone to say yes, but not one dollar more. And for people living in affluent zip codes, keep in mind that even a mere $10,000 is probably enough to get them to feel good about themselves so that they're not the only sucker paying full price and can run around town saying that their kid got an academic scholarship."

This is probably a bit too cynical. Then again, several years ago one of the biggest consultants got caught pitching a brilliantly evil bit of strategy based off a clever reading of the FAFSA form. On that form, applicants state which schools they want to receive their data. What the consultant discovered is that lots of families would list those schools in order of preference. Schools that found themselves on top of lots of lists could keep that in mind when considering how much aid to offer to families who seemed desperate to attend. Wink, wink. Nod, nod. Word got out, and within a few years, the schools could no longer see the order in which families listed recipient colleges.

But the enablers are not the part of the merit aid system that has the potential to be most problematic. Instead, the most disturbing element is probably the inequity that can result. One take goes like this: Taken to its extreme, merit aid uses money that could go to less affluent students and replaces them with people who could afford to pay but just aren't willing to do so. If your list price is $70,000 per year and you give $20,000 per year in merit aid to a student, that's $200,000 in revenue over four years. If it costs only $150,000 to educate that student over the four years, you're coming out ahead.

And that $200,000 student might replace one whose family can afford to pay only $100,000 over four years, thus requiring a $50,000 subsidy from the school to get to that $150,000 break-even number. Sure, the families who can pay more might have children with better grades and scores, but that's at least in part because of long-standing links between affluence and, say, the ability to hire an SAT tutor. By not only admitting disproportionate numbers of affluent students but actually throwing money at them if they come, the schools simply perpetuate the inequities.

Schools have a number of responses to that. Some are rather blunt, as when the financial aid director at Boston University demanded to know, in 1995, why she had an obligation to educate poor students in the first place. Wasn't that the federal government's job—one it was failing at, given how low the maximum Pell Grant for low-income students was and the fact that the student loan system didn't support borrowers properly? At the College of the Holy Cross in Worcester, Massachusetts, the financial aid director stated quite plainly that ethics in the field had shifted away from principles of egalitarianism. Instead, the need for sheer survival in the marketplace necessitated budgetary tactics that would have been unimaginable a few decades earlier.

Other schools maintain that they have committed no sins of inequity, and some of them may have a point. Here's their challenge: The marketplace has spoken, and there are only so many people in any given year who are able to pay full price. Willingness is another thing, especially in an environment in which competing schools have gotten into the habit of offering unpredictable discounts. As a result, if your school doesn't give a certain number of $15,000 discounts to people who can afford to pay your $60,000 list price but won't, you won't have enough people paying $45,000 to cross-subsidize the ones who can pay only $15,000 or less. Few schools have an endowment big enough to have un-limited numbers of undergraduates with lots of financial need, so they have to use tuition dollars from that same year to pay for the need-based aid. But there are very few private colleges that are enticing enough to attract lots of affluent people who are willing to pay full price or close to it. And so we get merit aid, which the schools hope will allow them to have a respectable mix come Labor Day of students from across the social-class spectrum.

Jerome A. Lucido runs the University of Southern California's Center for Enrollment Research, Policy and Practice and oversaw the universi-ty's enrollment operation in a previous role. He suggests thinking about financial aid in one of three ways. First, there is true merit aid, which is a scholarship that may come with additional opportunities, such as admission into an honors program and mentorship opportunities with faculty. "I think that is distinctly different from merit aid that is really a discount [the second kind], where they're using predictive modeling and analytics to determine how much people in your neighborhood are willing to pay while still allowing me to add to net tuition revenue at my school," he said. The third kind is the old-school financial aid that schools base entirely on students' demonstrated need.

There is an additional phenomenon to be aware of that has muddied the waters further: Many colleges, acting on their consultants' advice, give out merit aid and use it to cover part of a student's demonstrated financial need. The National Association of College and University Busi-ness Officers produces an annual discounting study that collects data from hundreds of member schools. For years now it has found that scores of colleges are using more than half of their merit aid to meet financial need. The organization sees this as evidence that the need-versus-merit discussion is a "false dichotomy."

I'd urge you to think about it differently. If there were no difference between how merit and need-based aid affected families, colleges would use just one term or the other or find a neutral one. In many instances, there doesn't seem to be any difference from an accounting perspective: A discount is a discount, no matter what it's called. But colleges know from the very data that their consultants help them process that patting people on the head and calling them meritorious will make them feel good about themselves. Their professors have studied it in fact, with one paper showing that if a scholarship has a name, it can materially affect a prospective student's decision-making. Perhaps the recipients should feel good. And perhaps they should also understand that these kinds of merit awards are, at least in part, about marketing. Marketing aims to make people feel a certain way.

However inequitable merit aid may seem in certain circumstances, I'm not here to argue that you shouldn't take it if a school offers it to you. I've never heard anyone else make that case, either. Take whatever you can get. The challenge here, which is an extension of the one we saw with need-based financial aid, is that it can be very difficult to predict if a school will offer you merit aid and how much. It bears repeating, and I'll say it a few more times before this book is done: Schools ask families to jump through several application hoops just to put themselves in the running to write some of the biggest checks they'll ever write, but you often don't get to find out the amount until several months into the process. That takes some nerve.

At least with need-based financial aid there are net price calculators that are reasonably accurate. But plenty of net price calculators do not predict how much merit aid a school might offer. College websites aren't always helpful, either. Large public universities may publish the tables they use internally, where one axis has test scores and the other has grade point averages. Then you look to the intersections to see how much of a discount you might expect. Less selective private colleges such as Wabash in Indiana are kind enough—or desperate enough—to offer this welcome transparency, too. Nearly every college publishes a list of statistics called the common data set (CDS) that offers some merit aid prediction hints. I'll walk you through a typical merit aid data hunt using the CDS in Chapter 31.

I spent a couple of years in a state of reportorial rage over the fact that at many of the more selective schools that offer merit aid, there is no surefire way to know even within a five-figure amount how much of a discount a school might provide. I made my case for change in the offices of twenty or so college and university presidents and vice presidents of enrollment, occasionally raising my voice in frustration. Did these people, I wondered, have any idea what it was like to try to pick schools to apply to or plot a financial strategy while having no earthly idea how much it might cost? They do and they don't. They certainly hear it from the few families who are bold enough to complain and ask pointed questions. Then again, many of the enrollment management professionals work for schools that offer tuition breaks of various sorts—often quite large ones—to the children of staff members. They are quite literally not operating in the same kind of marketplace that we are when they go shopping for colleges for their own kids.

The most reasonable defense that the schools offer up of the system's opaqueness goes something like this: "How would you propose we make this more predictable? Rely on test scores that wealthier high school students tend to do better on?" (This is ironic, given that some schools use merit aid specifically to make sure they have enough affluent students.) "And if not test scores, then we'd need to predict and hand out merit aid on the basis of high school grades. Be careful what you wish for there, because grades can mean wildly different things in different schools. Some schools use curves, while others use cutoffs. Plus, you probably want us to adjust for the degree of difficulty of the classes an applicant takes or correct any overly optimistic recalculation that a school does itself when it adjusts its own averages. And we also need to be fair to applicants from high schools that don't offer as many higher-level classes."

Case Western Reserve is a university with scientific backbone, given its historical strength in medicine and lab work. Its head of enrollment management, Rick Bischoff, is one of the more data-driven people in his field. When I met with him in his Cleveland office, he had a child on the cusp of applying to college himself. His wife is a college counselor at a private school. He gets it. "What else do you buy where you don't know the prices until you've already limited your choices?" he asked nonrhetorically, unable to come up with an answer besides higher education.

Yet he would not agree to my demand that he build a merit aid prediction engine to make the application process easier. It's not that it's impossible, he told me. It may not even be that it's too expensive, although it would take a fair bit of ingenuity to get the software code right. It's just that it's impractical. "An algorithm is a perfect predictor of what happened in the past. They're amazing!" he said. "Where you lose sleep is in the fact that they don't tell you anything about what the current environment is and if something is changing."

In other words, software can't help Case Western Reserve predict what a new enrollment management vice president will do at a competing school or how students will react to a new honors dorm at Ohio State. And it can't tell a family in October how Case might have to react in March when it becomes clear that market conditions have changed for that year's students. Indeed, any such merit predictor machine could not have predicted the market conditions in April 2020, a month after the pandemic hit and weeks before families had to commit to a college.

Objections to a merit aid prediction calculator are all quite sensible, but it's also quite convenient for the schools that don't provide one. Colleges and universities that operate this way get to shield their discounting formulas from the view of competitors. They also preserve the ability to offer whatever merit aid discounts they need to favor violinists and the deeply religious over French scholars and teenage entrepreneurs, depending on where an institution might feel depleted in any given year. Maintaining flexibility and the resulting campus-wide balance of talents is a reasonable goal; any accompanying lack of clarity for price-conscious potential consumers of the education is a feature, not a bug! But it leads naturally to the following logic: *I'd better apply to as many schools as possible in the hope that one of them will offer outsized merit aid. After all, I can't possibly guess which school might do that.* This is how the system creates more work for everyone, with high school juniors and seniors tearing their hair out and admissions officers up all night for months each year scouring an increasing number of applications and running thousands and thousands of numbers.

I'll give you a step-by-step tactical guide to finding out what you can about need-based and merit aid at the colleges of your choosing in Chapter 31. But for now let's dispense with a couple of big questions about merit aid that may have come to mind already.

If so many schools feel as though they have to discount, why don't they just lower their list prices permanently—or at least stop raising them each year?

There are at least two reasons. The first is that some families do pay the list price, and the colleges are always hoping against nearly all reason that they'll be able to find more of them the following year. If you live in a high-income zip code, you now know why your high school–age child gets so much mail from colleges. But who pays list price at schools that offer merit aid to lots of students but not all of them? Some families are simply relieved that the applicant has anywhere to go at all after a rough high school experience of whatever sort. Their full-size tuition checks come stained with sweat, printed on paper stock from the Bank of Thank God. Colleges also seek out affluent students who come from outside the United States. If they cut the list price, they give up money that those families would gladly hand over.

The second reason many colleges avoid big price cuts is due to something that people in the trade call the "Chivas Regal effect." As the legend has it (a Chivas representative said that the company was "unable" to discuss the actual facts with me and stopped responding when I asked why that was), several decades ago this middlebrow Scotch whisky raised its prices overnight only to find that the result was the sale of many more bottles. A tuition-setting strategy was born on the similar assumption that people believe that high prices signal high quality. Rice University, which has a giant endowment, subsidized its tuition for years with the earnings from it but came to believe that its low list price suggested that it wasn't as good as Harvard or even Emory. It raised its price dramatically and never looked back. Mount Holyoke College had success with regular double-digit percentage increases in the 1980s; the average SAT scores of students there rose in the wake of them. Even in the thick of the application process, plenty of families never learn what percentage of students at any given school are not actually paying the list price. So colleges try to maintain the glossy shine of a high retail rate as best they can.

A few brave colleges and universities, however, have dispensed with the charade. They came to the following conclusion: For every person who believed that price equaled quality, there were untold numbers of others who never gave them a second look because their list price was so high. After all, how were prospective applicants to know that the list price wasn't real? Even if they did figure it out, they'd then encounter a system in which the actual price wasn't easy to predict and the school wouldn't guarantee the total until after a student applied and won admission. So Drew University in New Jersey, feeling sheepish about the fact that its list price wasn't far from that of its much more prestigious fellow state resident Princeton, cut its price by five figures. The next year, enrollment of first-year students went up while it still received about the same amount of revenue per student. St. John's College, the liberal arts school in Maryland and New Mexico with a unique core curriculum, made a similar move.

Given how carefully colleges track prospective students, is it possible that appearing too eager will cause them to offer me a smaller discount?

No one wants to admit that this goes on, and the consultants say that they discourage this sort of thing. (Insiders who would like to confide in me can find me easily via my website.) That said, it has happened in the past. The *Wall Street Journal* documented it in a front-page story in 1996 in which it caught Carnegie Mellon offering less financial aid to students applying through an early admission program than ones who raised their hands later in the process.

This isn't all that surprising if you think about it. If you were an enrollment management administrator, what would you do? When high school seniors apply early decision, they are agreeing that they will come if they win admission. These students might as well broadcast that they are not all that sensitive to price. Given that fact, what reason is there to be generous with discounts that early in the admission season?

This raises a related question: Is it OK to walk away from a supposedly binding early decision offer if you don't get enough merit aid to make the school affordable, in your eyes? The answer is yes, with some qualifications. If a school won't predict merit aid in a grid or a net price calculator or a pre-application phone call, it can't very well expect you to come if it lowballs you on merit aid. Let's be crystal clear about this, too: Early decision is not a legal contract, and it's not binding. Pin the schools down (as I did a few times in 2021 and 2022—just search online for "Ron Lieber, New York Times, early decision, New York University, and Northeastern" to read more about it), and they'll tell you straight up that if you can't afford the quoted price, you can walk away from an early decision acceptance.

Also, these colleges won't hold it against future students from your high school if you walk away for financial reasons. If your high school counselor tells you differently, please tell that person to read my columns and then send me a note about it. I've searched high and low for years for proof of such vengeance, and I believe it to be a myth. I've asked admissions deans about it over and over, and they look at me cross-eyed; why would they want to get a reputation for behaving in that fashion toward people who can't afford the prices they quote when the market for the best students is competitive?

And one more thing: If a small group of applicants is opening every email from you within thirty minutes of receipt, are they the ones who would need the biggest discounts to convince them to enroll if they get in? Families who are price sensitive ought to think very hard before applying early decision, unless the target school is a well resourced one that guarantees to meet all of the need you've demonstrated in your need-based financial aid application. If you're not applying early decision, consider playing it at least a little bit coy. On the one hand, many schools give you extra credit in the admissions process for showing what is known as demonstrated interest. But if you're overly demonstrative, they may believe that they have you right where they want you financially.

Are we really to believe that schools that do not offer merit aid are not using targeted, more generous need-based aid to attract the students that they most want to enroll?

No, there are almost certainly colleges that use outsized need-based aid offers to win over some students. Katharine Harrington, the former chief enrollment officer at the University of Southern California, has presided over a huge leap in selectivity at the school over the last fifteen years. She describes the undergraduate part of her operation quite carefully as the most selective institution that "admits" to giving merit aid. "I think it's not a state secret that schools—all kinds of schools—give aid to people that they most want to come," she said. I asked her to clarify, just to be certain: Was she saying that colleges that claim that they give out financial aid only on the basis of need may offer $50,000 in grants each year to an applicant whose family could actually pay $50,000? She just smiled.

We have no proof that this is so—not exactly. What we do know is that families submit the same financial information to every college and get a bunch of different need-based aid offers in return. Sometimes we know why, and sometimes we have no idea why. Even the most storied undergraduate institutions will often raise a need-based financial aid offer if you present them with a better one from a school that they'd rather not lose you to. We'll discuss this and other bargaining tactics in Chapter 33.

Are colleges and the people who oversee them proud of this system—one that features semihidden wheeling and dealing and the kicking of asses that the gentleman from Oregon State mentioned? Not exactly, but nearly all of them arrived in their respective positions to find it fully in effect and gaining momentum. Sean M. Decatur, the president of Kenyon, looks at his budget and doesn't see any easy way to change what goes on. He runs a selective liberal arts college with an endowment bigger than what most other schools have, but it still doesn't produce enough income to cover more than a fraction of his budget for need-based financial aid. "Significant increases in the financial aid budget must come at the expense of raising tuition," he said.

That means that most schools must get every last bit of revenue they can from those with both the ability and the willingness to pay. As for the rest of the applicants, especially those students who have a lot of choices because they can make classrooms and campuses come alive in a variety of ways, there must be merit aid awards. "I wish it weren't necessary," said Brian Rosenberg, Macalester's former president. "It's a necessary evil right now. We're not a place that is so financially secure with a reputation so strong that we're just going to get all of those types of students. And I get impatient with people who think it's an easy decision or that schools that give much more merit aid than we do are somehow being morally corrupt. They're trying to keep their schools open."

Indeed, the chorus of critics is growing louder. New America, a Washington, D.C., think tank, has produced a fair bit of research making the case that merit aid, especially in public universities, comes at the expense of helping poor students afford college. Zakiya Smith Ellis, a former Obama White House staffer who also did a stint as New Jersey's secretary of higher education, lamented the state of affairs on the *Bad with Money with Gaby Dunn* podcast. She noted that she had grown up in the earlier era of student debt, when if you borrowed, it meant that you were doing something good for yourself. "Colleges actually, believe it or not, preyed on that," she said of private institutions. "There were whole colleges who had their strategy as being 'We are going to artificially increase our price, even if we don't expect people to pay it.' They increased their price, and then what they did is they gave people bogus scholarships to make them think they got a discount on the price."

The host, Gaby Dunn, who is not that many years out of Emerson College in Boston and its attendant debt herself, gasped repeatedly before concluding "This is evil."

Or hocus-pocus at least. La Salle University in Philadelphia is one of the schools that reset its tuition, cutting it by 29 percent in 2017. "We had a sticker price at that time, close to $41,000, that almost nobody was paying," Colleen M. Hanycz, La Salle's president, told the *Washington Post*. Quite frequently, families had to navigate what she described as a bunch of "Wizard of Oz nonsense" to figure out what the true price would be. She was especially upset at how hard it was for families who were sending a teenager to college for the first time to do the dance the school was leading them through. "I really couldn't stand the inequity in that," she added.

La Salle still awards some merit aid, as do Drew and other schools that have lowered the list price of their tuition. So they haven't exactly solved for the madness. Meanwhile, more selective schools show no sign of stepping back from it all, even if they find themselves saying "sorry" as they try to explain what is nearly unexplainable.

"I would argue that the merit arms race is designed to quietly apologize for huge price increases," said Michael Kyle, St. Olaf College's vice president for enrollment. "How do we explain this high-tuition, high-discount model? We're going to meet your perceived need by having this amorphous category called merit, and it is an arms race. Who is going to have the courage to say that this just has to stop?"

CHAPTER 5

But Wait, Isn't Tuition a Bubble, and All of Higher Education Is Going to Come Apart at the Seams?

Why bother scheming and saving for a six-figure expenditure per child if the system isn't going to look anything like it does now by the time your kid goes to college?

If you believe that the price of an undergraduate education is too high and that the discounting system is so fundamentally broken that things surely cannot continue as they have, you are not alone. Then again, insiders who are a lot more knowledgeable than you or I have been saying so forcefully for decades, and they've all been wrong so far.

In a 1971 report titled "The New Depression in Higher Education," the author claimed that the cost of college was reaching a "saturation point." The next year, Amherst's assistant director of admission worried aloud about the children of white-collar workers and possible anarchy if schools had to give out more financial aid. Stanford's dean of financial aid chimed in too and seemed ready to throw up his hands, owing to the fact that the financial sacrifices he was asking families to make "border on the ridiculous."

By 1984, insiders were predicting that somewhere between 10 and 30 percent of colleges in the United States would close in the next decade. In 1986, others became more pessimistic, thinking that close to 30 percent of schools were in imminent danger. Then one self-styled seer asserted that the right number was actually 50 percent. That prediction arrived in 2017 out of the mouth of the late famed business guru and Harvard Business School professor Clayton M. Christensen, the author of *The Innovator's Dilemma: When New Technologies Cause Great Firms to Fail*. He figured it would take until 2030 or so to happen.

Why have all of these members of the college cognoscenti been so off so far, and is it possible that the pandemic could make their predictions come true? And if it is possible, should you make a financial bet on their being right by not saving much for your younger children?

To try to answer, we should turn to facts before we get to feelings. Perhaps you're aware of the baby bust that took place starting in 2007, when economic conditions grew so bad that people had fewer children. Maybe you did the math on the child you had in a burst of optimism in 2009 and are now crossing your fingers that prices will fall dramatically by 2027, when the number of eighteen-year-olds in the United States will have fallen as well.

Many colleges and universities are also worried about these numbers, and when they want someone to explain them in more detail, they often call on Nathan D. Grawe, a professor at Carleton College and the author of a book called *Demographics and the Demand for Higher Education*. There he forecasted that there will be 150,000 (or 10 percent) fewer students in four-year colleges in 2029 than in 2018, when he published the book. But getting into the more selective schools may not get any easier. He believes that there will be 20,000 *more* students with the qualifications to attend a top-fifty *U.S. News & World Report*–ranked institution by that year and expects some trickling down of those students through the collegiate food chain. After all, the institutions that are hardest to gain admission to tend not to make space for more undergraduates, given the incentives that exist to maintain as much selectivity as possible.

The pricing projections aren't particularly promising, either. Even as the overall number of students falls, Grawe still expects the percentage of people who might be willing to pay full price or close to it to grow. How can that be? Blame income inequality and the richer getting richer. As a proxy, he looked at both household income (families in the top 13 percent) and the likelihood of having parents who are college graduates themselves. He expects the growth in full-pay families to be 30 percent from 2012 to 2025. Then, when the mini–demographic cliff hits, he figures the number of full payers will fall by 15 percent by 2029, leaving a net increase of 10 percent. As a result, the share of full-pay families relative to the college-going population will actually increase, from 6.5 percent to 7.5 percent. Among the families of students attending four-year colleges, it will jump from 13 percent to 16 percent.

What might these families be willing and unwilling to pay for? In the last two decades, we've had a partial test of this possibility in the more selective part of the higher education market. As more people have applied to the twenty-five most selective colleges, students who once might have gone to one of them and happily paid full price can no longer get in. Some of them default at that point to their flagship state universities, although admission is no sure thing in states such as Virginia, Michigan, and Texas and in the University of California system.

Meanwhile, private colleges and universities, especially ones close to popular cities, have buffed themselves up and attracted plenty of applicants from full-pay families or those who can pay most of the tuition. There have been so many, in fact, that their own admission rates have fallen accordingly. Witness what's happened at Northeastern University, Tufts University, George Washington University, New York University, Emory University, Tulane University, and the University of Southern California. These are nobody's safety schools anymore. Some of these schools, such as Northeastern and Tulane, have used merit aid pretty aggressively and are now trying to back off some, given how selective they've become. Others, such as Tufts, have not yet had to offer discounts for families who are able to pay.

But at all of these schools, plenty of families that are shut out of the most selective colleges and universities seem happy to pay double the cost of their state university or more to have their children matriculate a bit lower down the list of the most selective schools. Others will pay extra to send their teenagers to out-of-state public universities that have worked hard to make themselves attractive to teenagers from far away, sometimes in places they might not have considered two decades ago, such as Alabama or Delaware.

In March 2020, we got a different kind of test, one that almost no one saw coming but caused nearly everyone to ask pointed questions about what kind of value undergraduate institutions were delivering. Schools shut down as the coronavirus swept across the country, students went home, and everyone got a crash course in technology-enabled education.

It was an unfair proving ground for technologists who had been working on instructional design and software for decades and then had to roll it out widely in a matter of weeks. All sorts of professors who had never taught that way had to start calling on these experts (or ignoring them and just setting up endless Zoom calls) all at once. When it didn't go well, which it didn't in the majority of instances, the people paying the bills howled in protest. Students who did not have good high-speed internet service, a quiet place to work, or a home to return to suffered disproportionately. So did anyone who was struggling to keep up with college-level courses in the first place. The entire episode and the relentlessly bad publicity surrounding it, including a wave of lawsuits and petitions demanding partial tuition refunds, may well have set the cause of further adoption of online learning in residential universities back for years.

But in theory, it is also possible that the pandemic and schools' reactions to it could stoke demand for a radical alternative to the live-and-learn-on-campus experience, if someone could just manage to create one at scale. After all, consider just how much mistrust colleges managed to sow in a matter of months.

People choose a residential undergraduate program because there is something special about bunking down with your peers and being among your professors. And after spring break 2020, people were no longer getting what they'd paid for. Yes, there were prorated room and board refunds when people did not return to campus, but the education was no longer the same and neither was the kinship. Nevertheless, families didn't get any tuition money back. Moreover, with only a handful of exceptions, most schools kept their price the same or even raised it a normal amount for the fall semester, even though the undergraduate experience continued to be compromised. Sure, the schools had experienced increased costs of their own for technology and virus mitigation. But to many families, there appeared to be exactly zero sense of shared sacrifice coming from college and university administrators.

What followed felt even more insulting. Schools such as Columbia, Bowdoin, and Princeton told students that if they chose to sit out a semester or take an entire gap year to avoid what would clearly be a diminished experience, the school couldn't promise them reentry at the exact moment that they might choose or a dorm room on campus. At the same time, other schools were asking returning students to sign liability waivers or letting them know that they wouldn't get their housing fees back if the dorms closed in midsemester during an outbreak. The University of North Carolina gambled on reopening, at least in part because the state system, like so many others, desperately needed the tuition and fee revenue. Then, after hundreds of students tested positive for the coronavirus, administrators blamed them for gathering in groups. At Northeastern University, administrators kicked a bunch of students out for having a small party and refused to refund their tuition. Did these schools not expect that adolescents would gather on campus lawns when plenty of grown-ups were gathering outdoors on both sides of the protests that took place daily that summer? The overall frustration grew bad enough in August that one parent sought me out for advice on filing a police report. Her daughter's small liberal arts college wouldn't change her financial aid package after it pivoted to online learning only, and she wanted to pursue theft charges.

Where will this leave us, when raw feelings abate? To me, the hints are everywhere. Adolescents crave contact. The administrators who welcomed significant numbers of students back to campus—but then professed to be shocked when they wanted to hang out with one another—were delusional. At schools where students were not welcomed back to on-campus housing, plenty of students podded up to live together nearby anyhow, even though they could not enter campus buildings. Others rented cheap houses halfway across the country to do Zoom school from there.

Meanwhile, the recovery from that particular recession, during which low-income service workers were hit hardest, was K-shaped, with the top quartile of American families coming out of it in better shape than they went into it. After all, most of their savings rates have gone up due to their having cut travel, restaurants, and much new clothing out of their budgets. The emerging trust gap aside, these families may well line up to pay just as much or more than they would have in 2019 for the residential undergraduate experience that students so obviously miss, now that its short-term replacement has proven to be so unsatisfying. What other choice will they have?

A reminder: We are talking about just one segment of the higher education market here. Not everyone wants a residential undergraduate experience. Plenty of traditional-age college students live with their parents to save money, work twenty hours per week, commute to college, and graduate in six years instead of four. Many of the schools that educate those students were already doing plenty of teaching online, and the instructors there had the expertise to do it well. Plenty of parents with an older child who has a less-than-satisfactory experience with a virus-compromised attempt to live on campus for four years may be exhausted by resentment. A few of them might well order their younger kids into an online-only degree program at a fraction of the cost, just to spite the system.

But that isn't what true disruption is made of. And if you've read this far into the chapter, it's probably because you're rooting for someone to find a way to provide all of the good things about a residential undergraduate experience at a much lower price. It would need to deliver a mind-blowing education cheaply, provide kinship and contact with peers and potential mentors, and end with a credential that would be universally useful in the labor market.

So what are the odds of its happening in time to help a young child who is already living in your home? Perhaps a better question is this: What is the incentive for anyone to try to create a school that could do it? Sure, a great deal of investment capital has been aimed at reinventing higher education. But investors want returns, and that means producing revenue and earning profits. If you've read anything about for-profit education, you know that a fair number of bad actors provided low-quality classes while collecting a significant portion of their revenue from people taking out loans or using their military education benefits. Then the former students often couldn't get decent jobs in their fields after they were done, if they finished at all. This is not the solution you seek.

Now consider the gatekeepers. Sure, tuition-paying families are the ultimate deciders in higher education, but before a college can expect to thrive it almost always has to be accredited. The incumbent accredited institutions will not be so happy about interlopers who are shouting loudly about how they can do it better and cheaper. Any new state college or university will be jockeying with the existing branch schools in its system for resources. Private, nonprofit startup universities, meanwhile, need many millions of dollars to launch at scale. Then their graduates need to persuade employers to hire them, even though the school has no track record. There are very few schools in that category that have been successful in the last fifty years.

But let's say a bunch of startups tried anyhow. Any new school—university, college, company, institution, or whatever people might call it—would presumably need to rely heavily on technology. There would be software and template lectures and lessons and assessment tools that students could access from a single device or in some kind of flexible classroom setting anywhere. Those students (customers?) would presumably still want—and probably need, depending on who sets the school's standards—to make presentations to one another, learn to operate in teams, conduct lab work, and produce thousands of words of writing. Could they do that without a campus or something resembling one? And although ever-evolving software might well be able to assess some of their progress better than human beings could, students would still crave mentorship. These schools, then, would need to find teachers who wanted to work in such settings—settings that will presumably need to cut, for cost reasons, the total number of human professors and administrators that make college so expensive (but often so good) at present.

None of that would be easy. Sure, plenty of undergraduates could prepare, robotlike, for certain careers in this way. Would their parents make them choose it? Would they even dare to try?

One of the most reasonable visions for a great unraveling is the one Kevin Carey laid out in his 2015 book *The End of College: Creating the Future of Learning and the University of Everywhere*. He described that soon-to-come "university of everywhere" as a digitally driven experience that artificial intelligence will enable through "immersive digital learning environments." It will not make students feel isolated—and why should it, given how many real connections people already make in online communities? It will be "different but not solitary." It will lead, inevitably, to a "brutal unmasking" of many traditional colleges and universities that try to do too many things well but ultimately fail at training and teaching undergraduates. And it will happen well within the lifetimes of the children who are currently in grade school.

There is no reason to doubt the basic through line of the case Carey makes. It seems logical that anything that has changed so little over time yet costs so much money will eventually be run over by a freight train of technology-fueled innovation. But it didn't happen in the years after his book came out. So my question for him as I was finishing this book was this: Will the coronavirus be the trigger for dozens of colleges and universities to close each year, instead of a mere handful? And will any resulting consumer behavioral change leave undergraduate education looking more like the travel agency and independent bookstore industry? In those industries, plenty of good businesses survived in the wake of the internet onslaught. Or is this more akin to the record stores that were selling new music circa 1995 and experienced a kind of mass extinction event?

When I caught up with him in August 2020, he was on vacation in Vermont. That same week, by sheer coincidence, the out-of-business Green Mountain College was auctioning itself off down the road from where he was staying—the entire campus and everything on it. The notice had pegged the value at $20 million, and it had sold for just $4.5 million. But he wasn't ready to predict that there would be scores more similar scenarios in the coming years, nor is he rooting for that at all.

It can be hard to kill off a college, it turns out. Smaller branches of public universities are often major local employers and have strong political constituencies. Meanwhile, alumni often swoop in to rescue older and better-known private colleges that run into financial trouble. Perhaps you read a bit about Sweet Briar College's or Hampshire College's near-death experiences in recent years. Those didn't go the way of Green Mountain College because alumni came out of the woodwork to prop them up again. "I think people have a want and a need to be connected to other people," Carey said during our call. "Modern society is pretty atomized, and college-going people in particular don't have the same connection to regional identity, and families are all over the place. But you have an emotional relationship with your college, and that is part of what people are buying." And once they buy it, they will do a lot to preserve it.

Our idea—our ideal—of college will probably be similarly hard to alter in any kind of fundamental way. "There is an extremely strong cultural investment in a specific idea of college, where people don't just go to get a credential," Carey said. "It's a stage of life, a set of experiences that can exist only at the particular institutions that can provide them. Or at least people think that."

Think about it in another way too: If what you and your family seek from college is the credential alone, the traditional residential undergraduate experience may not have been a good value for you even before the pandemic. Schools from Southern New Hampshire University to Arizona State have spent years building digital infrastructure to offer bachelor's degrees at cheaper prices. If you believe—and the schools can persuade you—that employers in your chosen field will hire you based on that degree, you might extract the most possible value from the experience of acquiring it from them.

But will that way of learning and earning a degree become so popular that it will quickly crowd out the institutions that invite students to live there for four years? The answer depends in large part on a theory that Jon McGee laid out in his book *Breakpoint*. McGee is an administrator at the College of Saint Benedict and Saint John's University in Minnesota. It's a gorgeous place with some stunning architecture. Visitors are given a loaf of fresh-baked bread to take home with them after stopping in, and mine was so good that it did not survive a two-hour drive. It would be a shame if a place like that were to ever disappear.

To McGee, the persistence of his institution and others like it may well depend on how far higher education consumers move down a continuum toward viewing the overall experience as merely transactional instead of utterly transformational. If enough people continue to believe that college is a rite of passage—something to be experienced and not just checked off a list—there will continue to be many hundreds of residential undergraduate institutions charging something like the prices that they charge today.

Kevin Carey was already a father when *The End of College* came out. His child is growing quickly. And when it came time to put money on the line—to bet, in effect, on the medium-term future of college looking and costing something like it does right now—he did indeed start putting money away regularly in a 529 college savings account.

I wasn't surprised to hear it. These are our children that we're talking about after all—four pivotal (and yes, ideally transformational in my mind) years of their lives. They are four years that our parents perhaps made possible for us. Or maybe we spent years paying off debts and want to spare our children that ordeal, while giving them a more carefree undergraduate experience in which to thrive. Even if the robots come for us—come to us, arms extended—are large numbers of us going to turn our backs on a traditional residential college? Will we willingly turn our children into guinea pigs for the artificial intelligence conjured up by programmers in Silicon Valley in league with venture capitalists looking for a payoff?

Maybe. Someday soon, perhaps. But in the meantime, like Kevin Carey, I'm saving and planning as if the cut-rate $50,000 four-year solution—one that my kids will crave, that will seem safe to me and my wife, and will be blessed by employers and the federal government—isn't close enough ahead that it will be a realistic choice for children who are already alive.

PART II

The Unhelpful Feelings You May Feel

CHAPTER 6

Fear

If you happened to attend a selective college back in the day, you've probably heard the following come out of a former classmate's mouth in recent years: "I could never get in today." Maybe you've said it yourself. I know I have.

But what if your kid can't get in now, either?

Or maybe you went to your flagship state university. Perhaps it was undervalued back then, but it isn't anymore. As more parents in your home state and surrounding ones have become more conscious of price and value, admissions standards have tightened. Meanwhile, your child of above-average intelligence may also be one of above-average indifference or struggles with mental health issues or concentration. It could be that this child will need to consider completely different options.

What then? What now? Most of us become parents with the assumption—or at least the hope—that our kids will do better and achieve more than we have. Upward mobility is a sort of presumptive birthright. And in the world of private colleges, the preservation of status was nearly an entitlement not that long ago: If your parents attended a school, the institution would bend over backward to make sure you could, too.

But if you attended a selective college, this assumption has become nothing more than an emotional setup. Legacy admissions preferences don't provide near-guaranteed admission for mediocre students the way they once did. And although we don't really have any kind of a narrative of downward mobility in America, none of us wants to be a pioneer in that literary field, either. So if our kids don't attend schools as prestigious as the ones that we did, what will become of them? Will they do less, earn less, be less? What if the school they attend is less selective than the ones that the majority of other kids in our community get into? How will it affect our children's odds of being able to afford to return to the place they grew up if they want and raise a family there one day? If this is you or you're worried that it might be, it's not hard for your mind to end up in places that feel scary. And that's under the best of economic circumstances.

The fear of our children tumbling down the status, salary, and social class ladders that many of us have spent decades climbing or clinging to is a documented phenomenon. According to the Pew Research Center, 58 percent of Americans believe that the children walking around today will be worse off financially when they grow up than their parents are now. Just 37 percent expect them to do better, while the rest figure things won't change much at all. People over fifty are particularly pessimistic: Just 32 percent of them figure that the next generation will be better off.

That's a vague term, though, "better off." To some people, it means that their children will earn more money than they did. Even that word "more" is messy, given that most people don't have inflation calculators in their brains computing what they earned when they were twenty-three and how their own financial trajectories have changed over time.

To others, success means measuring themselves against those around them. If you live in an unremarkable house in a town with a middling school district, perhaps you hope your own child will live someplace better someday. And if your household income hovers around the mid-80s in percentile terms, with 15 percent of Americans earning more than you, perhaps you hope your kids will rise to the 95th percentile, where they won't have to think as hard as you do about what to pay for college.

However you define "better off," we have a lot more data than we used to on recent trend lines. If parenting is at least in part about prudent risk management, it pays to take a quick look at the actuarial data.

Let's begin with the first iteration of "better off": whether children at age thirty will earn more than their parents did at the same age. The leading research lab on these questions titles its paper on the matter "The Fading American Dream." People born in 1940 had over a 90 percent chance of earning more than their parents. Babies born in the early 1960s saw the likelihood fall below 60 percent. And by the early 1980s, we were close to 50-50. For those born upper middle class, the numbers were worse by then. Those people had only a 30 percent chance of earning more than their parents.

But what if your dream is for your children to have a better social class standing than you in relation to every other American—"relative" mobility, in economic terms, instead of the "absolute" mobility that those 50-50 odds represent? There the prognosis is a little better. Most young adults starting work as of the late 2010s had the same chance of improving their spot on the income distribution charts as the newly employed did in the 1990s.

Much does depend on where you start. If you were born into the top quintile of income, you have a better chance of landing there by age twenty-six, on average, than any of the people in the next four quintiles. Even so, just over 30 percent of people who were born lucky will remain in the highest quintile at twenty-six, so there are hardly any guarantees, at least for young adults. Just under 10 percent of the people born into the lowest quintile will jump to the highest-earning fifth of young adults. And race and gender matter, a lot. Of the black boys with American-born mothers who begin life in the top quintile of the income brackets, 42 percent of them will end up in the bottom two quintiles as adults. You can generate your own figures via an interactive graphic by searching for the following *New York Times* headline online: "Income Mobility Charts for Girls, Asian-Americans and Other Groups. Or Make Your Own."

These are the facts. Whether people channel them into anxiety over impending social-class demotion depends on the state of the economy at any given moment. Your politics may also have a profound effect on your fear. Every so often, Gallup asks Americans whether it's very or somewhat likely that today's youths will have "a better life than their parents, with a better living standard, better homes, a better education and so on." You know, all the expensive stuff.

When the pollsters asked in 2013, as President Obama was starting his second term, 64 percent of Democrats or people who leaned that way expressed confidence that the kids would do better than their folks. Just 30 percent of Republicans felt that way. Incredibly, that figure was 24 percentage points lower than it had been in 2010, when the economy had been much worse. Sure enough, once Donald Trump became president, the ratio flipped. By 2018, 70 percent of Republicans felt good about the prospects for their children, while Democrats had fallen back to 55 percent, even though the stock market was nine years into a bull market and the economy was humming.

We are not exactly rational in at least some of our biggest fears, and we are not using data to plot the trajectories of our children's success on blue-lined graph paper. But once we start contemplating letting them go and sending them off to somewhere unknown, the specter of disaster and fear does tend to take hold. The knowledge that a global pandemic can in fact reach our shores and cause enormous damage doesn't help the matter.

If our kids do not benefit from legacy admissions preference, if we are not rich or famous, if they aren't good at sports or especially desirable because of membership in some other desirable category, will anyone want them? Does a girl from an affluent suburb who would have had it so much easier in the admissions derby in the years just after coeducation have much of a shot now, when many schools are 60 percent female? Will a low-income girl from the inner city find a mentor, enough of a peer group, and a campus as tolerant as it claims to be? Will our disabled kids, our gay ones, our ones with mental illness and a 504 plan or an IEP find their place? And will the extra money we are so tempted to spend buy them some cachet that will help when others, later, are tempted to discriminate against them because they seem just a bit more "difficult"?

Fear enters the equation on so many levels. Has our unwillingness as parents to let them learn from failure rendered them ill-equipped to deal with a broken washing machine or a lost ATM card? Have we hovered like helicopters and then pushed ahead with the snowplow so much that they'll need us too much? Will they work even half as hard as we did, or are they just too soft from so many grown-ups' nudging them along?

We don't know. We *can't* know—not yet. The statistics above track young adults who haven't finished figuring out what kind of adults they want to be. And even if some of the more foreboding trends hold, it's not clear how the next generation will feel if they don't achieve whatever it is that their parents wished for them. The metric is just income, after all. What will any such number mean in an unknowable world with a spouse or kids or both or maybe neither?

When questions like these start to compound in my brain, I like to look at a drawing that my friend Carl Richards made many years ago now. It's just two circles, one labeled "Things We Can Control" and the other "Things That Matter." The circles overlap ever so slightly. Carl colored in the conjoined space and then drew an arrow pointing to it with a label that read "What You Should Focus On."

CHAPTER 7

Guilt

This looming bill, a six-figure bill, a $325,000 bill, a bill of unknown size for an as-yet-unknown school—it's our solemn parental responsibility to pay it in full, right?

The federal government certainly thinks so. Schools base their list prices on this same expectation, one that does not exist in much of the rest of the world, where college is free or close to it. Fellow parents in our communities seem to be just fine with all of this too, or at least they're not talking much about the financial side of college out loud because they're waiting for us to start asking the awkward personal questions first.

Our children may presume that we'll step up and pay, since few eighteen-year-olds pay their own way by working their way through four-year colleges anymore, and most students don't earn a full ride with scholarships. And if we haven't talked to them much about money, they may have no idea what we make, what college might cost, or what kind of strain it could cause for a family. Or perhaps they know good and well, and they assume that borrowing to make up the difference in cost between attending a four-year school and starting at a community college is a fine plan. If they have their eyes on a private college, this may involve another $50,000 or more in private student loans, over four years, beyond the federal undergraduate borrowing limit. If you don't cosign, they can't go. They'll handle all of the repayment, they insist, despite not having ever worked up a grown-up budget or having any idea what they might do or make (or need for graduate school, which may be necessary in any number of fields).

And if that is not enough, there are the stories we tell ourselves. Or perhaps we share them in tense, whispered conversations with a spouse or tense, not-whispered conversations with an ex. Our child will have and do more than we had and did; anything less is the opposite of progress. If our parents did not or could not or would not pay, we will pay whatever it takes, whatever the school. And if we knowingly settle for less, it will feel like failure. We will be guilty of not giving our kids what they need at the precise time they need it most.

It is, after all, the moment we've all been waiting for. Right now, before they leave home, anything seems possible. Potential, as Caitlin Zaloom wrote in *Indebted*, her anthropological study of borrowing for college, is sacred. If you take out loans, suspending all caution and perhaps most reason, you're paying tribute to your child's future, and debt becomes a kind of honorific. "Loans may be expensive, but potential is priceless," she wrote. Who among us would willingly crush our kids' dreams or at least forbid them to even consider their dream school with the high sticker price?

This is not meant to be a rhetorical question, and addressing it head-on is the surest way back from any guilt trip we preemptively send ourselves on. In the course of reporting her book *Squeezed: Why Our Families Can't Afford America*, about the economic precariousness of the middle class, Alissa Quart found that most of the parents she spoke with blamed themselves for just about everything. They had done it all wrong, pursuing a high-minded, potentially high-impact profession that came with career instability or low enough pay to leave them one surprise short of disaster. Perhaps they had bought a few nice things for themselves and then spent years living with regret. And throughout it all there was a fair bit of spending to enrich and cultivate and shape and mold their children, all to get them ready for college, hopefully a good one.

What does it mean to have made it in America? Part of the dream is a good education, and parents are supposed to have the money to make that a reality. But what if you don't? As Quart noted, so much of any given family's struggle isn't just for economic survival; it's also a struggle against shame.

Many families temper the growing sense of guilt with a very particular kind of hopefulness: Money will appear somehow, scholarships will come, schools will see the wisdom of investing in their offspring because, well, just look at them! How could you not love my kid? The late Lauren Berlant, an English professor at the University of Chicago, has a cutting phrase for this that turned into a full-length book: *Cruel Optimism*. It is the quality or state of being in which the thing you want most turns out to be a fundamental obstacle to your happiness. What nearly all of us want is for money to be no object when it comes to education. Few of us ever get there. So if we've failed to make it so—if it is a failing—we hardly have the standing to tell our kids not to go into debt for their own dreams, if we discover in the final weeks of the decision-making process that it is the only way to make that dream come true. That would be the real cruelty, not the optimism that makes us think that it will all turn out okay.

Is it possible that whatever acts of cruel optimism we commit in our own minds have something to do with our parents? If they put you through school or showed up in the financial aid office each year to haggle with the director, you may well feel as though it's your duty to do the same or better. Maybe your mother or father is in your head (and aren't they always?), urging you on. Or maybe they're in your field of vision, still alive and watching, perhaps even nagging you to work more and save more and sacrifice.

Let's begin our return from the guilt trip right here. If you're lucky enough to have parents who are still alive and in your life, perhaps they'd like to help save and pay for college, even just a little. Isn't this the perfect moment to help, not twenty years from now, when they die and you're reading the will as you close in on retirement? Ask them.

If that's not possible, be gentler in conversation with yourself. Our financial lives are just so different now. Maybe the parental units in your life understand this, or maybe they're cashing fat pension checks and can't fathom what it is like for you to be utterly on your own. And when it comes to the most expensive—and important—things in your financial life, your middle age is quite different from what theirs was. Real wages, adjusted for inflation, haven't gone up much in a generation unless you're affluent. Unions have less power, and employers push white-collar workers out of companies much more frequently than they once did. If you're lucky enough to have and keep a job, the majority of your retirement savings will probably need to come out of your paycheck via your discipline and good investing luck, not a pension contribution from a benevolent employer.

You may be spending a large part of your income on housing. Paying for a family-size dwelling in a good school district has become increasingly expensive. Out-of-pocket health care costs continue to grow beyond the rate of inflation, and that's if you're lucky enough to have employer-sponsored medical insurance. If you're buying it on your own without any federal subsidies, the cost has long since risen above $20,000 annually for many families (and that's before the four-figure deductible). And you already know about the costs of college and the fact that the state and federal governments aren't subsidizing higher education institutions like they used to.

This may sound like a laundry list of sadness, but it's actually the script for a reassuring conversation with yourself. Given what you are up against, you are under no obligation to make the same financial decisions your parents did, especially if that would require many more sacrifices.

If you're still inclined to feel guilty, consider the fact that choosing the highest-priced option for college is no guarantee that you'll be able to surround yourself with a guilt-defying force field. It is possible to feel guilty for spending too much, too. Inevitably, there will be times when you don't feel as though you are getting your money's worth. A professor will be an inadequate teacher or a dorm will have roaches or an administrator will be short with your child, and then you'll be That Parent on the phone seeking customer satisfaction. Or perhaps you will turn on your child, demanding good grades and accountability. You might mandate that there be no downtime, not for one single second, lest even $1,000 of the $300,000 go to waste. Really think about what four years of *that* would feel like, given that once you make a choice, you can't know if the less expensive one would have presented challenges that were any less bothersome.

Perhaps this is a moment too when leveling with your child about the precise nature of the sacrifice that is necessary will do some good. What will a more expensive choice mean during those four years in terms of the number of additional hours per week of paid work, the challenge of affording a fraternity or sorority, the lack of a car, or the elimination of family vacations? What would a postgraduation budget look like in a nearby city at the age of twenty-two with $300 in monthly student loan payments, and what would it look like with a $700 monthly bill? Pretend you're both recent college graduates, and together go tour a couple of apartments at both ends of the budgetary spectrum just to see. You may find that you are not the only party to this decision that doesn't want to set themselves up for bad feelings. Our kids may be more in touch with productive emotions than we might think.

In 2017, Marguerite Royo-Schottland found herself in an almost archetypal situation for high school seniors and their families who face choices like this. Her parents began their adulthood as artists, with her mother, Emily, founding a New York City dance troupe and her father, Thierry, working as a musician. Her mother eventually became an educator, while her father worked for a translation company. It was only in the latter half of Marguerite's childhood that her parents began earning a six-figure household income. So although financial aid formulas assumed that they had saved plenty, they had actually saved very little.

They'd only recently been able to afford to buy an apartment through a program for middle-income residents, and Marguerite's sister was already in college, albeit with some generous financial aid from Vassar College.

By April of her senior year in high school, Marguerite was considering two options in particular: State University of New York at New Paltz and Mount Holyoke College. New Paltz offered significant merit aid, while Mount Holyoke presented the family with a need-based aid package that would have left them paying between $15,000 and $20,000 per year more than they would at the state school. That gap seemed likely to increase each year. Thierry, who grew up in France, had uncomplicated feelings about the entire process, ones I've heard echoed by nearly every parent I've encountered who grew up outside the United States. Over lunch in Harlem a few months after the family had made their decision, Thierry told me the technical French term for how he felt about the process and the costs: "bullshit."

Emily did not curse, but over the course of many emails and phone calls, she expressed frustration with a nagging sense that perhaps they had somehow not done enough. "Don't I work sixty hours a week?" she asked. "Isn't Thierry up at six a.m.? The compromising position is in having to ask for help and then ask for more. There's a humiliating aspect to it too where you're just made to feel like somehow the choices you've made and what you do now still don't add up to what they are supposed to. That is just a terrible thing."

Still, they had to make a decision, and fast. How best to frame it for Marguerite? Emily and Thierry had not gone away on a trip together alone in twenty-four years. A modest amount of money was about to come to them through an inheritance, but their retirement savings were relatively meager and they were in their fifties. "How do you say to a kid, 'Well, Dad and I really, after two decades, need some cash. There are some things we need to do,'" Emily said, trying a script out on me one late night in April 2017. "How do you say to a kid who is trying to decide between a state school and a private school—how on earth do I say—that 'the money can't be for you'? The thought of asking us to pay double what New Paltz would cost, I think she's not sure how to ask, and I'm not sure if we can say yes."

Ultimately, however, Marguerite did not ask. Right before the May 1 deadline, I heard from Emily again. Marguerite had decided that choosing the more expensive school would not set her up for success. If the family spent more, she'd be expecting the perfect experience in exchange for the sacrifice. And if it wasn't perfect—and what is, really?—it would be demoralizing. "I didn't want to put the pressure on myself of always trying to make it worth it," Marguerite told me over lunch that summer.

Emily was relieved, given that they weren't going to have to zero out the family checking account in year one of Marguerite's undergraduate education. She also felt uneasy at not being able to send her daughter somewhere that might have offered her something a bit different. Mount Holyoke had certainly been aggressive about saying so when it had declined the family's appeal for more money and told Emily that the two undergraduate experiences were not really comparable. That, combined with the overarching feeling of incompetence that the family felt from not having been able to work the system better somehow, led her to start asking questions.

First, she asked with an arched eyebrow, isn't it in the best interests of private colleges to sell themselves as being the ultimate destination for curious teenagers but also totally, eminently affordable—even if they were not all that way once the inadequate financial aid offer arrived? Isn't that just laying a trap for those who are prone to feeling guilty?

And then there was this, as she put it to me via an email: "So many of these higher-priced schools are populated by students whose families have the wealth, means, and connections to ease them into their working lives. Is it the schools they go to that provide them with this mobility, or is it the fact that they are already members of the privileged class? I'm honestly not being a cynic; I'm just really curious about this."

Several years earlier, a couple of researchers had produced a guilt remedy in the form of an academic study. If you know anything about Alan Krueger, perhaps it's from reading his obituary. He died by suicide, a brilliant economist who seemed to have it all and lived to help others and was struck down by depression. Years before that, he had teamed up with a young student named Stacy Dale, who had attended the University of Michigan to play tennis.

Their work became known as the Dale-Krueger research, as well known in higher education as it is underrecognized outside it. Academics had always known that people who go to selective colleges earn more than people who don't. But it was never clear why that was, so people made assumptions that it had something to do what the college provided. Dale and Krueger, through an ingenious experiment, were able to provide a rebuttal in two different papers: By comparing people who attend more selective colleges with people who got into those same schools (or merely applied but did not get in) but chose to attend less prestigious ones, they found that most of them ended up earning the same amount of money on average once they were adults. The exception was alumni whose parents had very low incomes or were less educated, and Black and Hispanic graduates; people from all these groups saw their incomes rise dramatically as a result of attending the most selective schools.

So statistically, as a white family, the choice that Emily and Thierry made with Marguerite was probably not going to reduce her odds of succeeding economically in her chosen course of study.

Now a bit of a gender twist. Dale and Krueger included only full-time employees in their study, which meant that women who were raising children full-time were not counted. So more recently a different trio of researchers took another look at the question of how or if selective colleges pay off financially.

With men, the findings echoed Krueger and Dale's. But with married women, the results were a bit different. Women who attended those selective colleges earned 14 percent more than those who could have attended (because they got into them) but did not. And they were 3 percent more likely to work for pay and 9 percent more likely to get an advanced degree. They were also 5 percent less likely to be married, but if they did get married, their spouse was 13 percent more likely to have an advanced degree. That's a lot to unpack, but the researchers surmised that alumnae of selective colleges were more likely to work and attend graduate school and less likely to marry, perhaps because they had higher standards or better financial options. When potential mates did get over their high bar, they tended to be pretty ambitious, as evidenced by those advanced degrees.

Both of those studies used a database of people who had entered college in 1976. Harvard economist Raj Chetty and four colleagues used data from 1999 to 2013 and found that rates of bottom-quintile-to-top-quintile generational mobility were highest in what they described as "midtier" schools such as those in the City University of New York and University of Texas systems. Bottom-quintile-to-top-1-percent mobility was highest at the most selective colleges, including Ivy League schools.

Then again, there are metrics besides money and marriage that factor into the definition of "success." You may be worried as much about access as you are about take-home pay. At a more expensive school, will your children be more likely to find people they could not possibly meet in any or at least many other places? And will the gatekeepers of early adulthood, including graduate admissions boards and prospective employers, look askance at them if they choose the New Paltzes over the Mount Holyokes?

What we're talking about here has little to do with guilt and everything to do with other potentially unhelpful feelings, notably our own concern about other people's snobbery and elitism.

CHAPTER 8

The Pull of Snobbery and Elitism

I got my first job in the middle of a journalism recession, thanks to a listing I spotted on a bulletin board at Amherst. My future boss, who had also gone to Amherst, had sent it to the career counseling office. He had faxed it off to be posted on bulletin boards only at Amherst, Williams, and Harvard.

The chief of reporters at *Fortune* magazine was the next person to hire me. Her daughter had gone to Harvard, and she liked kids from "good" schools—a lot. My editor there had also attended Amherst, and he assigned and edited my first cover story for the magazine. During that period, an editor at the most high-minded literary publisher in New York bought my first book. Her résumé included Georgetown and Columbia.

A few years later, one of the founding editors of *Fast Company* took an interest in me and made me an offer. When I turned him down, he made some more offers until I said yes. He had gone to Amherst, too. (My other boss there had gone to Princeton and MIT.)

Few people ask where I attended college anymore, but it's awfully hard to argue that it did not matter in those first five years of my career. And really, why wouldn't it have? Hiring and mentoring people from your alma mater is a good way to reinforce the value of your own degree in the marketplace. Amherst was at or near the top of the *U.S. News & World Report* ranking of small liberal arts colleges throughout the 1990s. It meant something in the entry-level marketplace, especially around

Boston and New York, where I lived. When you're young and lack much of a track record, the name on your degree is the most convenient badge that others can read on you aside from race and gender. It faces out, at the top of your résumé or quite literally in public nowadays on LinkedIn. People see it, and, depending on what it says, many of them think they know things about you. Maybe you believe those things, too.

So what exactly was I benefiting from? Before we consider the value of any given college, it's a good idea to pay a bit of attention to the mindset that caused people to hire me and others like me—and determine how often it matters and to whom.

In his book *Snobbery: The American Version*, Joseph Epstein invited readers along on a winking romp. He had spent many years as a lecturer at Northwestern, and he cut loose on everything in his path, including higher education in an amusing chapter called "A Son at Tufts, a Daughter at Taffeta." He defined "snobs" as people who make themselves feel good at the expense of others and build their personal standards of success around where they rank against others after extensive jockeying for position. Although much of the book feels ever so slightly satirical, Epstein didn't shy away from the pain of living this way. "The true snob," he wrote, "can know no lengthy contentment."

To Epstein, elitism is a bit different—and something to aspire to. Elitists want the best in life; snobs merely want the things that everyone else thinks are best so they can swan around showing them off.

But what sort of corrosive effect might that have on someone who is inclined to think that way? In his book *Class: A Guide Through the American Status System*, Paul Fussell looked at elitism from a different angle: its outsized impact over time. "The number of hopes blasted and hearts broken for class reasons is probably greater in the world of colleges and universities than anywhere else," he wrote. "If no other institution here confers the titles of nobility forbidden by the Constitution, they do. Or something very like it."

So what is this "very like it" that a brand-name college can grant you in certain circles? Some of it, certainly, is parental pride, a statement to the world via a rear windshield sticker or a Facebook reveal that, yes, your child has indeed been granted admission into the kind of collegiate club that produced you. Or perhaps even better, your child has made it when you did not, thanks mostly to your parenting. But my reporting suggests that parents worry much more about the snobbery and elitism of other people, the gatekeepers and judgment wielders who will encounter our children in their first ten years after they graduate from high school.

Take the Swierczewskis, who live just outside Richmond, Virginia. Amy and John are both engineers, while he has an MBA as well. He has his own business, where revenue can fluctuate wildly. Though self-employment gives some families a certain amount of financial aid flexibility, the unpredictability of any given business cycle makes figuring out what you can afford to pay for college very tricky.

Their daughter got a nice needs-based financial aid package from the University of North Carolina, her dream school and one of the finest public universities in all the land. But her parents knew that the bill would likely rise in the following years, given that their business and income were likely to improve. Then along came James Madison University (often abbreviated to JMU and sometimes lengthened by snobs to Just Missed UVA, as in the much more selective University of Virginia) with an offer of free tuition for all four years, something that only a handful of incoming students receive each year. It was just too good to pass up, given that there was still one more child at home to educate.

That option did not sit well at first. According to Amy, their daughter focused for a bit on how hard she'd worked in high school, wondering why she had taken a bunch of International Baccalaureate classes if she didn't need them to get into college (forgetting that her stellar record was what had gotten her the pile of scholarship money). "She felt like she lowered herself," Amy said.

That changed quickly as classmates approached her in the hallways at school to thank her for helping to inspire them to make similar choices. But Amy felt funny about it once she started telling her own peers. "No one ever asks you where your kid applied and got in," she said. "They only ask where she's going. And it would kill me. I'd want to say that she got into all of these other places. I wanted to say she got a full scholarship."

So many more of these college decisions each year are based partly on money. But in communities and among casual acquaintances where people just don't talk about their finances, college conversations end up being fundamentally dishonest, or at least highly misleading. And isn't it wild that we can talk about achievement all day long but we can't talk about money, even if the giant tuition discount was itself a result of achievement? I mean, when was the last time you saw one of those braggy lists of college matriculation plans that many schools post late each spring about their seniors that came with a spreadsheet of who got what kind of merit aid?

The Swierczewskis never regretted their decision. "It was the perfect place for her, and she never would have gone there had it not been for that scholarship," Amy says now, five years out from the choice. "I had such joy watching that graduation ceremony, because I felt her joy. It was kind of an indescribable feeling. And I don't know how to tell people not to be scared. Just because a school seems 'lesser than,' people have to get over this idea that their child will not be able to find happiness there."

Amy's daughter is now in graduate school for occupational therapy. At one interview when she was applying, she found that she was among a tiny number of undergraduates under consideration who were coming straight from college—an indication that her choice of undergraduate institution was not going to affect her life going forward. Which naturally raises the question of just how much we know about whether any given child will have the best possible shot at the best graduate schools or the most selective early-career jobs in all the land. Just how elitist are the people at Goldman Sachs, Teach for America, McKinsey, or the startup incubators in Silicon Valley who make the decisions at those sorts of places?

It isn't just parents who ask these questions; the answers are a source of intense interest among both academics and authors of book-length nonfiction. Lauren A. Rivera, a sociologist and professor at the Kellogg School of Management at Northwestern University, is herself an alumna of highly selective schools and one of the most elite consulting firms for entry-level employees. At the same time, she is a person of color and received need-based financial aid throughout her undergraduate career. And she wanted to know: How do hiring managers in the most prestigious investment banks, consulting firms, and law practices select their future colleagues? Whom do they pick, and whose résumés do they never even bother looking at?

She embedded herself inside a prestigious consulting firm she would not name and spent years on research for what became a book called *Pedigree: How Elite Students Get Elite Jobs*, which will confirm many of your worst fears about how things work in that particular part of the world. The number of schools that the firms drew from was so small that they made distinctions even among the Ivy League, looking down their noses at the students from Dartmouth, Brown, and Cornell while devoting disproportionate attention to Harvard and Yale. Quoting directly from the recruiters she observed, she wrote, "Many evaluators believed that high-achieving students at lesser-ranked institutions [even among the top fifteen in the country by various rankings] 'didn't get in to a good school,' [or] must have 'slipped up.'" Moreover, any decision to go to a lower-ranked school (because it was perceived by evaluators as a "choice"), was often interpreted as evidence of a moral failing, such as faulty judgment or a lack of foresight on the student's part.

Apparently, none of the evaluators had ever heard of merit aid, or maybe none of them had ever had to make a decision based on money. Indeed, Rivera concluded that membership in those employment clubs is "formally reserved for graduates of a handful of prestigious schools dominated by the nation's most affluent families." Such hiring practices can stack the odds high against college seniors of color. Not that many interviewers cared much for diversity in the first place, according to Rivera. "Many evaluators were more forceful in their dismissal of diversity as a valid hiring criterion, saying that the sheer act of considering diversity meant 'lowering the bar.'"

If you head over to McKinsey's website these days to see whom that elite consulting firm is rolling the red carpet out for, the Harvard page shows a five-person recruiting team and a listing for fifteen events. Search for Pomona, long one of the most selective small liberal arts colleges, and there is one recruiter and no in-person events on a generic page titled "West Coast Schools." Other equivalent schools display an application deadline that is weeks later than the one for the more prestigious schools, which suggests that McKinsey hires first from what it considers the cream of the crop. (And, yes, the system treats Stanford differently from other schools near the Pacific Ocean.)

Over at Bain, another top consulting firm, sixteen events are listed for Harvard students. Type in "Middlebury," and there is a generic page inviting you to introduce yourself. There is no page at all for Carleton, which, like Pomona, is one of the most selective small liberal arts colleges in the country.

The firms make the case in Rivera's book that this is merely expedient elitism, although they don't call it that exactly. In effect, they are relying on the admissions officers at the colleges and assume that their examination of seventeen-year-olds was entirely meritocratic. As a result, the firms choose employees in part based on how they performed as teenagers and pay no mind to outstanding students who chose to go elsewhere or reached their full adolescent superpowers at twenty-one instead of sixteen. It's certainly efficient, and if it was affecting their revenues or how their customers feel about the quality of the advice the firms offer, they presumably would have made changes long ago.

If Rivera's findings make you uncomfortable, the best antidote is Frank Bruni's book *Where You Go Is Not Who You'll Be: An Antidote to the College Admissions Mania*. There my former *New York Times* colleague stated what should be obvious but bears repeating as ever more high school seniors apply for the most selective colleges in the country each year: You don't have to attend one to be happy or successful. In fact, as he pointed out, the majority of chief executive officers and members of Congress did not go to schools like these.

I ran my own set of numbers in August 2019 and attempted to add a few categories of prestigious jobs beyond the coveted entry-level roles at Goldman Sachs, McKinsey, Bain, Google, and Teach for America. To establish a baseline, I counted as "selective" any undergraduate institution where the average SAT score for incoming first-year students was at least 1400. This list included forty-five schools, including the entire Ivy League and three flagship state institutions: UC Berkeley, the University of Michigan, and the University of Virginia. Under 3 percent of first-time, full-time undergraduates start school at a place like these each year, so the basic question is this: What percentage of college graduates hired by prestigious employers come from this collection of schools?

Startup-minded young adults may attempt to shape their business idea in what is known as an incubator. Others may pitch their business plans to venture capitalists and try to get investments from them. The best-known incubator is Y Combinator, which makes the names of the people in its incubator "classes" public. I found that 43 percent of the most recent group had gone to one of the forty-five schools on my list. Among the recent founders who had received money from Kleiner Perkins, a highly-regarded venture capital firm, 58 percent had attended those institutions.

As for people farther along in their careers, there are similar patterns. In the U.S. Senate, 33 percent come from one of the forty-five schools. In Congress, it's 22 percent. In the boardroom, according to a study by University of Arkansas assistant professor Jonathan Wai, 21 percent of Fortune 500 chief executives hail from a similar list of schools.

Each year the MacArthur Foundation gives out no-strings-attached $625,000 awards that have come to be known as "genius grants," and 45 percent of the 2015–18 classes got their undergraduate degree from one of the forty-five schools.

Running a sports team these days has become a bit of a nerd gig, given all the data analytics that are now in play. Among baseball general managers, 57 percent came from the chosen forty-five. In football, it's 13 percent. The basketball chiefs show a 30 percent figure, and hockey comes in at 33 percent.

So are these statistics, or "status-tics"? On the one hand, the data prove that Bruni was right: No less than 42 percent and as many as 87 percent of people in these exalted professional jobs come from schools that are not highly selective. On the other, it sure looks as though the gatekeepers are paying outsized attention to people from the most selective schools. Again, less than 3 percent of first-time, full-time college students attend one of these institutions, but we've now determined that their alumni fill between 13 and 58 percent of these prestigious roles. And that's not counting the employers who won't share their figures, because their numbers are probably even higher.

As Bruni put it in his book, what these schools give your children is the benefit of the doubt. They may have been geniuses or National Football League general manager material from an early age, but certain gatekeepers are going to give them a first look—or a longer one or an extra one—if they have the right college on their résumé. At the very least, they'll spend four years rubbing shoulders with classmates who will fill these exalted positions sooner or later themselves, which makes for a mighty fine network.

So if you're a parent who wants a child to have the best possible shot at doing any kind of work, these data may matter at least a little when you're considering whether to pay full price for one of these institutions or a lot less someplace else. It also may matter to you that the twenty-year-olds who commit to Goldman Sachs or Bain are often earning more than their parents within a few years in the workplace.

Still, we are talking about a tiny fraction of 1 percent of the jobs available to recent college graduates. How much is it worth to you to be sure your child is competitive if he or she chooses to make a play for one of these types of roles? Is it worth an extra $100,000 in tuition to vault him or her from a state school to a selective private one that offers some merit aid? Or maybe $200,000 more to attend one of the forty-five schools that feed the sports teams and Congress?

If you lack a recognizable last name, status, other than whiteness, isn't something you get to pass down. College may be the last chance to buy a bit of it for your child. My family did with the money that it had, and it probably helped me get my first few jobs (and maybe my current one too, given that 52 percent of *New York Times* staff writers came from a 1400-plus-SAT school as of 2016, according to one study). I'm glad they did, and my wife and I are trying to save enough that we will have the option to make the same choice for our own daughters when the time comes.

But I'm also cognizant of this: At my first real internship in my first real newsroom, it was pretty clear that the crew there didn't think much of Amherst College kids. The school was just five miles or so away, but they had hired mostly state school interns. It took many mornings of writing obituaries in the predawn hours before I started to win people over.

And although nobody has yet been able to prove it with data, all of the social trends—the mistrust of higher education among many Republicans, the admissions scandal involving Rick Singer and several universities, and the feeling that admission to selective colleges is rigged or random or discriminatory or otherwise unfair—suggest a possible turning of the tide. Is it possible now or soon that hiring managers will look askance at people from the exalted forty-five? I hear this more than a little in New York City these days—that Harvard or Yale graduates are now on the raised-eyebrow list for hires. I expect to hear even more of it going forward.

Gallup found that only 9 percent of biased hiring managers see the undergraduate degree nameplate as being very important. That leaves a lot of great jobs for young adults who don't attend the most selective or prestigious schools. Now, did those Gallup respondents tell the whole truth? Parents of children of color tell me that their consideration of other people's snobbery is even more relentlessly practical, given that a certain number of hiring managers might give their children a second or more careful look if those children come from a college that is more selective.

I would not try to talk any of those parents out of that conviction. Nor can I quite shake the most uncomfortable observation that Joseph Epstein made in his book: that snobbery often takes deepest root in the areas where substance is absent. We don't know much about what students learn at Northwestern or say about it afterward, but we know a fair bit about how hard it is to get into the school. And after decades of teaching there, he came to the conclusion that snobbery about higher education may be more pervasive there than it is anywhere else in the United States.

I don't doubt it anymore. And if you're privileged or confident enough that you couldn't care less about it, count yourself among the lucky.

PART III

Value

Things Worth Paying For

Classrooms Where Experienced Instructors Have Time to Teach (and Actually Want To)

Think of a college that is best known for the quality of its teaching and faculty mentorship.

Having trouble naming many? Well, so am I, even after years of trying to figure out what sort of undergraduate classroom experience is worth paying extra for. But we the customers want our children to learn. We want them to meet adults who will help them become the adults they are meant to become. This is indisputable, but we don't do a very good job of flexing our muscles in the marketplace in a way that would force these institutions to measure the quality or even the quantity of teaching and mentorship.

This is true even though some of the best research on higher education outcomes that does exist proves that mentors matter more than nearly anything else in finding life satisfaction as a young adult. And it is true even though countless prominent insiders at the schools that top the *U.S. News & World Report* list have not just admitted but lamented the haphazard approach they take to teaching undergraduates. Once upon a time, teaching was their core function, but they don't seem to care very much about it anymore. Those that do ought to say so and prove it.

Here are some opinions on the matter from people who know this terrain very well.

"If universities truly compete with one another, why do they neglect their teaching so? At least part of the explanation is that rewards for excellent research far exceed those available for excellent teaching. . . . Small wonder that so many professors concentrate more on research than on teaching."
—*Derek Bok, former president, Harvard University,* Universities in the Marketplace: The Commercialization of Higher Education

"Professors are chosen for their specialized knowledge and receive no serious instruction in the art of teaching."
—*Anthony Grafton, professor of European history, Princeton University*

"Somewhere along the way, we spiritually and emotionally disengaged from teaching and mentoring students. . . . While teaching undergraduates is normally a very large part of a professor's job, success in our field is correlated with a professor's ability to avoid teaching undergraduates."
—*Jacques Berlinerblau, professor, Edmund A. Walsh School of Foreign Service, Georgetown University,* Campus Confidential: How College Works, or Doesn't, for Professors, Parents, and Students

"The profession's whole incentive structure is biased against teaching, and the more prestigious the school, the stronger the bias is likely to be."
—*William Deresiewicz, former Yale University faculty member,* Excellent Sheep: The Miseducation of the American Elite and the Way to a Meaningful Life

"Most of the rewards a professor can receive are for research success. Professors gain little—not salary, not free time, or promotion—by

becoming better teachers. They gain all of these things by becoming better researchers."
—*Andrew Roberts, associate professor of political science, Northwestern University,* The Thinking Student's Guide to College: 75 Tips for Getting a Better Education

What on earth is going on here? Colleges and universities care about prestige, but good teaching is hard to measure. It's easier to measure the return on academic research, whether it's a patent that the university owns in part or the number of times other scholars cite social science research that originated on a particular campus. As a result, when people are up for tenure, promotion, and funding from their home institution, research often matters more than any reputation they have for doing well by their undergraduates.

Research takes time. Teaching takes time. Scholars have only so much of it. And if research is what administrators measure and where the rewards are, many professors will naturally try to spend less time in the classroom and more in the lab or the library. Meanwhile, as the overall costs of running colleges and universities rise and tuition subsidies for the state institutions fall, it has become ever more tempting for administrators to let somebody other than the most experienced professors teach the undergrads some of the time. They could be graduate students, or they might be part-time faculty, like the adjunct professors you may have heard about who roam from school to school in any given week.

In an ideal world, most college teachers would be full-time employees fully available to our children. The reality is a bit different, although the severity of the situation depends on how and where you do the counting. The American Association of University Professors (AAUP), which advocates for more hiring of full-time faculty with the possibility of tenure and less use of adjuncts, uses federal data to conclude the following: At all U.S. colleges and universities, 73 percent of teaching positions are not on the so-called tenure track, which means they may not be around for all four years of an undergraduate's education. At two-year colleges, including most community colleges, it's more than 80 percent, while a tad less than half of teaching positions at institutions that grant bachelor's and master's degrees are not full-time jobs in line for tenure. Some jobs are full-time but not tenure track; that can be a bit better for students who seek availability and ongoing relationships with their teachers. It's not ideal, however, for the instructors, who would prefer something more than a year-to-year contract.

At a small liberal arts college, faculty are more likely to be full-time, so if those are the only schools your family is considering, you can safely skim the rest of the chapter. If your child's goal in school is to learn workplace skills and build a network, part-time teachers who spend most of their waking hours at full-time jobs in your child's chosen industry might be preferable. At any given university where half of the teachers are part-timers, they may turn up more in some academic departments than others. And they tend to teach certain kinds of courses, perhaps disproportionately populating introductory classes.

This is where common metrics such as the student-faculty ratio start to get funky. Would you like to know what the ratio is at any given school if it removes graduate students who are preoccupied with finishing their dissertations and adjuncts who are rarely on campus? The schools probably don't know, and if they do, they may not tell you. Ditto if you'd like to know the average number of classes in the first half of an undergraduate's education staffed by instructors who are not full-time or tenured or tenure track.

Meanwhile, a few words about adjuncts. Many of them are miserable. They make an average of perhaps $3,500 or so per class per semester. They often can't pick up more than a handful of classes at any given school, so they're driving around the region all week to make ends meet. They often don't get medical insurance or other benefits. A 2015 report from the UC Berkeley Center for Labor Research and Education found that one-quarter of part-time college faculty qualify for food stamps or some other form of public assistance.

Adjuncts may not have an office. They're probably not included in faculty meetings and may not be included in department ones, either. They may not know what they're teaching until a week before the term starts, and they can be terminated then if too few students register. And because of the overall precarious state of their existence, they may be less likely to push the envelope by doing creative teaching or expecting more than average effort from their students. Unkind reviews or complaints, after all, may affect whether their bosses will offer them more classes the next semester.

Perhaps you want nothing to do with supporting a system that seems so exploitative. Or you may want to know if there are any data there are to support steering clear of schools that depend heavily on adjuncts. Logic would suggest that there is plenty of reason to demand clarity on this point. If adjuncts are teaching many classes, they may not have enough time or energy to devote to class preparation, extensive office hours, and emailing back and forth with students. They may be great teachers, but they are working under compromising conditions. Moreover, they may be gone in a matter of months and will be unavailable for building deeper relationships. Plus, if they don't have a tenure-track job, their recommendations for jobs or graduate school may not be worth as much as a good word from a full professor. The working conditions of the teachers are the learning conditions of the students, as the AAUP put it.

The same thing goes for instructors who are graduate school students. They may be early in the process of learning to teach and are probably preoccupied with getting their dissertations done and not ending up as adjuncts themselves. Undergraduates are a distraction; teaching them is often a way to make ends meet and to make life easier for the faculty and the departments they report to.

There are additional distinctions that we should draw here too. Many schools have full-time "lecturers." Many of them do focus full-time on teaching and students and are included in department and faculty meetings, and they often win teaching awards as well.

There are some data on whether people learn less from adjuncts or graduate students, but the results are mixed. Plus, it isn't always clear whether it's the teachers who are the cause of any inferior knowledge acquisition or curricular progress. One intriguing study out of Northwestern University examined whether students who took classes that non-full-time faculty taught were more likely to take the next, more advanced class in the department. In this way, the study checked to see if the original teacher had turned a student off entirely to a topic (and perhaps a department or a major). Then it examined the grades in the next class and compared them to students who had taken the previous course in the sequence with tenure-track faculty instead. The study found that the non-tenure-track teachers were the outperformers, both in the number of students who studied at the next level and in terms of the grades they received there.

That said, Northwestern can hire the very best non-tenure-track professors due to its prestige and pay them well, too. Several other studies have come to the opposite conclusion. One showed that when the percentage of faculty that is part-time is increased or the percentage that is not on the track for tenure is higher, graduation rates fall. Another study, based on a survey of part-time faculty, found that they used teaching techniques that took up less of their time and were also likely to be less effective.

Science may not be able to answer definitively the question of whether tenured or tenure-track professors are the best teachers, and anyone who studies this issue is probably rooted in academia and prone to some degree of bias. But the question is also too narrow, given that what goes on outside class is just as important as the formal transmission of knowledge.

What we're talking about here is mentorship, and there's one reason why it's a buzzword among academic administrators these days. When Mitch Daniels, Jr., the former governor of Indiana, became president of Purdue University in 2013, he was aghast at the lack of accountability in higher education. After freezing tuition and pledging to keep it frozen for several years, he set about looking for new data that he could use to measure the value of a college degree. He also wanted to track the university's progress under his leadership in making a Purdue degree more valuable than average.

He didn't find much, and soon it became clear that he would have to commission a study himself. Eventually he found his way to Gallup, arguably the country's premiere polling firm. There he met Brandon Busteed, a young executive fifteen years removed from his time at Duke. Gallup had wondered about doing more work in the higher education industry, and when I caught up with Busteed in the summer of 2018, right before he left for a new job, he summed up his five years of work on the project in this way: "I continue to be amazed at how opaque the system is."

Busteed had told Daniels that what he sought wouldn't be cheap, but at least Gallup had the infrastructure to conduct nationwide polling. It began by surveying 1,000 people a day in order to create its initial sample of 30,000, asking them a list of questions about aspects of college that had contributed to their overall satisfaction in life.

The 2014 Gallup-Purdue Index Report, the largest poll of college graduates in history—reported the following: Having a good job is a crucial factor in overall well-being, given how much time people spend at work. Sadly, only 30 percent of Americans feel fully engaged at their workplace. We all want our kids to be among that 30 percent and want their undergraduate education to improve their odds of landing in that group. So what did the survey respondents say about the aspects of college that had contributed to their engagement at work?

They listed six crucial factors: involvement in extracurricular activities; an internship or job where they could apply what they'd learned in the classroom; an academic project at school that had taken at least a semester to complete. (We'll come back to this one in Chapter 20 on the College of Wooster.) And then came the three things that depend on the human beings that the colleges and universities employ: Did the graduates have a professor who cared about them personally, made them excited about learning, and encouraged them to pursue their dreams?

In other words, were they able to find a mentor? It's a word that means something different from "teacher," and it may not always be a professor. A dean of students, career counselor, spiritual leader, or financial aid officer can fill the role, too. But a mentor is much more likely to be someone you spend tens of hours in a classroom with. And then, hopefully, the relationship will extend further. Herb Childress, in *The Adjunct Underclass: How America's Colleges Betrayed Their Faculty, Their Students, and Their Mission*, laments the increasingly fleeting prospects for undergraduates seeking out people in academia who reveal "the pleasures and richness of a culture in ways that make it seem attainable to another." In *Excellent Sheep*, William Deresiewicz described students longing for teachers who both challenge and care. "You have to assign a lot of work, and you have to comment on it carefully," he wrote. "Caring about your students takes time: you need to be willing to talk to them, if only about their work."

Of the six crucial factors that contribute to overall well-being, the three related to mentorship turned out to be the most important. But Gallup found that the vast majority of undergraduate instructors aren't making enough time for mentorship or simply do not have it to give. If respondents felt strongly that they'd had a professor who'd made them excited to learn, cared about them personally, and encouraged them to pursue their dreams, it doubled the likelihood that they were engaged with their work as adults and doing well overall.

Just 14 percent, however, strongly agreed when Gallup asked if they had actually experienced the three aspects of mentorship. The firm does not name names as a matter of course, but Busteed did let slip to me that the so-called R1 research universities—mostly big, mostly public—had scored second worst on mentorship, with Ivy League schools coming in dead last due to their propensity for hiring famous researchers who are not good teachers. Also, people with arts and humanities degrees were twice as likely to "strongly agree" with the mentorship statements as business majors were. In 2019, Gallup published additional research in which current arts and humanities undergraduates confirmed the findings, giving the "strongly agree" answer at nearly double the rate that both business and science and engineering majors did.

All of that was surprising to Busteed. The overall lack of mentorship is, as he put it in an essay for Inside Higher Ed, "perhaps the biggest blown opportunity in the history of higher ed."

Morton Schapiro, the president of Northwestern University, recognized that something like this was true long before the Gallup research emerged. He came to the university from Williams College, which has about one quarter the number of undergraduates as Northwestern. Having taught economics at Williams, he knew how powerful it was for a sophomore or a junior to do research with faculty members, but he also knew how intensely inefficient it could be. "My science friends tell me, if it's a post-doctoral fellow working for you, it's 24 hours, 7 days a week," he said. "If it's a PhD student, it's 23/7. And if it's an undergraduate, it's 2/1." Given that faculty at bigger schools might just as soon avoid undergraduates altogether if left to their own devices, Schapiro knew what he had to do: subsidize the cost of employing Northwestern undergraduates so they could get that exposure and a shot at making better connections with their teachers. "Certainly, it's not in their research interest to have undergraduates in the lab," he said. "They say that to me over a drink all of the time. But then they tell me they are doing it as a service, and God bless them for that."

Today, the more conscientious college and university administrators are making similar efforts to encourage greater levels of faculty access and mentorship. Busteed told me that the initial Purdue report is the most downloaded work that Gallup has ever published. He and his staff have run searches, and hundreds of universities have now incorporated Gallup's findings into their strategic plans. And, yes, Gallup sold survey work to individual schools as a result. Given how little the schools seem to know about themselves, why wouldn't they hire the firm to help? Here's what a vice president at Bentley, the business university in Waltham, Massachusetts, near Boston, told the *Chronicle of Higher Education* about its work with Gallup: "We all believe that a residential experience and all that goes along with a traditional higher education is valuable, but we have never measured it."

Butler University in Indianapolis has gone out and bought mentors on the open market, paying them to serve in the role for the school's undergraduate business majors. This is something that a school in a city the size of Indianapolis can do, given the number of people around town (including alumni) who enjoy helping young people. The roster includes a former chamber of commerce president, retired executives from the health-related and other industries that help drive the regional economy, and an ex-judge. The moment those 275 or so students from each class declare a business major, they get a mentor who meets with them a minimum of twice per semester. All of this is touted under the headline "Lifelong Relationships" on the school's website for any prospective family to see.

Butler is a Gallup client, so the institution knows how well the mentorship program should sell to prospective students. "Career mentorship is far more important than placement rate," said Stephen Standifird, the business school's dean, even as he was quick to note that 99 percent of recent alumni of the program are gainfully employed or in graduate school or fellowships. "We're not just placing but making sure it's the right placement. That can get lost in the placement arms race. We don't know of anyone else who does this, the reason being is that it's pretty expensive to set up."

There is some reason to be skeptical of this overall movement. It's possible that the people who find mentors already have the sort of people skills that would allow them to connect in any event. Maybe their undergraduate education has nothing to do with it. Busteed said that Gallup added ten questions to try to screen out extroverts and evaluated them separately but found that their results were no different.

Whatever the circumstances, we probably all want our kids to be able to take advantage of such campus relationships. So how best to evaluate any given school's odds of providing them?

For starters, consider whether this is actually the most important question for you and your family. If college for any given teenager is about obtaining a credential and nothing more, opportunities for mentorship could come in the workplace via internships or a first job. But everyone else needs to ask schools for better data. If the tour guide knows nothing besides the student-faculty ratio, move on to the group information session. There you're likely to encounter a full-time admissions staffer who probably understands that the student-faculty ratio may not tell the whole story. You could ask what percentage of classes are taught by graduate students or non full-time adjuncts, but even these can vary dramatically by major. The best thing to do is to ask even more specific questions.

First this: Let's say my child is going to take sixteen courses in the first two years of college. On average, what percentage of them will be taught by instructors who are not full-time faculty or lecturers? If this varies by department, can you please list the outliers? To Herb Childress, the author of the book about adjuncts, this question is clarifying for a couple of reasons. First, remember that nationwide, 19 percent of freshmen do not become sophomores. Is a school really using its more vulnerable and least-supported teaching community to try to educate or at least retain its most vulnerable students? All too often, the answer is yes.

Then consider the possible experience of a junior or senior in the three academic departments that your child is most interested in. Go to the websites and examine the roster of professors. Look for words such as "adjunct" or "visiting." Take a peek at the course catalogue to see what percentage of the classes are taught by people who might not be around for four years or even two.

Jacques Berlinerblau, the Georgetown professor quoted above, offers a few urgent questions of his own in his book. First, he sees no reason why families shopping for a school should not ask precisely how it awards tenure. Generally, there is a pie chart formula with three pieces, representing research prowess, teaching skill, and a catchall category called "service" that measures participation in departmental administrative work and campus-wide initiatives of various sorts. And when a school inevitably answers, "Well, there is no formula here," families might ask, "Can you state definitively that teaching matters as much or more than research here, in every case or the majority?"

Finally, put your tour guides to the lasagna test. "Time and again, a single dinner at a professor's home . . . seemed to have an outsized impact on the student's success—for very little effort by the professor," wrote Daniel F. Chambliss and Christopher G. Takacs in *How College Works*. They examined the phenomenon at Hamilton, where one of them teaches. "It seemed almost magical to them, a kind of talisman." Many colleges use a standard off-the-shelf survey to track such encounters, and Hamilton does as well. A deep dive into its own data showed just how much they matter to students, as there was a clear and strong connection between attendance at a meal and an affirmative answer to a question about whether they would choose the school again. In fact, the dinners mattered more statistically than did the difference between a B-minus and an A-minus grade point average.

Hamilton responded to this data by offering to reimburse any professor who wanted to have students over. Dartmouth College offers vouchers for students to take faculty to lunch. Denison is happy to pick up the check when professors are out with students. Given the impact, every college ought to do the same thing. So ask: Does the school you're considering encourage faculty student meals? Are they counting how often this goes on?

David Coleman runs the College Board, which administers the SAT, a problematic test that many colleges are now happy to do without. Whatever you may think of his organization and its tests, however, he does seem to know something about the relationship between faculty and students. "Finding great teachers and insisting on learning from them is a form of resistance," he wrote in the *Atlantic*. "You must push the rules and the system. One of the most misleading things we say in education is that a good school will 'give you an excellent education.' A great education is never given—it is taken."

Good information about how teachers deliver that education is also rarely easy to find. Now you know how to do that, too.

CHAPTER 10

Schools Where Students Learn (Because Many of Them Don't)

In 2011, two professors at schools that most parents would be thrilled to have their kids attend published a book called *Academically Adrift: Limited Learning on College Campuses*, and it hit like a bomb in the offices of undergraduate administrators all over the United States. One author, Richard Arum, was a sociologist at New York University at the time with a joint appointment in that institution's education school. The other, Josipa Roksa, was in the sociology department at the University of Virginia. "How much are students actually learning in contemporary higher education?" the pair asked. "The answer for many undergraduates, we have concluded, is not much."

The result was shocking, even more so because so few people had bothered to investigate the question quite the way they had. To answer it, they assumed they could draw on basic facts about the background and performance of college students over time. Yet here was what the authors found: The data they needed did not exist. Like, at all. The very institutions that employed some of the world's best researchers hadn't gathered any useful data on themselves.

The authors weren't the first to notice this. In 2006, the U.S. Department of Education published a report making the following observation: "Parents and students have no solid evidence, comparable across institutions, of how much students learn in colleges or whether they learn more at one college than another." The report did, however, point to the promise of something called the Collegiate Learning Assessment (CLA). This is a test of critical thinking, complex reasoning, and writing skills—the ones that would often matter more in many future endeavors than pure subject knowledge, which can be of more limited use. Through in-class discussion plus writing and feedback, students ought to get better at these things in college, and the test is designed to measure any improvement. But most undergraduates never take it, either on the way into college or on the way out.

Arum and Roksa tried to fix that, tracking 2,322 students from a variety of backgrounds during their first two years at twenty-four colleges across the spectrum of selectivity. The subjects took the CLA soon after arrival on campus and again in the second semester of their sophomore years. In a follow-up book, the pair kept tabs on 1,600 students from the original group to see how they did on the CLA at the end of college and what happened to them in their first few years in the workforce.

The headline finding was this: For at least 45 percent of the sample, there was no statistically significant gain in the first two years when it came to measurements of complex reasoning or critical thinking. African Americans had lower CLA scores at the beginning of college than did white students and experienced just one-sixth of the modest overall growth that did occur for white students in the study. The news wasn't much better for all of the students at the end of four years, either: About one-third of the students hadn't made any progress at all.

Why so little achievement? One possible reason is that the researchers found that, on average, students spent just twelve hours per week studying. This is much less than students labored over homework in other decades, less than what both the federal officials who define "credit hour" believe to be necessary for learning and less than the amount of time that students outside the United States spend studying.

The low number of hours may have something to do with how little the faculty asks of the students. The researchers asked whether students in the previous semester had written twenty pages or more for a single class during the term or read more than forty pages per week for a given class. A quarter of the students had not taken any class that required either. Only 42 percent had experienced both requirements in at least one course.

Given what we have already learned here about institutional priorities that favor faculty research over classroom teaching, it's tempting to sweep all this up into a tidy generalization. Arum and Roksa quoted Indiana University professor emeritus George D. Kuh, who described a "disengagement compact" that professors and students often wordlessly agree to. Georgetown's Jacques Berlinerblau made a similar point but went so far as to refer to it as an actual conspiracy, albeit an unspoken one.

The compact goes like this: If professors don't assign too much work, they won't have to grade too much and can get back to the research that their overlords reward them for. Then students can give the professors nice feedback in their evaluations and press on with the delusion that they learned as much as they could have. Here's how Arum and Roksa summed it up toward the end of the first of the two books that they wrote together: "No actors in the system are primarily interested in undergraduate student academic growth, although many are interested in student retention and persistence.... The institutional actors implicated in the system are receiving the organizational outcomes that they seek, and therefore neither the institutions themselves nor the system as a whole is in any way challenged or threatened."

The news is not all bad for parents paying six figures of tuition who hope for a bit more. The students who ended up in the highest-performing decile on the CLA test improved so much that, on average, if they'd been in the 50th percentile at the beginning of college, they would have improved their scores to the 93rd percentile of incoming freshmen by the time they took the test at the end of their sophomore year. The researchers found that this group included students from a variety of races and social classes and different levels of preparation for college.

Moreover, the data suggested that the range of performance improvements on the CLA test *within* any given institution was much wider on average than the ranges *across* institutions. In other words, it was possible to improve quite a bit at all sorts of schools, even if it was also possible to participate in a conspiratorial disengagement pact with professors there as well.

Still, given that the research does suggest that you get out of college what you put into it learning-wise, it's worth noting that at the highly selective schools in the study, 68 percent of the students had experienced both twenty-plus pages of writing assignments and forty-plus pages of weekly reading in at least one class. And students attending those schools did improve their scores more than did people with similar backgrounds who attended lower-selectivity schools, although the researchers still labeled their gains "modest." Students in more traditional liberal arts fields also improved more, on average, than did business students.

One other more recent bit of data comes from a study of one hundred students at Hamilton College. Students lucky enough to gain admission often saw their writing improve measurably in just the first few weeks in the classroom, with the weakest writers improving the most. Eventually, objective readers were able to place essays that the subjects wrote in high school and in college in sequential order, from late in high school through junior year, although the essays from junior and senior years in college were too hard for the readers to tell apart.

So what have we figured out here? Sometimes people learn a lot, and all kinds of people can learn a great deal at many different places. In subject-specific classes, they may even achieve a kind of mastery. Graduate schools value that kind of learning, and some employers do, too. But when it comes to the overarching skills that the CLA measures—thinking, processing, communicating—there seems to be no guarantee of any progress whatsoever, even though it is these skills that give adults the ability to interpret whatever comes at them in the workplace and pivot when necessary.

Perhaps a guarantee of measurable learning is too much to expect from schools, given that students, through their own efforts or lack thereof, play a direct role in their own success. But we have every right to be irritated at the shrug-emoji nature of the way schools evaluate their own educational competence. Again, to put it bluntly and in Arum and Roksa's words, "The measurement and understanding of learning processes in higher education are considerably underdeveloped." Given all the brainpower that colleges and universities warehouse on their payrolls, is developing this understanding as hard as curing cancer? Is it possible that nobody wants to know if they're doing a horrible job of educating undergraduates because then they'd have to change a whole lot in order to fix it?

Here are some other related questions that you should ask in your wanderings on campuses.

Start with the general: Can you please describe how your institutional research office or the individual academic departments measure progress in learning? If you get cross-eyed looks in response, maybe try some specifics: Do you attempt to measure how much time students are studying outside the classroom? If not, why not? Have you quantified the average amount of pages or words that professors assign them to read and write and compared that with peer schools? Or tried to measure the quantity and quality of feedback that they receive from teachers? If you don't think these are useful measures, what measures do you use?

Now a counterintuitive question: What will your professors do here to make my child's life harder? So much about the tours and brochures and group information sessions on campus is about smoothing the path. But we want our kids to think harder and work harder and eventually think and work smarter. How do they get from here to there? Which professors are best known for it?

Purdue president Mitch Daniels made a point in an appearance on the *Freakonomics* podcast that's well worth repeating: Knowledge advances through the clash of ideas. So here's something to ask of every undergraduate you meet, from your tour guide to your neighbor's child who is a recent alumnus: Tell me about the biggest clash of ideas that you've witnessed inside the classroom. Now tell me about the most interesting debate that's occurred outside class. Were the opposing sides predictable? And when was the last time you changed your mind about something important as a result of your academic experience?

CHAPTER 11

Undergraduate Mental Health Centers That Are Not in Crisis

Every so often, a group of college presidents visits the *New York Times* and the bosses trot out one of the writers to provide lunchtime entertainment. Several years ago I had my first turn.

After telling the group a bit about how and why I covered higher education through the prism of money and feelings, I asked one of the questions I always put to people in power: "What has surprised you most about your job?" There was a beat of silence, some murmuring, and then one of the guests burst out with this: "Nobody told me that a double-digit percentage of the undergraduates were going to show up with prescriptions for psych meds." More murmuring—and then suddenly we were off and running down a conversational path I had not expected to be on.

I had clearly missed the memo, but a few years later, in 2018, the *Wall Street Journal* published it. Nearly a quarter of new undergraduates are now disabled, owing largely to their mental health diagnoses. The figure was 22 percent at Pomona College, up from 5 percent just four years earlier. At Amherst and Smith Colleges, the figure was about one in five. The University of Vermont came in at 16 percent, and Oberlin College clocked in at a full quarter of undergraduates. So many students at the University of Minnesota qualified for special accommodations during final exams that it had to rent 10,000 square feet of temporary space in a hotel.

In some ways this is good news. Teenagers are getting care, receiving prescriptions for mental health drugs when they need them, and making their way to and through college when they might not have even tried a generation ago. The challenge comes when parents expect to hand off care to someone on campus—or believe that a college will step in and manage the care for a student with a new diagnosis. "Many times parents have told me during orientation events that their child was just diagnosed with a mental-health condition. Their expectation is that the college will have the services on campus to fully support their child's success while dealing with this new diagnosis," wrote Kathleen Baker, a doctoral student and the director of housing and residence life at Seattle University, in a piece in the *Chronicle of Higher Education*, where most parents would never see it.

"Well," she continued, "we don't."

That bit of honesty ought to give you pause, given how utterly elemental mental health is and how often adolescents experience anxiety, depression, and other related conditions. Sure, "We don't have the services" is a bit of an exaggeration; just about all colleges have some form of a mental health counseling center. But as I've lapped the country these last few years asking college presidents uncomfortable questions of all sorts, none seems to make them more uncomfortable than this line of inquiry: "When demand for mental health care appears to be nearly limitless, what level of service should a family paying up to $80,000 per year expect from a residential school?"

On the one hand, as Pomona's president, G. Gabrielle Starr, put it to me in her office, she has every sympathy for every student who presents themselves with symptoms. "People call them snowflakes?" she asked incredulously. "They've gone through stuff that would make your hair curl. They survive. And suddenly they are in a place where there is no rhyme or reason as to why you got in. And maybe a mother has bet all her chips on this middle son, and he's the one leaving home and the rest of the family."

On the other, it's hard to define where a college's duty of care ends. "It's hard to answer the question of what to expect. The costs are ballooning at such a high level that it will only drive up the cost of college further. And you cannot expect colleges to do what the entire mental health system can't seem to manage," Starr continued.

So what do colleges actually do for undergraduates with mental health conditions? The people who do this work are pretty good at quantifying it, and they do so through two annual reports. One, from the Center for Collegiate Mental Health at Penn State University, provides a visceral sense of just how much demand has grown for on-campus counseling services. In just the six years ending in 2015, utilization increased between 30 and 40 percent overall at counseling centers, while enrollment at the survey respondents' schools was up only 5 percent. A large amount of that growth came from undergraduates who arrived with "threat-to-self" indicators, and those patients tend to use 20 to 30 percent more services than other students who seek help.

Most counseling centers don't have enough staff to handle growth like that, and their schools lack the generous budgets that would allow them to add full-time employees quickly. Already a school is lucky if it's able to afford one full-time therapist for every eight hundred students; many have a ratio nearly twice as high. So the growth in demand has forced them into a series of compromises that can affect both the quality and the quantity of care. According to the report, the pressure "to prioritize rapid access instead of treatment" in many centers means that therapists "actively seek to 'shed' or terminate existing clients in order to accommodate new ones." As a result, "our findings suggest that de-prioritizing treatment in favor of access may have significant negative consequences for students in need," including significantly less reduction of depression and anxiety symptoms.

Nobody wants his or her kid to be shed. So what are the markers of a counseling center that might feel pressure to push patients out? The 2018 Association for University and College Counseling Center Directors Annual Survey offers a hint: There are six pages of survey results alone that measure all of the ways that the centers must establish limits. Often they'll cap the number of counseling sessions that any one patient can have, put new patients on wait lists before they can begin any therapy, or both. Two-thirds of centers have no wait list, and there you can get an appointment in 6.5 business days on average. At centers that do keep wait lists, however, the first appointment will be an average of 17.7 business days away—at least three weeks. In spring 2018, Ohio State's wait time was more than a month. Almost no centers offer weekend appointments, and only a single-digit percentage will see someone in the evenings.

This survey does provide some revealing data about school size. The smaller the school, the more likely you are to be able to schedule a weekly appointment if you need one instead of once every two weeks. At schools with more than 2,500 students, utilization of the counseling center falls by a bit more than half. The larger the school, the more the counseling center directors express a need for a psychiatrist to spend a higher number of hours there. The clinical load index, which measures the number of full-time employees and clients, goes up about 50 percent from the smallest colleges to ones with 7,500 to 30,000 undergraduates and has nearly doubled by the time the 30,000-plus schools report in. As a result, the student-to-counselor ratio is lowest at smaller schools, although they have the disadvantage of having a smaller number of therapists to choose from if a patient is having trouble finding a good fit.

The data raise some additional questions: Does a school have any relationship with a psychiatrist who comes to or works on campus? If not, getting a prescription for necessary medication may be more complicated. If a matriculating student already has a relationship with a psychiatrist or a counseling psychologist or both, will that professional be willing to work via video, even if it's across state lines? And if not, will the home-state therapist be willing to coordinate care with an on-campus practitioner and vice versa? Put all of these questions to the people in charge, to be sure. But you might get a more visceral sense of the goings-on by seeking out the campus chapter of Active Minds, a student-led mental health support organization. And if a school doesn't even have a chapter (there are over 550 around the country), that could serve as a warning signal—or a sign that your child should go there and start one.

The better data ratios at the smaller schools haven't kept students from breaking into open revolt in recent years. One notable protest came at Harvey Mudd College, the engineering-focused school that's part of the Claremont Colleges consortium in California. Overwhelmed by overwork and infuriated by a faculty report that seemed to cast aspersions on the aptitude of minority undergraduates, students led a march around campus and then a sit-in. Administrators canceled classes for two days as part of a cooling-off period. Then students issued demands: a doubling of the counseling center's budget over four years and five new mental health counselors, including three people of color. Harvey Mudd's president lamented in an NPR interview that it now seemed to the world as though students of color at the Claremont Colleges needed to commit suicide to get attention. She added that Harvey Mudd administrators had been tracking a watch list of sixty people at risk of breakdown or worse. She said she had had nightmares every night for a month after graduation that year.

At Tulane University the conversation got more visceral and more detailed. An undergraduate who had attempted suicide started a Google doc inviting anyone with experience with mental health care at the school to leave a note for Tulane's president about the experience. After fifty-some single-spaced pages, she finally cut it off. I've read them all, and although there are some reports of good experiences, it's mostly a catalogue of horrors that would set prospective parents' hair on fire. There are forced—and unwanted and possibly unnecessary—trips to psychiatric emergency rooms, fury over caps on counseling sessions, complaints about the inability to schedule an appointment in the first place, vivid descriptions of what seem like counterproductive therapeutic techniques and overall lack of warmth, and on and on and on.

Tulane responded by increasing the cap on sessions, starting an evening hotline for people in crisis, and assigning an administrator to work full-time helping students find nonuniversity therapists and other professional help in New Orleans. It has also rethought how it manages each case, which can free up therapists to do more actual therapy.

When I met Dusty Porter, Tulane's vice president for student affairs, he was not at all defensive about what had gone on. Tulane had, after all, listened and pivoted where it could. But he did offer a few pleas, first to students. Your first month in college, he said, is not the time to decide to take yourself off your meds without telling a medical professional first just to see what happens. Nor is it the time to try your roommate's meds. He wasn't being flip; he was speaking from hard-won experience.

As for the message to parents, he remains baffled by people who don't tell Tulane that a student had been, say, hospitalized for suicidal ideation six months before coming to campus. The school then comes to find out only once the undergraduate reaches a crisis point again. "Why wouldn't you have told us?" he wondered. It may, he continued, be some combination of fear or shame that doing so might cause the school to yank its offer of admission. Or perhaps it's just magical thinking—that everything would work itself out if the student just got to New Orleans, where he or she wanted to be. But mental health is not magic.

If the Tulanes and the Harvey Mudds of the world struggle so much, what hope is there for schools with more students and lower endowments? One possible solution is to focus on prevention. "In an ideal world, every freshman would come in and do a wellness plan," said Paul Granello, an associate professor of counselor education at Ohio State. Until then, he runs the SMART Lab, SMART being the acronym for "Stress Management & Resiliency Training." Students can stop by and plug into computer-mediated breathing exercises to train themselves to become calm and stay that way. I spent several soothing minutes there teaching myself to breathe in such a way that the tracker monitoring my heart rate would create a pattern of rolling hills as I inhaled and exhaled.

Denison has hired a first-year care coordinator to become immersed in the cases of people who arrive with preexisting needs. Meanwhile, an entire subcategory of treatment known as the "single-session approach" is the subject of conference sessions for overwhelmed mental health workers from across the country who are hoping to solve patient problems in fifty minutes or less.

Assessing all of this as a parent isn't easy, but you can often learn something simply by taking a careful look around and listening. At Bowdoin, the admissions office tour stops at the counseling center for a straightforward explanation of who works there and what they do all day. At Colorado College, students with mental health conditions appear on posters with their real names and encourage others to end the silence and stigma around the issue. Many student newspapers report aggressively on mental health issues, and their websites are often searchable. When I visited the University of Pennsylvania admissions office in August 2019, it had mental health brochures on display in the wake of a series of suicides. A few weeks later, the head of the counseling center took his own life.

Now that you know what a challenge it is to provide good mental health care on campuses, you should certainly try asking for schools' data. "Any counseling center worth its soul will have some kind of outcomes research," said Paul Granello, the Ohio State professor. "They should have a pie chart showing what conditions—depression, anxiety, relationship issues—people came in for. They should be able to tell you what success meant and what the outcomes were. And it is perfectly reasonable to ask."

What happens when the counseling center gets too busy? Darlene Compton, the associate director of counseling services at Denison, suggested asking about referrals. When I talked to her in 2018, the school had never had a waiting list but had moved to a sort of triage system with a brief thirty-minute initial assessment. Sometimes staff counselors refer students to local practitioners, but that didn't always work out so well. "We have people within one-mile walking distance down on River Road near the coffee shops," she said. "Students will walk there for coffee but not for counseling."

Those referrals beg other questions: Just how inconvenient will those local referrals be for students? Will the counselor on campus who did your intake hand select a good match for you nearby or just hand you a list that may be out of date of people who may not take your insurance? Students who are saving money by attending state schools in big cities may have no problem rolling the dice on the possibility of needing to spend more for necessary care off campus. But parents who are spending more to send a child to a school in a smaller town may want to ask tougher questions, especially if that child is already in treatment and is hoping to find a new counselor at school. Compton also advises people to consider the privacy issues around insurance, keeping in mind that privacy-minded undergraduates might avoid off-campus therapy if it means that a parent might find out about their sessions and then ask about their troubles.

At some level of severity, we'd hope to find out about our children's mental health struggles whether they want us to or not. But federal laws such as the Family Educational Rights and Privacy Act of 1974 (FERPA) and the Health Insurance Portability and Accountability Act of 1996 (HIPAA) often give undergraduates the right to keep those problems to themselves, no matter who is paying the tuition bill. There are some exceptions, and schools may interpret them differently. G. Gabrielle Starr, Pomona's president, suggested asking schools about these situations straight up—for example, "What is the process for figuring out whether a student goes home or stays, and under what conditions would you get a call?" You might consider asking your child to sign a waiver for both FERPA and HIPAA, while making it clear that you'd use it only in case of emergency and perhaps coming to an agreement on what constitutes one before they leave for college.

You might also ask for details on how colleges monitor undergraduates who are in treatment and are having more trouble than most. Harvey Mudd is not the only school with a watch list. Brian Rosenberg, the former president of Macalester, brought this up unprompted as we chatted in his office in St. Paul, Minnesota, in the summer of 2018.

"It's a group that meets every other week," he said. "It's essentially all the people on campus in the best position to know which students are in distress. It's based on residence halls, hearing from faculty members, from coaches, the dean of students, the director of residential life, the registrar—who we need to watch out for and, in worst-case scenarios, who we need to intervene with. If a kid has been in his dorm room for three days, we're going to know. If a friend says someone is cutting themselves or not eating, we're going to know that."

It is, he continued, quite literally what you're paying for. "I do think one of the things that we sell at a place like this is that we will take care of you. You are now part of a community with people who will take care of you. And if we make that promise, we have an obligation to deliver on it."

Yet he too struggles with how far the obligation should extend. When I spoke with him the first time, the most recent Macalester suicide had been someone who had not been on anyone's watch list and had brought drugs to campus from home. And he, like Dusty Porter at Tulane, practically begged me to tell every parent to tell him and his colleagues at other schools if their child is in any kind of trouble. Sometimes schools just don't know and can't catch it.

So even at the small liberal arts colleges, the system is not foolproof. The core competency of a college or university was never to provide mental health care. They're doing it because they must, and plenty of the students need care on an ongoing basis. Which puts leaders such as Brian Rosenberg, at a school that charges nearly $300,000 to the families who pay full price, into a bind.

"We keep ramping up, and we cannot get ahead of the demand," he said. "I just don't think, unless we dramatically change the way we allocate resources, that we can become the kind of place where students go every two weeks for therapy for four years. We don't have the resources. Does that nag at me? Yeah, it does. But I'm on the board of the largest health care provider in the state of Minnesota, and they can't keep up with the mental health needs, either."

It doesn't seem right to end a discussion about something so fundamental with a warning that you'll need some luck to navigate these shoals: luck for good health, for availability of appointments at a campus health center, for a good fit with a counselor. But if $300,000 doesn't buy a guarantee against cancer or a car accident, there's no reason we should expect it to shield us from mental illness. Warn your kids about all of the above, watch for warning signs as best you can, and be ready to help them make the treatment choices if you're able. And, most important, ask the right questions ahead of time so you have a realistic sense of what to expect.

CHAPTER 12

Peers Worth Friending (or Marrying)

You'd like your child to meet some new people. What sort of school will help best?

Let's start with a declaration of shamelessness. If kinship is your highest priority as you shop for college, it does not make you or your child shallow. Remember: The schools themselves, if they are even remotely selective, consider peer quality to be an urgent matter. If they didn't, they'd admit more people and expand enrollment instead of maintaining offices of rejection.

But despite the evidence that the institutions believe that teen friendship curation matters plenty, the research in the field of so-called peer effects is underdeveloped when it comes to undergraduates, just as so many areas of proof we seek are when we try to figure out what is worth paying more for. Nevertheless, let's pick through what we do know so you can increase your ability to determine which schools will give your child the best odds of finding their people.

The introductory unit of friendship analysis for most first-year students at residential colleges and universities is the roommate. A bad match can make life hard during the transition from high school to college, and administrators' creative attempts to play matchmaker don't always work so well. They are also sometimes sort of brilliant. I did not know any football players before I ended up living with two of them—

one from New Jersey and one from Texas via Taiwan. It's not a choice I would have made, but I sure learned a lot. And I respected the stir-stuff-up spirit that lay behind putting the preppy guy down the hall from me with the two lower-income young men of color.

Nowadays, social media allow future first-year students to meet one another online within hours of getting an offer of admission. Inevitably, high school seniors go shopping for new best friends in those forums, and also inevitably colleges give in to their requests to pair themselves off in one-room doubles. Why not fix yourself up with a roommate rather than letting a stranger make you the subject of a social experiment? Lots of people try that now, with the stress over admission immediately being replaced by the anxiety over finding the right roommate match. One teenager I know referred to this as "girl flirting," which is the quality or state of engaging in mild stalking of other admits' Instagram or VSCO accounts in search of commonalities.

By 2017, nearly half of new Duke University students were indeed pairing themselves off on their own. One possible rationale for letting the college pair people off is that the matchmaking experts actually do know what they're doing—and are better at this than your kids are. In early 2018, Duke stopped allowing first-year students to pick their own roommates, alarmed by how little appetite people seemed to have for living with someone even a bit different from themselves. Instead, it decided to take sleep and study habits into account but otherwise make the pairing random, although it made exceptions for athletes and people with certain medical conditions. By December 2018, it had data: Nothing was different. The number of students who had asked to switch roommates during the year hadn't changed at all.

So which policy should you and your child prefer? Dartmouth College sociologist Janice M. McCabe, who spent five years studying friendships at a large unnamed midwestern university, concluded in her book *Connecting in College: How Friendship Networks Matter for Academic and Social Success* that roommate pairings were indeed consequential: People stayed friends with their first-year roommate (and floor mates) at a rate greater than chance would suggest.

But McCabe found that the friendships that persisted didn't necessarily cross racial lines. Earlier research from a 2008 study set in a large, relatively diverse university found that 15 percent of mixed-race roommate pairs didn't make it through their first year before one party requested a split; 8 percent of all-white pairings did not end the year together and 6 percent of all Black pairings met the same fate. A 2009 examination of daily questionnaire data found that roommates in mixed-race rooms reported fewer positive emotions and less overall intimacy than did pairings of the same race. Overall, however, mixed-race roommate groups were successful on one count: Black students who earned a score of at least 24 on the ACT or 1040 on the SAT earned higher grades, on average, when they lived with white roommates than with Black ones.

There is a risk for people of color when it comes to this important relationship at the outset of college. At Duke, Black students were intuitively aware of what the administration seemed to be asking of them, according to press reports at the time. In essence it wanted some of them—and other people of color, people of faith, gays, lesbians, and people with nonbinary genders—to do the work of education by osmosis or even direct instruction. They were there to create awareness of differences and, if necessary, teach tolerance and respect one-to-one in their own bedrooms and living rooms.

If this makes your family uncomfortable, it's worth asking any school that demands random assignment why it puts some students into that spot. Cite the studies and ask them to defend their oppositional approach. It's also worth asking schools that allow roommate requests just how little diversity exists within those pairings and how it defends that result. The answer to either set of questions will tell you a lot about what a school stands for, where your child might fit into it, and what sort of investment you'd want to make in that culture.

Now to the dorm. Depending on the school and its rules, sometimes students get to pick their residence hall or at least make a request. In *Paying for the Party: How College Maintains Inequality*, a book-length study of how people sort themselves into buildings and groups, we learn first and foremost about the so-called party pathway anchored in sororities and fraternities. The two sociologist authors, Elizabeth A. Armstrong of the University of Michigan and Laura T. Hamilton of the University of California, Merced, set their study at Indiana University. There they followed fifty-three young women from their arrival at a particular dorm until graduation.

The party pathway is something that an individual can choose and leads almost inevitably to association with certain kinds of peers. Most people who attended a residential undergraduate institution can probably identify one likely place where it can take root: a fraternity or sorority member, living in that Greek organization's residence, enrolled in one of the easier majors. Those students need to prove that they made it through college but may not need to excel to get a job, thanks to their connections through friends and family. Relative affluence reduces the need to borrow or work for money during the school year, which leaves more time for parties.

At a place such as Indiana, many of these students come from out of state and pay higher tuition, which can net the school five figures of extra revenue per student, per year at a time when the state government doesn't subsidize the university budget the way it once did. There is a sort of implicit agreement between the school (which demands little of the students other than not to misbehave too much and not to bounce those extra-large tuition checks) and the students (who don't want to work too hard or have campus security arrest them for underage drinking).

The authors identify two other prominent pathways. The first group consists of undergraduates from middle- or working-class backgrounds who put their heads down and grind through a more vocationally oriented program such as nursing or accounting in order to land in a profession with some degree of stability. Then there is the professional pathway—for future engineers, lawyers, and doctors—where there is heightened competition, more culling along the way, and not much time for a lot of fraternity and sorority hijinks.

The danger here is for the wannabes. They want to spend four years on the party pathway but can't really afford it. If they end up majoring or working in lower-paying fields such as marketing or fashion, they may not be able to afford their student loan payments and the rent in urban areas. So they move back home, where they end up away from some of the good labor markets and also isolated from the best marriage markets.

No one wants to think of his or her child as a wannabe. But if you are stretching financially for a school—if every additional social event or fraternity or sorority dues payment means additional financial strain—danger signs should be flashing. Following the party pathway when you have fewer financial resources can put you into more debt than you might otherwise get into. And if that debt constrains postgraduate choices, it could mean certain cities or fields are off limits. That will be true even if your child spent four undergraduate years establishing ties to peers whose connections could otherwise have helped them get established in that place or career.

So be somewhat wary of the party dorms. As Laura T. Hamilton, one of the authors of *Paying for the Party*, told the *New York Times*, not one of the mixed-social-class roommate pairings ended well. None became friends, and in most cases the roommate with more money moved out at the end of the first semester or even sooner. Hamilton offered some blunt advice via Inside Higher Ed: "Prospective college students who are working class and not wealthy, whose parents do not have extensive social connections—those on the mobility pathway—should be wary of attending a four-year residential university" where sororities and fraternities dominate the social scene.

Another related question that parents often wonder about is this: If we send a child to a college where they will be a top academic performer, perhaps to take advantage of a merit aid offer, how will being at the head of the class affect them? Some scholars refer to this as the "big fish in a little pond" effect, and there have been few studies of its impact on undergraduates specifically. Many researchers believe that at least some high-achieving students become intimidated in the big ponds and end up thinking less of themselves. So does swimming in a smaller pond actually help their confidence? One 2018 study of schools in a variety of countries was able to prove that it does in math and science classrooms, and it was equally true for men and women. The researchers took pains to point out that they do not see this alone as a reason to send a child to a less selective school, given other advantages that might come from whatever prestige, resources, or connections may exist in the more competitive institutions. Meanwhile, there appears to be no study that measures the quality or persistence of friendships that big fish form in smaller ponds.

Now, about those special friends. Long ago, even before we parents all went to school, families of a certain stripe referred to college—or at least certain colleges—as a place for nice young ladies to go to get their MRS degrees ("Mrs." as in going-to-college-only-to-find-a-husband). I recall one bad joke about this during my undergraduate years, but that was it. A few of my friends paired off, and we all made fun of Middlebury, where everyone supposedly married everyone else.

But in 2013, an open letter that a mother published in the *Daily Princetonian* ripped across the internet and caused the newspaper's website to crash from all of the traffic. There, a mother of two Princeton men and an alumna herself offered up advice she would give to daughters if she had any: Hunt for a husband while you're still an undergraduate. (She had no specific advice for lesbians.) "Smart women can't (shouldn't) marry men who aren't at least their intellectual equal," she wrote. "As

Princeton women, we have almost priced ourselves out of the market. Simply put, there is a very limited population of men who are as smart or smarter than we are. And I say again—you will never again be surrounded by this concentration of men who are worthy of you."

Young female Princeton alumnae of the scribbling set picked her argument apart bit by bit in essays all over the internet. Not everyone wants to get married, after all. And who was it that declared that a woman could not be smarter than her spouse and still be happy? Still, there was this bit from a young Princeton alumna writing in the Daily Beast: "I've overheard plenty of former female classmates express regret for not appreciating what an eligible pool of men we were surrounded with for four years (though, none would say it on the record)." And, she added, there are others who try to avoid mentioning their alma mater for fear of spooking potential mates.

I have no beef with families who care about this, nor would I argue with people who find the discussion totally retrograde. Let's at least stipulate this: The special-friend question clearly matters to enough people that a variety of entities track it. In *Aspiring Adults Adrift*, Richard Arum and Josipa Roksa noted that among the individuals they studied, the selectivity of a partner's alma mater tended to be highly correlated with one's own, with that selectivity serving a sort of "protective" function.

And yes, there are most-likely-to-marry-within-the-alumni-base statistics. All the snickering about Middlebury was much ado about nothing: 15 percent of its alumni are married to another alum, according to the school—nowhere near the top of the league table. Facebook published school-by-school rankings in 2013. First it looked at the percentage of women attending a college who married a man who shared their alma mater. Topping the list was the engineering school Rose-Hulman Institute of Technology in Indiana, with 70 percent of alumni marrying someone from the school. It was followed by, among others, the United States Air Force Academy, Faith Baptist Bible College and Theological Seminary in Iowa, and Brigham Young University in Utah.

The United States Military Academy, the United States Coast Guard Academy, and Harvey Mudd, the engineering college that is part of the Claremont Colleges consortium, also made the top twenty-five.

When Facebook flipped the genders, the types of schools were similar—lots of engineering schools and religiously affiliated ones. Faith Baptist was on top of this list, with 68 percent of male alumni marrying someone from the school. BYU made the top five again. The others at the top were Harding University in Arkansas, Martin Luther College in Minnesota, and Bob Jones University in South Carolina. Almost all of the rest of the top twenty-five were religiously affiliated schools, with no household names among them such as Notre Dame.

Though Facebook published only the top twenty-five schools for both genders, many other schools have done their own in-house marriage census somewhere along the way. If your admissions officer doesn't know the results, consult the office of institutional research or the fundraising team. They are generally quite proud that this goes on, and there is nothing wrong with harboring some hope that your child will walk away from college holding hands with a life partner.

As for forging lifelong friendships, there are a few metrics that may matter. What percentage of students live on campus? Must they live there, at least for a few years? If people scatter each afternoon or are gone on the weekends, it is harder to bond. And perhaps more important, how do they live if they are bedding down in university housing? This is a design question as much as anything else, according to the authors of *How College Works*, who suggested looking for what they call "high-contact dorms." These are the more traditional sort, with long hallways and a series of doors leading to shared rooms, plus communal bathrooms that the entire floor uses. The suite setups that are increasingly in vogue keep people more isolated. Christopher G. Takacs, one of the book's coauthors, encouraged families to conduct a geographical survey on top of the architectural one. "How residential is the campus?" he suggested asking. "Not just do people live there, but is it close or is it diffuse? How long does it take to walk across it? How sore are your feet by the end of the tour?"

When investigating friendship, don't take the official adult voice of the institution at its word. This is one place where glossy brochures or the sixteenth PowerPoint slide from the assistant director who visits your school won't tell you what you need to know. When your tour of any given school or your student-led group information session comes to an end, ask your hosts the following questions: Who are your three closest friends here? How did you find them? Was it easy? How are they different from your high school friends? See if they light up immediately or struggle to answer.

Some students find their friends in or around the classroom and through their field of study. Another list of questions that you can and should put to the administrators includes: How does the school make efforts to bridge classroom learning with residential living for undergraduates who have finished their first year of school? Are there theme houses for sophomores and beyond? Honors dorms? Get a list of them and contact information for people who live there, then find people with passions like yours and see if they've figured out a way to live well in close proximity to one another.

There may be fraternities and sororities at the schools you're considering—lots of them, even—and that may be exactly what your family wants most. Still, ask some questions, such as: What percentage of the campus is Greek? If this doesn't interest you—or on the off chance that your child will arrive and find that Greek life is not for him or her after all—ask a few other pointed questions of any dean: What investments have you made in the social lives of people who are not in the Greek system? Anything in particular in that realm that is unique to your school? Do you take a hands-on approach to the budget in this area, or do you let the students spend fees as they see fit?

Even the most confident sociologists in this area eventually conclude something like the following: "We can give you only so much in the classroom. For most undergraduates, it's not just what you know but whom you know. Certainly whom you know may have way more than a little to do with what you know, since you learn a lot from the people who are part of your group."

I gave a speech near San Diego not too long ago in which I talked about how and when and why to talk to kids about money and what to say when you do. I explained that much of what we do and say and teach our kids about money from years zero to seventeen is to get them ready for the enormous decision that the family makes together when the kids are eighteen. I lamented how little we know about how much real learning takes place at college and whether college friendships last. Afterward a former colleague, Tom Herman, walked up and introduced me to his close friend of fifty years, someone he'd met as a Yale undergraduate. His friend, Steve Treadgold, shook my hand, looked me in the eye, and said, "At Yale, I met the sort of people who I never could have imagined actually existing in the world."

Every school should do everything in its power to introduce you to those kinds of people. And every question you ask and every visit you make should be centered around figuring out whether or not a school can pull that off.

CHAPTER 13

The Special Power of Historically Women's Colleges

When I first met Smith College president Kathleen McCartney over breakfast, I figured we'd be talking about her school's singular traditions. There are the Friday-afternoon teas in the residential houses, so beloved that many alumnae now hoist a cup with one another via Zoom each week. Or maybe Mountain Day, a surprise announcement by McCartney on a random fall morning when bells ring, classes are canceled, and everyone plays outside.

Instead she issued a simple challenge when I asked her what made her college worth a whole lot of extra money: Imagine a place where every single position of note is held by women. Then she fell silent and let it sink in.

So I did, conjuring up my daughters at just such a place. The president of the student body is female. The captain of every sports team. Every single one of the teaching assistants in the labs. All the study group members. The person who talks the most in every class. The lead in every play. If your daughters haven't had an education like this so far, thinking about it this way is enticing. It feels, in fact, like an opportunity.

Which is of course exactly what McCartney wants you to think. Now that you know how challenging it is to fill a first-year class of any students in this day and age, imagine what she's up against. Half the population is off limits right from the start. Much of the rest wants no part of a college like hers. Many high school girls and their families assume that such a college is unaffordable. Other potential applicants may want to be in choruses and classes with men, for any number of reasons. According to the College Board, less than 5 percent of high school–age girls will even consider applying to a women's college.

Given how hard these institutions have to fight to be competitive in the marketplace, they have long known that they need to prove themselves. As a result, they produce more and better data than the coeducational institutions that are their peers. Yes, most (but not all) of it makes them look equal and sometimes superior. Still, their data deserve an airing, given that plenty of other social science research suggests that gender often puts young women at an overall disadvantage once they leave the classroom for good. Unless otherwise specified, all of the data below come from surveys that a coalition of women's colleges has run in recent years.

Most women's colleges are small. (In the chapter title, I used the more modern phrase "historically women's" to be inclusive of trans and other students who do not identify as or with the formerly standard definition of female. I've shortened the phrase to its more traditional usage in the body of the chapter though. If your child is trans, you're likely already aware of the experience of trans applicants and undergraduates, but if not, now's the time to familiarize yourself with both and ask questions of current trans students.) At flagship state universities, just 18 percent of alumnae say they benefited from small classes of fewer than twenty people. At women's colleges, 84 percent answered affirmatively, 8 percentage points more than women who graduated from coed small liberal arts colleges. The teachers at women's colleges are more likely to be female as well: 61.4 percent versus less than half at all coed colleges and universities.

Once upon a time, some women's colleges had a reputation as finishing schools for the white-glove set. That has flipped around entirely, with the students entering women's colleges now coming from families whose median incomes are well below those of a large group of coed peer schools. The incoming students' academic ambitions are also pronounced, with higher percentages of them expressing a desire to attend graduate school than young women elsewhere. They also come in with a healthy—and appropriate—sense of entitlement, given the higher prices they may pay beyond what a state university would cost. A higher percentage of these women expect to communicate with professors and work on their research projects than do students at peer schools. And those who attend women's colleges are much more likely to say that the schools helped them become politically or socially aware than women who attend coed small liberal arts colleges or larger public universities.

Then there are the outcomes. One crucial bit of outsized difference is what happens to the women who bring an interest in science to a single-sex institution: They stick with it. By the end they are 50 percent more likely to major in math or science or fulfill the requirements for medical school than are women at coed schools. And their outperformance in high-profile positions later looks similar to what we saw in the snobbery chapter: Whereas alumnae of women's colleges make up just 2 percent of the population of college graduates, in recent years they've made up over 20 percent of the women in Congress and one-third of women on the boards of directors of the nation's largest public companies.

A large National Survey of Student Engagement study summed these statistics up like so: "In terms of gains, women's college respondents reported making more progress in every measure tested. Specifically, women's college students indicated greater gains in understanding themselves and others, general education, ability to analyze quantitative problems, and desire to contribute to the welfare of their community. . . . More specifically, women at women's colleges engage more frequently in effective educational practices at levels that exceed those of their counterparts at coeducational institutions. Indeed, on almost every engagement measure, women at single-sex colleges scored higher."

Now a bit about who and what fall on the other side of those "almosts" in this category of school. Over the years researchers have found that students at women's colleges are more likely to find their social lives wanting. They're also less likely to be on a varsity sports team or join an intramural one. And if your child is a person of color, you once again need to ask additional questions. Research has shown that women's colleges are not immune to some of the same overall challenges that coeducational schools face. First-year and senior Black students are less satisfied with their college experience than are white students, and Asian American students are less satisfied overall. And in the all-important mentor-teacher-access category, African American and Asian American seniors at women's colleges reported fewer interactions with professors than white students did.

Despite the "almosts," too many people categorically refuse to even consider women's colleges. If you're anywhere near one, just go check it out. If it's a few years before senior year of high school, fine. Consider it practice or a warm-up. Plant a seed at least. Listen to what the tour guides and admissions officers say. Note how much more data they tend to give away. Keep that in the front of your mind as you visit coed colleges and demand that they produce the same data. Ask those schools what research they do on women specifically, or women of color, and their level of engagement and satisfaction. If they can't or won't answer or if they promise to follow up and then don't, that ought to tell you something.

My very first newspaper job was in Northampton, Massachusetts, and I could practically walk to Smith from the front door of the newsroom. The one class I took there through our five-college consortium positively crackled with energy. It's such a terrific part of the world that I've long fantasized about moving back there someday, something I confessed to President McCartney.

She just wishes more people would show up to check it all out for themselves. "Is it a cloister?" she asked. "No. It's a four-year intervention where students see that women can lead."

CHAPTER 14

Diversity in All Its Forms

Students benefit in many ways from living and studying in diverse environments as undergraduates. In this context, diversity is about race, but it's about a lot more, too. Any given family may wonder about gender, social class, sexual orientation, political leanings, faith, dominant social groups such as fraternities and sororities, or whether there are lots of other first-generation college students on a particular campus. Perhaps you want your teenager to meet the widest variety of people along the continuum in every one of those categories. Or maybe the teens themselves are tired of what they see as the unbearable homogeneity of their high schools. And it's possible that not everyone in the household agrees on the importance of seeking out diversity and questioning the value of a high-priced institution that lacks it, in which case a frank conversation about it all may be necessary

The United States is growing more diverse, not less, and the long-term economic trends in the world are likely to tilt toward more trade and the need for more cooperation. The more that college students learn about the perspectives of others, the better prepared they will be. This isn't necessarily self-evident to teenagers. It certainly wasn't for me. But think back to your own college experience. Which peers did you learn the most from? The Black guy from Virginia who had just spent a few years at an overwhelmingly white boarding school; the Filipino American young woman from the elite public school on the Upper East Side of Manhattan; the parochial school kid from Toledo who ditched the law to become an Episcopal priest, since she couldn't very well do that as a Catholic; the out gay man from Texas; the Republican from Colorado and the other one from Brooklyn; the Sephardic Jewish immigrant whose family came to Arizona after fleeing terrorists in Algeria and making pit stops in Israel and Paris; the people who had more money than me and the people who had less (all of whose families showed equal generosity toward me over the years, hosting me at beachfront homes or for casseroles near the Hartford airport)—these are some of the people who are still in my life decades later or who helped shape me most. I don't think it's a coincidence that they were all in some way different from my eighteen-year-old self.

And I don't think I'm alone. There is a rich body of literature going back decades that shows the impact that diversity has on college students. There is the meta-study (a collection and analysis of previous research) that concluded that diversity has positive effects on both minority and majority groups. In the classroom, curricula that examine modern social issues can help different groups of students agree on the definition and promotion of social justice. Encounters with diverse groups led to better leadership skills later, according to another study. And Gallup found that recent college graduates who strongly agreed that they'd regularly interacted with people different from them were 2.2 times more likely to think that their degree was worth the cost than those who had not had similar encounters.

If you want to begin to consider your teenager's numerical odds of having those kinds of encounters, one good place to start is with the raw data that exist in the common data set, or CDS. That's the form that colleges and universities fill out to hand off to the main list makers and ranking operations such as *U.S. News & World Report*. Section B2 tells you the gender, racial, and ethnic makeup of the student body. Right below that you learn about graduation rates by socioeconomic status (including people who borrowed and people who received Pell Grants for especially low-income students). The student life section will tell you what percentage of the students are members of fraternities or sororities and will signal the presence or absence of campus ministries, theme housing, international student associations, and Reserve Officers Training Corps groups. Section I provides the percentage of faculty who are members of minority groups and the gender split.

This gives you some information in isolation, but it doesn't give you much context. The enrollment management consulting firm Ruffalo Noel Levitz reported in its 2019 Discounting Report for Four-Year Private and Public Institutions that the more selective a private college gets, the lower the percentage of Pell Grant recipients in its student body tends to be on average. How low can that Pell figure go? In 2014, my *New York Times* colleague David Leonhardt shook up the world of undergraduate education by publishing a proprietary college access index that aimed to measure how much effort top undergraduate institutions were putting into attracting and graduating low- and middle-income students. At Washington University in St. Louis, it turned out, just 6 percent of its undergraduates were Pell Grant recipients. The institution was so embarrassed that it soon pledged to double that figure within five years, and it succeeded.

Though the *Times* has not updated the index in several years, these trend lines usually don't change all that fast, given how expensive it can be to provide aid for lower-income students. So a look at the data in the *New York Times* archive under the headline "Top Colleges Doing the Most for the American Dream," which lists 171 of them, is well worth your time. If what you see alarms or delights you, ask schools for updated data.

In 2017, the *Times* published yet another sort of ranking. This one, drawn from a unique set of data that the economist Raj Chetty and his colleagues had obtained from the federal government, listed thirty-eight colleges that had more undergraduates from families who are among the top 1 percent of earners in the United States than people from families in the bottom 60 percent. Washington University in St.

Louis was there at the top again, as ranked by the ratio between the two income groups, with a startling gap between those from the top 1 percent (21.7 percent) and those from the bottom 60 percent (just 6.1 percent). Colorado College, Washington and Lee University in Virginia, Colby College in Maine, and Trinity College in Connecticut rounded out the top five. The story, which is online under the headline "Some Colleges Have More Students from the Top 1 Percent Than the Bottom 60. Find Yours," allows you to do just that by plugging in other schools for which there was enough data to see where they ranked. Have a look if social-class equity and diversity are on your mind.

All of these numbers raise two overarching questions: What is the definition of "success," and how much is enough? When is a school sufficiently diverse, and what measures exist to prove its progress or lack thereof? Washington University answered that for itself: Being last was simply awful. Six percent wasn't enough. Doubling the Pell Grant number would at least get it out of last place. But shouldn't a school with an enormous endowment such as Washington University do even more? A 2016 *Chronicle of Higher Education* article asked the question, and Dorothy A. Brown, a law professor at Emory who examines race and class issues, put it this way: "As long as they're in the range of their peers then everything is good. Somehow mediocrity was fine when we're talking about diversity." Emory is aiming to hit a 20 percent Pell Grant figure in the coming years. Pell Grant recipients have to meet income requirements; if colleges were to enroll as many in rough proportion to the number of people in the Pell Grant income bracket in the overall population, the percentage of any given undergraduate population receiving a Pell Grant would be 35 percent.

None of the most selective private colleges and universities that I am aware of has pledged to hit that number, although Amherst did recently enroll a first-year class in which 29 percent of the students were Pell Grant recipients. Its target was likely a few percentage points below that—and not because it dislikes poor students. As we've learned, small colleges are expensive places to run, and the math on enrolling the poorest students is not favorable. Chances are that Pell Grant recipients are getting $50,000 or more in grant aid directly from a given selective private college each year. Moreover, unless a college expands—and most haven't done so all that much and don't want to—that low-income student may be replacing someone who would have paid $75,000 each year. If you run those numbers thirty-five times for every hundred students you enroll, things get very expensive very quickly. That is the primary reason why hitting 35 percent has not been a priority for any of the most selective colleges, although plenty of the ones that accept most or all applicants have hit numbers that are higher than 35 percent.

Some administrators dislike the Pell Grant metric. It doesn't account for people who are undocumented and living in the United States (who can't qualify for Pell Grants due to their lack of citizenship) or low-income students who come to a school from their home outside the United States. Moreover, it fails to give a school credit for enrolling and subsidizing a disproportionate (to other competitive schools, at least) number of students from families who earn up to $50,000 more than the Pell Grant cutoff. This is a reasonable point, since few schools want a student body that is mostly either lower income or affluent. Still, I did not interview a single president who did not hope to do better. "Students want to go to diverse colleges, and if you aren't going to provide that, you're not going to enroll the students that you want," said David R. Anderson, the president of St. Olaf College. "That's a thing we know from the admissions office, especially from students who go someplace else."

I put many of the questions in this chapter to people of color with years of experience counseling students. One of the first was Marie Bigham, who spent years working as a college counselor in private schools before helping to start ACCEPT (Admissions Community Cultivating Equity & Peace Today), a group for admissions professionals that is trying to make the system more racially equitable. I did so with some wariness, knowing that for many people who are not part of a majority

one of the few people whose family was from the Middle East who was actually involved with the culture. She threw herself into campus activities, and she jokingly described integrating a sorority that was made up mostly of blond-haired women. But she too had a lot to learn. "There was so much about equity and inclusion that I didn't understand," she said. "I was a very conservative Muslim girl. I didn't even understand the concept of different sexualities or races and their hardships."

Abboud crossed all sorts of lines at Wooster, happily, but not every undergraduate does. Another big question for any student hoping to truly engage with people who are different is this: How atomized is the undergraduate population, and if it's more than zero, is the college doing anything to change it? Does it give money or extra money to campus groups that, say, jointly sponsor events? "I can attest to the fact that the benefits of diversity do not spontaneously arise merely from the presence of a varied student body," wrote Ronald G. Shaiko, a senior fellow at Dartmouth, in a *Chronicle of Higher Education* article. "It is amazing to me the amount of effort undertaken to create diverse incoming classes while comparatively little is done to create a 'choice architecture,' to borrow a phrase from behavioral economics, that would 'nudge' students into interactions outside of their comfort zones."

Abboud also spoke to the complexity of navigating life just off the College of Wooster campus. For a while she was exploring the possibility of becoming a pharmacist, and she worked at a local drugstore. There a customer kept insisting that she tell him what she really thought of life outside Saudi Arabia. He either didn't believe that she was Lebanese American or didn't understand that the two countries' borders don't even touch one another. "You know how you sometimes go online and see white supremacists' and racists' comments, and you don't think people like that are out there?" she said. "There is a very big gap between the college and the community, and the college actually set up a board to help fight ignorance and racism."

Many undergraduates, no matter what group they belong to or identify with, do not want to feel duty bound to serve as an official representative of it. That's why we shouldn't be too quick to dismiss schools with less diverse populations out of hand. Sometimes they struggle to break out of self-perpetuating cycles that may owe at least something to their surrounding areas.

The questions in this chapter are a road map to the places that are at least trying. If being a bridge on that road is a role your teenager would relish, it's important to think hard about how difficult it can sometimes be to build bridges. Maybe the school ought to be paying you to do so, in the form of merit aid. But if every answer to the questions above makes you think that you could find a truly nurturing community there, that place may be worth more to you in dollars than the other schools on your list.

CHAPTER 15

How and When Small School Size Matters

When it came time for Anabel Mydland to pick a college, she had plenty of good choices. Colgate and Hamilton wanted her. A less selective liberal arts college in her midwestern state was practically throwing merit aid at her. And her flagship state university offered to pay her to attend: Her tuition, room, and board would be free, plus she'd receive an annual stipend.

But she turned them all down because she wanted to attend a truly small school, one that was going to cost a lot more money. She needed it, in fact; her high school had 4,000 people, and she had struggled with mental health issues at times. When she contemplated the Big State University, it frightened her. "I thought I'd get lost in the fray and be alone and sad and that it would be weird and awful," she said. Her psychiatrist endorsed her choice. In fact, that big state university employed her psychiatrist. "I figured that must be a good opinion," she told me over coffee as she took a break from studying for a linguistics exam.

It all makes perfect sense, right? How can any big place, with all of its competing priorities, be truly great for any undergraduate? Small must be better than big—small classes, first and foremost, and more contained campuses, too. Size matters to *U.S. News & World Report* and the millions of people who treat its rankings guide as a college-shopping bible.

There are seventeen factors that go into any school's *U.S. News* ranking, and class size makes up 8 percent of the overall score. The publication defends using this factor at all by saying that class size is a proxy for whether students will be able to engage with their instructors. Schools get the most credit for the fraction of classes with fewer than twenty students. For those with a significant proportion of classes between twenty and twenty-nine students, there's also credit, and decreasing credit for class sizes with thirty to thirty-nine and forty to forty-nine people. Any classes with over fifty students get no credit at all, and *U.S. News* pointedly added that it doesn't tell anyone how it weights these scores. Why not? Well, back when the publication was more transparent, schools tried to game the system; Northeastern had particular success doing so, and others capped a lot of classes at double-digit numbers that ended in eight or nine.

So why twenty? Why fifty? No reason at all; the magazine doesn't point to studies that show some sort of deterioration when more than twenty students are in a classroom or overall devastation once the fifty-first walks in. Puzzled skeptics such as Mark Salisbury have run their own mini-experiments with real undergraduate data. Before he started TuitionFit, which helps applicants pick and pay for value-priced colleges, he ran institutional research at Augustana College in Illinois. In a blog post in 2017, he mocked the "mythology" that had emerged from *U.S. News* rankings around the superiority of classes with nineteen or fewer students. He used his school's own survey data on self-reported learning plus satisfaction with the instructor and the course to prove that the most meaningful cut is at thirty students, not twenty.

Perhaps the biggest class-size data set comes from a 2013 effort from the IDEA Center, a nonprofit at the University of Notre Dame that researches how students learn. (The acronym stands for "Innovation, De-Risking and Enterprise Acceleration.") It gathered information from over 490,000 classes at four hundred schools, measuring some of the same things Salisbury had. (He was using IDEA survey data from his own campus.) Class-size groups were ten to fourteen, fifteen to thirty-four, thirty-five to forty-nine, fifty to ninety-nine, and one hundred and up. IDEA concluded that students in the smaller classes did in fact report the most progress, worked the hardest, and had the most desire to take the course. They also said their instructors did more to establish rapport, inspire students, and encourage them to collaborate.

All good, right? Still, this study is like many others that we've already seen wherein the authors can't claim that one thing causes the other. For starters, there are no exam results here—just self-reported declarations of academic progress. It's also possible that only the most motivated students take the smaller-class-size courses or that weaker ones hope to blend into the crowd in larger lecture halls. Certain teachers—say, those who have much less interest in interacting with lowly undergraduates or grading their messy prose—may also shy away from teaching smaller classes.

Though not all studies show a link between smaller class size and student satisfaction or other positive learning outcomes, there are several that seem rigorous enough to raise the antennae of parents tempted to pay more for a more boutique experience. One look into the records of 60,000 students found that when class size goes up, undergraduates tend to drop out of school more often and take longer to complete their undergraduate degrees. This study is noteworthy for the researchers' use of techniques that led them to conclude that larger class sizes were in fact the cause of the negative effects.

Another study looked at four classes at California State University, Chico; Cornell; the University of Puget Sound; and the flagship University of Minnesota campus in Minneapolis. Slightly larger classes were the subject, starting at 40 students and going up to 239. There, as the size grew larger, women did worse than men on exams and final course grades, although they performed better than men in other areas that contributed to their final grades. The researchers looked for similar effects for people of color but did not find any. Other researchers homed in on gender effects in STEM courses and found that when classes grew from 50 to 150 people, women's participation in class fell relative to men's by 50 percent. Smaller classes make it easier for professors to find students with promise or who are perilously underperforming as well. One eye-opening essay in *Forbes* by Chad Orzel, a Union College physics professor, explained how much easier it is in a smaller class to identify a talented quiet student, even one who isn't making As, who would outperform in a lab as a summer research assistant. In a class of 200, he said, he'd probably never find that person.

If you find all of this evidence convincing or even merely intriguing, it stands to reason that all the data you need can be found in the admissions brochure.

But it turns out that average class size doesn't really tell the whole story. At the 2018 conference of people who work in institutional research—the professionals who help colleges and universities study themselves and generate data that college shoppers often never see—the best single breakout session that I witnessed was also among the least well attended. Maybe fifteen people turned up to hear Mark Umbricht's presentation "Perception Isn't Everything: The Reality of Class Size."

Here was the revelation, which Umbricht, a project manager at the University of Michigan, also outlined in a manuscript by the same title with coauthor Kevin Stange: If the point of the exercise is to capture students' experiences in any given classroom, merely looking at a standard average class-size number is inadequate. That's because this metric doesn't reflect the time students actually spend in class. At Michigan, 84 percent of courses have under fifty students and 57 percent have fewer than twenty students. Not bad for a big state school, right? But if you measure by time spent in class, only 19 percent of any given student's time is spent in classes with fewer than twenty people, while he or she spends nearly 30 percent of the time in classes with one hundred or more peers.

In short, Umbricht concluded, class size is measurable, but it isn't necessarily meaningful. "Therefore," he and Stange noted rather drolly, "there is a disincentive for a single college, or a small group of colleges, to recalculate their class size based on the student experience." There is, however, absolutely an incentive for all of us to march into every admissions office and ask for class-size data that are based on the actual time spent in small or large classrooms, as opposed to averages that insiders such as Umbricht and Stange have proved can be pretty misleading.

Perhaps you're tempted to use the student-faculty ratio as an anchor or proxy for size and attention. The most eloquent assessment of this metric that I've seen comes from Georgetown professor Jacques Berlinerblau, who referred to it as "a bullshit statistic if there ever was one" in his book *Campus Confidential*. Often people mistake a 15:1 ratio for victory on average class size, but just because there is one faculty member for every fifteen students doesn't mean that each class will be that small. Some faculty go on leave frequently, while others don't teach much if at all. Some professors teach only graduate students. And it isn't always clear how "faculty" is defined. Does it include adjuncts, who may be teaching at two other schools to make ends meet and aren't on campus much? Does it include graduate students? It's not always clear.

Alas, the more reassuring the answers to questions like these are, the more expenses a school faces. Faculty can teach only so many courses, and every student generally needs to take at least four each term. If most classes are smaller, a school needs more classrooms and teachers and office space to put them all into. Meanwhile, good numbers can turn bad on a dime. In the wake of the 2008–09 economic collapse, 56 percent of large public universities reported consolidating sections into fewer and larger classes. We can be reasonably sure that we'll see more of that during the next extended recession. When you rely on adjunct professors for a chunk of your teaching, it's easy enough to cast them off when times are tough. Private colleges with more tenured faculty may not have that flexibility, even if fewer students are willing to come (and pay) when economic times are tougher.

Let's turn to the overall size-of-school question. This is a good point at which to discuss some of the best, most basic data on undergraduate outcomes that exist. As we've already discussed, there isn't much good statistical school-level information on what happens to people while they're in college and afterward. We can learn, however, exactly how many people stick around any given campus after completing their first year (versus dropping out or transferring), and we also know how long it takes them to graduate (if they do). These data are crucial; when lots of people leave a school after a year, it can be a sign of a troubled institution. And if it takes longer than four years to graduate, that will probably cost more money (negating any savings from possibly lower tuition) and will delay a student's entering the workplace for however long it takes to finish. On average, this is another area where small schools shine.

You'll also want to ask about these so-called first-year persistence and retention data by department or program, since they can vary widely within a large university that has many different undergraduate tracks. The Council of Independent Colleges, which exists to promote private schools that are generally smaller but nevertheless use standard federal data that schools of all sizes must report to the government, has noted one extraordinary difference in STEM fields: When you examine the percentage of undergraduates who complete these degrees in four years or less, the figure is 80 percent for people at private nondoctoral institutions (small liberal arts colleges, mostly). The figure is 81 percent at private schools that also offer doctorates, which tend to be bigger schools. At the larger public doctoral schools, meanwhile, the figure falls to just 52 percent. So it's basically a 50-50 proposition whether you will get out on time if you want to major in chemistry or computer science at a big public university. Though we cannot know for sure whether school size is the sole cause of the lower odds, the risk is that the normalization of the five-plus-year stay on campus may affect any teenager who arrives intending to finish in four.

Another consideration when evaluating size is the perception that large schools may seem superior to smaller ones due to the sheer size of the alumni network. Be careful here, though. When Gallup asked 5,100 college graduates how helpful their alumni networks had been in their careers to date, just 9 percent said they had been very helpful or just plain helpful. Just over two-thirds of respondents said that the networks had not been a factor in their careers at all. Even if you are inclined to believe that fellow alumni can help your child down the road, it's hard to know what metric to examine. Often people use the percentage of alumni giving as a proxy for satisfaction, which then becomes a potential predictor for the likelihood that someone might throw the rope back for someone younger. If you believe that, the larger schools that score well here are Notre Dame, the University of Southern California, the University of North Carolina, Clemson University in South Carolina, and Georgia Tech.

If your child's aim is mostly to find likeminded people and have a blast with that group, the more undergraduates, the merrier and the easier it is to find a niche, at least in theory. The bigger schools are also more likely to have a thriving Greek system, which can be a quick way to form tight bonds as long as you can sort yourself out and into the best-fitting fraternity or sorority before and during the rush period. Not everyone does that successfully, and others can't afford the dues and parties. Still more want nothing to do with the party culture. Joining up isn't strictly necessary, however; at Northwestern, which is 40 percent Greek, those students score high on the university's internal engagement scores, but so do people who participate in singing groups, theater, and Christian organizations.

If it's the classroom that's most important to your family, listen carefully to the way that the big schools talk about themselves when they're trying to persuade students to choose them. You take a tour, and they want you to know that the average class size is smaller than you might think. You read the brochure, and the student-faculty ratio sure seems reasonable. "There is a reason every R1 [research-intensive] university in the country sells its undergraduate education as being like a small liberal arts college," said G. Gabrielle Starr, Pomona's president, using the higher education term for the most productive research universities. "There is a secret sauce in the now largely romanticized idea of a scholar-teacher sitting in a room with six or twelve brilliant students with nothing off limits that they can talk about."

That is true to a point, as long as students don't want to declare a pre-professional major. There are no business majors at many small colleges or nursing degrees or engineering departments. But that is a point of pride for these schools, take it or leave it. You know what they are and what they stand for. "The challenge for a large contemporary university is that it is trying to be five or ten different things at once, and trying to do everything at a high level of excellence is next to impossible," said Macalester's former president Brian Rosenberg.

If you're running a state university, you spend 30 percent of your time dealing with the government, 30 percent fund-raising, 30 percent on Division 1 athletics, and 50 percent of your time on the hospital that the school also oversees. Given that those numbers add up to way more than 100, there's not a lot of time left to focus on the teenagers on campus. "We do one thing," Rosenberg continued. "We educate undergraduates. When I gather with my team, we talk about undergraduates. Others talk about the basketball team scandal and whether to merge the hospital. We educate undergraduates at the highest possible level of quality, and those types of organizations are more likely to excel."

At this point you may be wondering: *Those administrative teams, those educators—many of them have kids of their own. Where do they go to college?* In 2006, a couple of cheeky economics professors at Vanderbilt University in Nashville decided to find out, and they published their results in a prominent economic journal. They studied 4,742 faculty kids and compared them with teens from similar backgrounds who did not have a professor parent. And for those of you on the inside who know that some faculty have access to tuition benefits that will pay for some or all of their children's college education, the professors studied only faculty families at private colleges and universities whose benefit was equal at any school they chose. They also excluded families whose children attended the institution where one or both parents taught.

The two economists found that faculty families make "dramatically different" choices than do similarly affluent members of the general public, and there is a "substantial" preference for smaller liberal arts colleges. That wasn't true just for families where a parent teaches at one; it was also true for families where a parent teaches at a large research university. They seemed to know something about what goes on at bigger schools, and an unusual number of their children ended up choosing smaller ones. "The tilt toward liberal arts colleges by faculty families is unambiguous," the authors concluded.

Is the case closed, then, for the families who are focused first and foremost on the actual education? After all, smaller colleges are in the business of paying close attention, of trying to make it very difficult for students to escape notice. But for Anabel Mydland, that turned out to be unexpectedly suffocating. There was only one dining hall at her college, and walking in alone felt oppressive. She'd been on a preorientation trip with some nice people, but in the days after it ended she thought they were all secretly hanging out without her. "No one sits alone, and I needed to eat," she said. "So I would sit in my room and eat sunflower seeds like a rodent."

When she fell into a depression and missed her small classes, she worried about returning and having well-meaning peers ask after her, since everyone would notice that she had been gone. "Everyone knew who I was, and it was really hard for me," she said. There was some bad luck, too: an unpleasant dorm, a bad roommate. And there was also some bad planning that she now admits to, such as not having a strong enough mental health treatment plan in place when she got to campus. Before long, she withdrew from the school and eventually ended up thriving—

and paying full price—at the same large state university whose scholarship she had turned down. Now her math class has seventy-five people. "No one talks to each other or is expected to make friends," she said. "You're here to get a grade." And that's just fine by her.

We—parents, kids, well-meaning mental health workers, and college counselors—can know our kids and ourselves only so well. And sometimes, acquiring that self-knowledge is damn expensive. It's one reason why sending eighteen-year-olds straight to college in the first place is a questionable move, and I'll have more to say about gap years in Chapter 25.

There are a couple of blunt questions we ought to make our kids answer again and again in the years leading up to college. I particularly like two that the college website Unigo published in an article about the small-versus-big question: Are you more likely to skip a class if you're just a face in the crowd? If so, perhaps small classes would provide needed discipline. That cuts to the heart of the social anxiety that is a natural part of any transition to college but may become overwhelming if your school doesn't match your answer to this question: When you enter a dining hall, do you want everyone to know you, some people to know you, or no one at all to know you?

Then there are the questions we can put to the colleges that really ought to tell us a bit more about class size. When they broadcast the average class size to you, ask about the percentage of time that students spend in classes with more than fifty or one hundred or two hundred people. If they don't know, ask them if they'd please start calculating it. If the consumers of their product don't request better information, schools are not going to offer it of their own accord, since there's a decent chance it will make them look worse. While you're at it, ask them to break it down by year. Are first-year students vulnerable to going unnoticed or dropping out when spending most of their time in large classrooms? If so, does the school think this is ideal? If your child has a strong academic interest, ask the same thing of the chair of that department. The good ones will have a clear sense of which classes are large and how much time their majors spend in them. And if you send an email or two or leave a couple of phone messages and nobody calls you back, that should tell you something.

Then follow up by asking "What have you done to change the number of large classes or the dynamic within them?" Plenty of schools are indeed trying new strategies. Arizona State is one leader here, with hundreds of technologists and designers helping professors take their courses apart and re-create them. Introduction to Biology can often be quite cutthroat at a large school, with premeds slugging it out among themselves and the merely curious often struggling. When the ASU class was a traditional lecture class for three hundred, 20 percent of the students dropped the class before the end of the semester and another quarter flunked. Once upon a time, academics might have deemed that an appropriate result. It should be hard, after all, and there should be a weeding out. But ASU didn't think so, and after changing everything about the course to make both taking it and teaching it more intimate, under 2 percent of students withdraw and 90 percent pass.

Ask for specific examples of classes like this at schools that you're considering. If no one can cite any, that's a telling sign. If someone in admissions provides you with a list, have your applicant make arrangements to visit one of the classes. Or suggest that your son or daughter pick a large introductory class at random in a topic that most interests them and ask to visit. This may feel a bit aggressive, but it's also elemental. If learning is any part of the undergraduate agenda and your applicant has never been in a classroom with more than thirty-five people before, it is important to see what that feels like. That's doubly true if parents are tempted to save money by sending their child to a school with many classes that large.

CHAPTER 16

Amenities
(but Is a Lazy River a Plus?)

Most colleges promise small classes and engaged professors. They maintain websites featuring fresh-faced undergraduates. The students work hard and play hard, and then in the summer they get paid to do meaningful work. They graduate in four years flat and contribute to a 101 percent alumni employment rate. And at a certain point this particular college story starts to blur together with all the others, and the colleges know this. But what if a school builds a lazy river around the campus that students can enjoy after class in an inflatable tube? Now, that is memorable—singular, even. Enter an infinite number of outsized campus amenities.

Let's be crystal clear about what is going on here: Colleges are trying to manipulate you and in particular your teenage children. Lazy rivers and climbing walls and the campus steakhouse are marketing, plain and simple, and it works quite well. In a 2013 paper, curious professors at the University of Michigan—a prestigious place that is not particularly amenity laden—attempted to quantify how well the sell job works. They found that market demand for "consumption amenities," including dorms and student activities, can explain at least 16 percent of the differences across colleges in their ratio of academic-to-amenity spending. And as the author and higher education policy expert Kevin Carey put it to Inside Higher Ed in 2015, "In the way they decide to market themselves, colleges teach naïve students what to desire."

Let me take you on a guided tour of what the colleges spend those millions of dollars on when they divert it from the academic spending pot. We'll begin with exterior architecture, since it provides so many obvious clues as to what an institution hopes to stand for. Consider the University of Southern California, known in past decades as the University of Spoiled Children or the University of Second Choice. The institution worked hard to obliterate those handles, throwing merit aid money at top students to lure them from the Ivy League. Now its admissions rates are in the teens, approaching Ivy League levels of selectivity.

Or maybe you have a vague sense that the school is not in the best of neighborhoods and that student housing, on or off campus, has never been its strong suit. To compensate, USC spent many years buying enough land—fifteen acres, no easy feat in an urban area—to increase the amount of undergraduate housing by almost one-third in one fell swoop to the tune of $700 million. With that budget, the school could have had its pick of the stalwarts of modern architecture. Instead, it made a telling choice: It went Gothic. If it weren't for the Trader Joe's and the smorgasbord of casual restaurants tucked discreetly into the ground floor of the buildings, the new USC Village could be one hundred years old. It practically screams: TAKE US SERIOUSLY. And the first-year honors students get some of the very best real estate.

Collegiate interiors have evolved quickly as well. At the most selective end, Amherst had to dismantle some of its first-year dorms and put them back together again in a different configuration. People were choosing archrival Williams instead, owing to Amherst's numerous, undersized two-room triples. Upperclassmen at less selective schools have come to expect suite-style living: a common space, often with a kitchen, surrounded by small single rooms plus a shared bathroom. No more long halls, open doors, and bathrooms shared by everyone on the floor—and no more of the social mixing that comes with all of that.

Probe tour guides a bit, and they'll talk endlessly about dormitory features—which dorms have air-conditioning, just how stifling the others are for how many weeks each year, how this compares to the rival school up the road. And then there's the laundry. At first, coin-operated machines started taking credit cards or maybe student IDs linked to a cash account. Soon the machines could text or email you when your cycle was done. Colleges that hoped to stand out then made all laundry free, and if doing it yourself is too much to handle, the laundry service can now deal with it for you. That bit of outsourcing is not free, by the way, but some schools will probably make it so before too long.

The institutions that wish to maintain some whiff of egalitarianism try to push back on what feels like progress to many undergraduates. When a developer built off-campus student housing near the University of California at Berkeley, it advertised its "state-of-the-art fitness center" and "gaming lounges." If you're on financial aid, you're probably not going to live there without accruing significant debt. Nevertheless, when a Bloomberg reporter showed up and started looking around, a university spokesperson practically sniffed when insisting that the new housing was not a "luxury" facility. Income stratification is not a good look for any school, but it is truly off brand for Berkeley, the flagship state university in a progressive state. Nevertheless, simply being able to afford to live close to campus is beginning to qualify as luxurious.

Brandon Busteed tried to figure out whether all the new buildings had made anyone any happier. The Duke alum, who spearheaded Gallup's research on the undergraduate experience, kept scratching his head over the fact that his alma mater had increased its square footage but hadn't enrolled many more students. "I've tried to measure it," he said. "Is there a better outcome if you lived in a dorm or no dorm? But on outcomes there is no relationship."

What about leisure time? The climbing wall was perhaps the first campus amenity that really raised eyebrows among parents and faculty members who worried about misplaced priorities. Its history extends at least as far back as the 1970s to the famed Husky Rock at the University of Washington. In fact, the concept is so old that the school recently replaced it with a new and improved indoor climbing center. Even though intrastate rivalries abound on the climbing wall front—the University of Texas at San Antonio's wall is one foot higher than the one at the University of Houston, which is one foot taller than the one across town at Baylor—a professor at Furman University in South Carolina discovered that of the 467 students he surveyed at his own school, 23 percent didn't even know that there was a climbing wall on campus.

On top of mimicking urban health clubs, some schools have decided to replicate a resort experience. If floating down a lazy river on vacation is an utter delight, why not make it part of everyday life? These "leisure pools," as they are known in the trade, are expensive to build and maintain. Students don't seem to care, though; often it is they who vote to pay for them through hikes in the extra fees that show up on each semester's tuition bill. At Louisiana State University, students hit the road to check out facilities at the Universities of Texas and Alabama before deciding that their lazy river should spell out *L*, *S*, and *U* and be visible from space, or nearly so if the aerial photos that abound on the internet are to be believed. I was not able to confirm whether they also did due diligence at the University of Missouri, where tour guides note that the school modeled its indoor grotto on the one at the old Playboy Mansion.

Upon opening, LSU administrators took pains not to use the word "leisure" and certainly not "lazy." It is just "the River," like the one you'd dive into in a Bruce Springsteen song after a long day of hard labor. "There is nothing lazy about the pursuit of health and wellness," a recreation director told a local reporter. The university's president was a bit looser with his words at the wellness river's ribbon cutting. "Quite frankly, I don't want you to leave this campus ever," he said. "So whatever we need to do to keep you here, we'll keep you safe here. We're here to give you everything you need."

In this hierarchy of needs, food scores quite high. And any conversation about campus dining halls with higher education diehards almost inevitably leads to a dissection of a now-infamous Malcolm Gladwell podcast from 2016 contrasting the good food at Bowdoin with the bad food at Vassar. Gladwell drew a straight line between meal quality and the fact that Vassar enrolls a higher percentage of low-income students who are eligible for Pell Grants. According to Gladwell, instead of spending money on socially important programs, Bowdoin was spending its money on too-good food. In fact, the food at Bowdoin is fine but not extravagantly so. One July day in 2019, I had garlic scapes fresh from the on-campus gardening plot pretossed in creamy cider dressing. From the hot line, there were serviceable polenta cakes with a "spicy" (but not really) tomato chutney. Also whoopie pies, kind of a thing in Maine. And Fritos on the sandwich bar.

To Gladwell, all of this adds up to some kind of moral failing, but he didn't do much math on the topic. In the wake of Gladwell's viral podcast, Robert Kelchen, an associate higher education professor at Seton Hall University in New Jersey, did run some numbers and estimated that if Bowdoin spent about $1,000 less per student per year on food (an average school charges $4,500 per year for food per student), it might subsidize some additional low-income students. That said, how many others might attend a different school in the wake of a four-figure budget cut per student in a category that many people believe is important? Something else that emerged in my own reporting: Lots of affluent Vassar students skip the subpar dining hall meals, potentially resulting in a dining hall where social classes do not mix.

The market eventually gets what it wants, and it is forcing most of the laggard schools to make at least some effort on the food front. In my travels, nearly every dining hall—even the ones where third-party outsourcers run the culinary show for the college—had posters or maps showing the farms and local suppliers that the chefs were buying from. Regional specialties abound, such as the excellent bratwurst of the upper Midwest at Macalester. Penn has a multistall food hall to rival pioneering ones in New York City, Los Angeles, and Lisbon. It features some of the best falafel in the United States, an outstanding pizza operation, and Philly cheesesteaks, of course. And because parents still can't seem to get comfortable with Penn's urban locale, it has a uniformed security guard to make visiting families feel better. She was very busy reading the newspaper and checking her phone the day I dined there.

Now that better food is a commoditized baseline, schools have turned to the newest amenity, the most elemental of them all: sexual intercourse. Colleges don't talk about it quite that way. Instead, easier sex is dressed up somewhat chastely in a bid to upgrade the bedding. If you went to college and lived in a dorm, you well remember the mysterious extra-long mattresses and the pre-internet hunt for sheets that would fit them. They were always twin size, just at the moment when you were out from under your parents, raging with hormones and hoping to finally have a real grown-up sleepover party for two. No wonder moving off campus as juniors and seniors became a thing.

Colleges are onto this, and now an increasing number of them offer double beds in on-campus housing. Butler, Syracuse, Oklahoma State, and Texas Christian (!!) all feature them in at least some dorms.

That's all rather nice, but we should probably invoke the late University of California at Berkeley chancellor Clark Kerr here. When someone asked what he was doing about the perennial parking problems at the school, he had a ready bit on the tip of his tongue. His job, he said, had come to consist of "provid[ing] parking for faculty, sex for the students, and athletics for the alumni." And so it goes.

While most teenagers want more sex, some will be more swayed than others by the overall amenity package, according to the study that those Michigan professors conducted. Few places put it all together quite like High Point University in North Carolina. The tour of the place is an experience unto itself. You arrive at the campus gates, and a security guard checks you off a list. There is a parking spot with your name on an LED sign next to it. Nearby—unmistakably so—is the president's spot. He drives a Mercedes with HPU vanity plates.

The tour participants ride in shaded golf carts, so no one has to walk or sweat too much. The itinerary includes swimming pools and stops at the desk of the concierges, who can book your free trip to the airport or help with other everyday errands. For a few minutes there is a visit to the on-campus steakhouse, part of the life skills development program. Construction cranes are everywhere, building more and better. My hour-plus tour did not stop at the library, which was the first and last time any tour I took skipped that building.

High Point does this because of where it sits in the market. It accepts more than three-quarters of applicants, and it attracts what the University of Michigan professors described as "wealthier students much more willing to pay for consumption amenities." But at the more selective schools, administrators "have a much greater incentive to improve academic quality since this is the dimension most valued" by the sorts of students they would like to attract—the ones who tilt more toward having their minds blown and their minds grown than floating on a raft after class. In fact, according to the professors, less selective schools actually harm their ability to enroll more students by spending more on instruction.

Kevin McClure, an associate professor at University of North Carolina Wilmington, is perhaps the leading scholar of such things. He said that he does not have reason to doubt these conclusions, although he wishes there were narrower data sets that measured amenity spending more precisely. He's also not a fan of the "arms race" and "amenities war" rhetoric, and I think he's right. As we've seen already, these schools might as well be businesses competing for customers. Like any good business, they innovate—or try to. When they do, they want to talk about it. Amenities may or may not be useful for connecting students and keeping them on campus and enrolled; again, there just aren't enough good data to say for sure. But they are definitely useful marketing tools. They exist to make a school attractive and attract attention.

There is no shame in wanting nice things or having them and enjoying them, too. But ask yourself this: If you're visiting a college that will allow your child to live lavishly, what might be missing because of the choices the school has made? As Kevin Carey put it in the *Chronicle of Higher Education*, if there's any sin around climbing walls and the like, it's this: "They're *cheap*, compared to the cost of improving the quality of instruction that many undergraduates receive. If colleges want consumers to make choices differently, then colleges have to take the lead in creating, promoting, and standing behind different terms of consumer choice."

CHAPTER 17

Genuinely Reinvented
Career Counseling Offices

In the world of undergraduate career counseling, all roads seem to lead to Andy Chan, and they have for years. He has two decades of name-brand experience, first at Stanford and now at Wake Forest University in North Carolina. Plus he knows the real world that students want to inhabit, given that he did time at Bain, a top-tier consulting firm; at Clorox in brand management; and as a chief executive of two tech start-ups. A feature article about him in the *New York Times Magazine* inspired both awe and a tad bit of eye-rolling among his professional peers.

What makes him so instructive for our purposes is that he is also a blunt truth teller about the way things have been in his field for far too long—and how urgently they need to change. In a TEDx talk called "'Career Services' Must Die" that he gave at Lawrence University in Wisconsin, he laid it all out for any family that is worried that undergraduate institutions are failing to help undecided teenagers find meaningful work.

"Can you hear it?" he asked the crowd, wondering aloud if they were aware of the audible din that the angry people coming their way were already making.

"In my work I talk to lots of students, recent graduates, and their parents," he continued. "And beyond the fact that they did enjoy going to college, there is one thing that most of them will say, and that is that they're pretty pissed. They're pissed because it was such an anxiety-ridden process to figure out the path from college to career. They're pissed because many of them feel underemployed or are unemployed. And the bad news is, they are actually angry at us."

Their strong feelings, he said, show up in the choices of their younger siblings, who decide they have to choose quasi-professional undergraduate programs in health care, business, or engineering. Chan also sees it at larger universities such as Wake Forest, where the liberal arts departments struggle to compete for students against other undergraduate offerings that seem to offer better career prospects. "There is huge angst for students not in the business program, because they think they are unemployable," he pointed out.

If your child isn't dead set on law school, accounting, or the health care professions and could use a whole lot more guidance, these schools hear you loud and clear, even if they don't speak with the same kind of force as Andy Chan. In the past several years, nearly every liberal arts college and many universities with lots of undecided first-year students have attempted to turn their career advice operations upside down and inside out. St. Olaf College set a stretch target, which it described as a "very public commitment to becoming the best in the country among liberal arts colleges at helping students discern their vocation."

But in an environment in which every career office claims to have reinvented itself, how can you tell what's real and what's worth paying extra for? Who actually has expertise helping undergraduates find their way to jobs and careers? What has any given school done for its history and religion majors lately?

When I first met Clayton Spencer, the president of Bates College in Maine, she summed up this competitive landscape with the kind of sarcasm that works only when it has the ring of truth. "The better the college, the worse the career services," she said. "Because why would you sully things up with crass commercialism?"

From the beginning of her tenure in 2012, Spencer sensed that the market was shifting and that Bates was not above it all. To her, one fundamental factor was the power of purpose, a word she used repeatedly in her inauguration speech. Based on several years of work and some polling help from Gallup that studied college graduates nationwide, Bates came to a couple of conclusions. First, it was clear that a sense of purpose in the workplace mattered a lot. Only 6 percent of people who felt low levels of purpose in their work reported high levels of overall well-being, while 59 percent of people with high levels of purpose at work experienced high overall well-being. Bates also identified what it now refers to as a purpose gap: 80 percent of college graduates want to have a sense of purpose in the work they do for money, but not even half actually feel they have it. And just 23 percent of respondents to the poll that Bates sponsored with Gallup said their schools had given them realistic expectations about their job prospects.

What is purposeful work? It begins with a look inward at an individual's values and passions and a clear-eyed assessment of the things they are actually good at and the skills they could still acquire inside the classroom. Then the gaze turns outward in an attempt to connect with something larger than themselves. For it to work, it has to start early. So Bates had to figure out how to promote this sort of reflection at the earliest possible moment in its students' time at college. Finally, it had to develop a process to connect students with industries that they might never have considered without giving them too many highfalutin expectations about what kind of jobs a recent college graduate could actually get.

When Priscila Guillen arrived at Bates, she was reasonably certain about her career trajectory. The daughter of a single mother in Santa Fe, New Mexico, she had come to Bates because it had offered the best combination of generous financial aid and being far away from home. As a child she had loved going to the dentist, and as a high school student she had been at the top of her class. Fulfilling the predental science curriculum as an undergraduate, going on to dental school, and earning a good living to support her family seemed like a fail-safe plan.

But her classes at Bates were much harder than the ones she had aced in high school, and when she flunked a biology class, it gave her pause. Should she borrow money to retake the class during the summer? Or might it be time to consider the parts of the Bates course catalogue that she had barely glanced at so far? Sociology looked interesting, and so did psychology. But then she stumbled on gender and sexuality studies, and she was transfixed. The coursework combined with her summer experience working as a tutor and then as a tour guide persuaded her that she still had a desire to pursue some kind of helping profession. But helping whom and doing what?

To answer that question, she drew on all of the traditional career counseling office resources. She met repeatedly with her counselor, Peter Osborne, whom she enthusiastically described as "The bomb dot com." She got lots of advice about her résumé and job applications and met repeatedly with a small group of students who were similar to her and also seeking employment. A relatively new tool called Handshake helped her find the kinds of job openings that come from employers that don't have the time or money to conduct on-campus recruiting. One post there led to the job she eventually took, working as an advocate for a Wilmington, Delaware, organization that helps clients of public defenders connect to social services.

This is a far cry from dentistry. But perhaps the more important distinction is a narrower one that Bates helped Guillen draw on her own. For part of her senior year, she seriously considered taking a paralegal gig as her first job. It would, after all, give her more exposure to the law and helping people, and it would certainly pay the bills. But as she read various job descriptions, she was able to deduce just how little client contact she might have. She'd be helping only lawyers in any direct way.

Throughout my conversation with her, she kept referring over and over to her conversations with "Purposeful Work." The office wasn't some acronym, such as OCC for the Office of Career Counseling. Instead, the name was designed to convey not just a message but a mission, a standing order, really. And the question that Guillen said she found herself asking more than any other was this: Is it going to mean something? There are plenty of ways to find meaning and derive it from jobs of all sorts, but not every undergraduate will have had the four years of analysis necessary to even pose this question.

Denison also took its career counseling redesign cues from an extensive data collection effort, which revealed that there were some practical skills that it could do a much better job of providing. It's no violation of the liberal arts covenant to give people better training in Excel spreadsheets, for instance. So the school is aiming to use the months of January and May more effectively to drill students in the basics of business and perhaps a bit more, too. It also wants its career office to be more useful and available for alumni one to five years out, to help them when they reach their first big career pivot and are seeking a promotion or a job change. It has started virtual coaching circles for people in that situation.

Perhaps its biggest leap, however, has been into the curriculum itself. For years Denison has lost students to Indiana or Ohio State—students who, echoing Andy Chan's comments, felt compelled to default into an undergraduate business program given their desire to improve their odds of employment after graduation. Denison didn't want to offer a business degree, though. "We spent 18 months talking to employers and asked, 'What do you need from fresh, brand-new college graduates,'" the school's vice president for enrollment management, Greg Sneed, told its alumni magazine. "Not one employer said 'We need more people graduating from business school.'" Instead, he explained, what they wanted sounded a lot like a traditional liberal arts graduate with some practical spreadsheet and basic balance sheet–reading skills bolted on.

Denison president Adam S. Weinberg put a challenge to the faculty: Could they invent new academic programs rooted in the liberal arts that would prepare students for the direction in which business was heading? One response resulted in what came to be known as the global commerce program. You don't take accounting, but you do take economics. You don't take marketing, but you do study a language besides English. You must choose a region of focus. Then the course of study ends with a team-based, data-driven senior project. Within four years, it was the fifth most popular major. "We want to create a new generation of liberal arts programs that have more of a pragmatic edge," he said. (Do remember to gently probe how the school does its own survey research on what happens to people after they graduate.)

As we've seen, measuring the learning that goes on in any given major—let alone comparing it to majors across campuses—isn't easy. But colleges do publish at least one bit of data on recent alumni. In fact, you can't miss it on campus tours, since it's a fixture of nearly every career office and is often hung on banners or appears on highway billboards in the area. It's a percentage number that represents the proportion of the most recent graduating class that is gainfully employed, in graduate school, doing a fellowship, or engaged in some kind of service work.

"It is one of the most gamed numbers in all of higher education," said David R. Anderson, St. Olaf's president. How have schools gamed it traditionally? Anderson and others explained it to me over the course of the time I spent reporting: If you count only the people who respond and only people with good employment news bother to complete the survey, your numbers will look pretty good. Maybe you're reporting average starting salaries because medians won't show well. Perhaps you have a loose definition of employment. Possibly you leave international students out of the numbers while your competitors do not. Or maybe your school puts recent graduates to work itself at times when the job market is tough. And so on.

Anderson pulls no punches when describing his own college's career development offering in the not-too-distant past. "It was located in a modular building, tucked away in a corner of campus and staffed by people who had gotten their training in the 1970s and 1980s," he said.

"It just wasn't very good, and people didn't go there and didn't get a lot of help." He went on like that for a few minutes, growing increasingly animated. He described staffers who had told him that there were no companies coming to recruit because nobody did on-campus recruiting anymore. The office didn't even have basic data about how many students came through its doors.

That has changed as the institution itself has made an overall commitment to much more transparency. Now if you're concerned about the prospects for a person with a particular major, you simply click "What can I do with a major in . . . ?" on the career counseling office's website and choose a major. Once you pick one, a list of "first destinations" appears on the screen. I do wish St. Olaf would let outsiders behind their paywall as George Washington University does through its "Undergraduate Employment & Education Outcomes" web page, where you can see that its religion majors, for example, are serving in the Peace Corps, working for the United States Conference of Catholic Bishops, and working for GW itself.

Any school that asks for tuition that is higher than what your state university charges ought to hand this list of first destinations over to prospective families. "I would 100 percent print that list out for you," said Mindy Deardurff, the dean of the Career Exploration department at Macalester. "That would tell you a great deal about an institution—if it has that data and if it will share it."

Geography ought to be a consideration as well. At Macalester, Deardurff has taken to hiring specialists and deploying them around campus so that the science majors, for example, can't help but encounter the staff expert who literally sits next to their departmental offices. "The students are so busy that we can't rely on them to come to us, so we are out in the space that they are in," she said. "We try to think about it as a Minute-Clinic, where you don't have to make a specific appointment with the doctor."

Then there is the external geography. Macalester is the rare selective liberal arts college located in a city, and the Minneapolis–St. Paul area is chock-full of a diverse array of corporations. Career staffers can round up students at noon, take a Lyft, visit a company for lunch at 12:30, and be back on campus in time for sports team practices or an afternoon in the library. Students at more remote schools have to take field trips to big cities or rely on recruiters and alumni to visit campus, which can be hit or miss. If vocational exploration makes up a large portion of your reason-for-college decision pie, geography ought to be a consideration. More distant locations make in-semester internships more challenging, too. "If you're going to pay for something, pay for access," Deardurff said.

About those internships: Does a school guarantee that you can get one? What percentage of people do? Do the people who get them tend to be interested in just a handful of industries? And what happens if you can't afford to work for free? Someday a brave college or university will ban employers who refuse to pay their interns. Until then an expensive school should subsidize internships for people who are on financial aid or can make some other good case for getting some funds to cover internship programs. And it should do everything it can to make sure that first-generation college students and others who come from families with less experience in the college-to-career pipeline know what to expect—and extract—from a career counseling office.

There is a school of thought that suggests that this focus on workforce preparation is just so much foolishness. Let colleges be colleges; studying English or astronomy is no way to prepare for a career in marketing or data analytics, nor should we expect it to be. And rebuilding undergraduate education around the needs of employers doesn't make much sense, either. That takes time—years at the halting pace of the higher education industrial complex—and who knows what the job market will value most by the time it's done, anyway? Let employers handle the training.

The thing is, schools don't get to decide what the job market values, and neither do students. For now, we're working within a system where a lot of what professors teach doesn't match up neatly or obviously with what employers need. Someone has to smooth the transition and act as a translator, and sizing up this potential at the colleges you are visiting has to be part of the search if you're tempted to spend a whole lot of money for an undergraduate education.

CHAPTER 18

Places That Create Better Odds When Applying to Grad School

For all of the bragging that colleges do about internships, career networks, and entry-level jobs, they usually don't have much to say about the people who keep studying after they get their bachelor's degrees.

That's too bad, because there are some excellent data on the undergraduate institutions that are sending the most people on to even more education. If you're a parent of a child with a passion for a particular topic, paying extra for four years at a good feeder school may well be worth considering. They're not always the schools that you might guess, either.

Let's start with PhD programs. The National Science Foundation maintains a public database called the Survey of Earned Doctorates that anyone can search online. If you were to take an educated guess, the most selective large universities would probably be high on your list of schools that send the largest number of alumni on to PhD programs overall—at places such as Berkeley, Michigan, and UCLA. And you'd be right about that. They're in the top five. Also in the top ten are other large universities, including Brigham Young and Penn State.

The first small liberal arts college to make an appearance is not Amherst or Williams (regulars on the top of the *U.S. News & World Report* list) but Carleton, albeit more than eighty spots down the list that includes all schools. Amherst and Williams don't even make the top ten for smaller liberal arts schools that feed PhD programs. But St. Olaf does. (St. Olaf is a bucolic school so infused with Minnesota niceness that when I went to visit, the president himself gave me a tour of the campus.) Also ranking higher than Amherst and Williams: Calvin, a Christian school in Michigan that recently signaled its growing ambition by changing its name from "College" to "University." And in line with what we learned about the overall outperformance of women's colleges, both Smith and Wellesley make the liberal arts college top ten, too. Five of the top-ten PhD candidate–producing small colleges struggle enough in the marketplace that they have to offer merit aid even as they outperform so many other schools in making and launching scholars.

The names change a bit when you look at the overall list of alumni admitted to PhD programs in the humanities and arts. There, Berkeley and Brigham Young stay, but Harvard and Yale join the top ten. Swarthmore is the first small liberal arts school to appear. In engineering, some of the schools that make the top ten besides Berkeley and Cornell include Georgia Tech, Purdue, and the Universities of Florida and Illinois. Harvey Mudd, part of the Claremont Colleges consortium of colleges in California that includes Pomona, is the first smaller college to appear there, followed by Lafayette College in Pennsylvania.

Examining the schools one by one is a bit like treasure hunting, given how many pockets of excellence exist at all sorts of undergraduate institutions. Numbers exist for fields as small as anthropology (where the University of Delaware; Lewis & Clark College in Portland, Oregon; and Scripps College in California, another women's college, do well), biology and biomedical sciences (Juniata College in Pennsylvania is among the top small liberal arts colleges supplying its graduates to PhD programs here), history (with William & Mary, Macalester, and Reed all sending a high number of students along), and psychology (here, Vassar sends the most graduates to doctorate programs among the smaller colleges).

The Association of American Medical Colleges produces a handy table of all undergraduate institutions providing at least fifty or more applicants to medical schools during any given academic year. (An internet search for "institutions 50 or more medical" should turn it up.) Big, prestigious state schools top the list, with UCLA on top followed by the Universities of Florida, Texas, and Michigan, and then Berkeley and UC San Diego. Cornell is the first Ivy League school to appear. Wellesley, Wesleyan, and Pomona supply the most applicants among small liberal arts schools.

Which colleges and universities feed the most applicants to law schools? The Law School Admissions Council reports that the top five, in order, are the University of Florida, UCLA, Florida State, the University of Texas at Austin, and UC Berkeley. The small liberal arts colleges and smaller universities that rank highest are Tufts University, Spelman College, Wesleyan University, Morehouse College, and Amherst. An internet search for "feeder schools lsac" should turn up a recent version of the list.

Whether or not good data exist on who goes on to study these subjects in graduate school, nothing is stopping any of us from requesting school-level data. If your child has a passion for a particular topic, have him or her scan the research interests of faculty members and email them to set up a meeting or a phone call. How (or if) they respond should reveal a lot about a place and how it views its undergraduates. It's also helpful to find out where recent majors applied for graduate school and where they got in (and were rejected). Is there a pipeline to certain graduate schools?

With medical school, things may be a bit more complicated. The data cited above are only for the number of applicants from particular schools. Actually getting in can be awfully hard. So take a look at various colleges' websites and see what data they post about any success they've had. If you need to, find the premed adviser at the schools that interest you and ask about the number of students and young alumni who applied to medical school in recent years and the percentage that got in. Since some people attend medical school outside the United States, ask for a breakdown of those data, too. Also, what percentage of people who declare themselves to be premed actually stick it out and apply to medical school at all? The science courses can be rather cut-throat in some places, while other schools' premed programs may not be strong enough. If you want to be a doctor and are considering paying more to attend a college that could give you better odds, your school should tell you exactly what those odds are. Does it produce undergraduates with better average scores on the standardized test that medical school gatekeepers use? Who from the school does not get in when they apply, and what do those people have in common?

CHAPTER 19

Better Salaries When You Finish—*if* You Finish

What percentage of people at any given college finish in a reasonable period of time? And how much money do they earn when they graduate?

The good news is that we have some answers to these questions. States and the federal government invest a fair bit of money in higher education, so they have an interest in measuring their return. They demand the data as an accountability measure, which means we get to see it, too. The information can be useful to a point, so let's spend a bit of time learning what it means and how to consume it wisely.

The best place to find these data is in something called the College Scorecard, which the U.S. Department of Education maintains online for every school. It is a mandatory stop for anyone shopping for any kind of college. When it was first under development during President Barack Obama's administration, policy makers imagined it as a sort of rating system. Colleges complained loudly, with the president of Rochester Institute of Technology protesting that the proposed rating system "falsely equates a quality education with gainful employment upon graduation." What eventually emerged was a searchable database whose results render no judgments—just facts.

First come the facts on retention and persistence—the percentage of students who stick around and graduate. The first thing you see on the College Scorecard for any given school is the graduation rate, which is generally the percentage of full-time students who started at the school and finished there within eight years. If you click "Graduation & Retention," you can figure out what percentage of students returned to the school after their first year of college there. You can also see whether the people who left the school dropped out altogether or transferred elsewhere.

Here's what the persistence and completion data don't tell you, though. None of it is broken down by demographics. So if a state school graduates only two-thirds of the people who start there within six years, is it a failure? Or does it deserve a pat on the back for enrolling way more poor or first-generation students than most private colleges ever would—and trying its best to get as many of them over the finish line as possible in an era of diminishing state support? And if you're not from a low-income family or the first person in your family to go to college, do way more than two-thirds of all students like you manage to get through the place relatively quickly? Also, do the hard-core engineering students drop out at a higher rate than the English majors—or do they just take a lot longer because the classes are hard or it's difficult to get into all the ones they need and in the right sequence for satisfying prerequisite requirements? What about people of color?

None of this is in the College Scorecard. That doesn't make it useless, but it does make it incomplete. Nearly every school posts a common data set on its website; it's a collection of data that magazines and others that publish college rankings or lists ask for. There, in Section B of the common data set, you can pick up data on retention by social class; it tracks retention by Pell Grant status (only low-income students qualify for those) and by borrower status (generally upper-middle-class students and below).

Now to the salary data. On any given school's College Scorecard home page, under "Salary After Completing by Field of Study," it posts a range of median annual earnings that people earned—but only from those who used at least some federal student aid to attend school. Sometimes the data fields for certain areas of study are blank if there are not enough data. Nevertheless, this is good fodder for family discussion (and discussion with the colleges) if your child will need to borrow and the median starting salaries in any given major look rather low.

Why does the College Scorecard track only people who borrowed money? Currently the federal government doesn't have the right to match enrollment data with salary data from the Internal Revenue Service or Social Security Administration. So we don't learn anything about what the children of more affluent families—the ones who didn't need to use aid from the federal government—are earning. That's about 30 percent of the overall college-going population that is missing.

Even the most accurate schoolwide income data are problematic on a couple of levels. They don't say much about the types of students a school is producing. After all, a college that produces a disproportionate number of the best teachers and social workers won't look so great if you compare it with a school churning out subpar engineers or accountants who still get jobs in their higher-paying fields.

Some states, including Texas, have produced their own data and have been doing it long enough to have studied it carefully. What Texas found was that its nationally renowned flagship campus in Austin didn't necessarily outperform the regional campuses when it came to postgraduation salaries. Instead, it was the academic major students chose that tended to matter a lot more, even after a team from the University of Texas system and the Georgetown University Center on Education and the Workforce controlled their analysis for the race and family income of recent graduates. Architecture and engineering majors were at the top of the heap, earning nearly $40,000 more than biology and life sciences majors, who were at the bottom. People who majored in computers, statistics, and mathematics; health; and business also did quite well. Arts, psychology, and social work were also near the bottom of the income rankings. (Texas has data for all students, not just those who received financial aid.)

Here's one thing that even the state data cannot tell us, however: How many more hours are the engineers working each week than the social workers? Here's another: How much more satisfaction do they get out of their jobs? And remember, it's only the first few years in the workforce that we're talking about. David Deming, a public policy professor at Harvard, extracted some eye-opening details from the U.S. Census about how things change later in life. Yes, early-career computer science and engineering majors make 37 percent more than do people who earn history or social science degrees (including economics, political science, and sociology). But by age forty, the men who started off earning less are earning about $131,000 on average, nearly $7,000 per year more than the comp sci/engineering majors are earning. Women don't quite catch up, although they do come close; the STEM-focused majors are earning just 10 percent more annually between ages thirty-eight and forty.

Institution-wide data can help answer a simple question, though: Do people who start at a certain school end up earning more than they would if they had never matriculated in the first place? In theory, everyone who attends college ought to earn more than the average high school graduate, but things don't turn out that way for a shockingly large number of people. Some drop out, sure. But others attend schools that simply don't help enough people earn a living. For a few years the College Scorecard published this so-called threshold earnings data— the percentage of people who begin at a school who end up earning more than the average high school graduate some reasonable number of years later, as long as they aren't still in graduate school and not earning money for some other reason. But in 2018, it stopped doing so, claiming that it wasn't fair to compare people who had started college in the past decade with high school graduates who might have been in the workforce much longer.

Michael Itzkowitz, who ran the College Scorecard operation as a federal employee from 2015 to 2016 and helped create it as well, republished the data in 2019 under the auspices of the public policy organization Third Way. He took a look at all of the higher education institutions that received federal funds, including community colleges, for-profit trade schools, and old-fashioned public and private four-year undergraduate programs. Students at more than half of them ended up on average with lower income than the $28,000 that an average high school graduate earns. Many are for-profit schools offering vocational certificates of various sorts, but plenty of others are community colleges. And a few of the better-known names include some private colleges in New England such as College of the Atlantic, Goddard College, and Marlboro College, which is now closed. Itzkowitz helpfully published a spreadsheet with every college on it, and you can look it up on Third Way's website under the headline "Higher Ed's Broken Bridge to the Middle Class."

There is a decent chance that all of this talk of money will leave you cold. What happened to the romance of college? How do you measure the economic value of having your mind blown even if you don't earn much early on in your career? As human beings, do we really add up only to whatever value the labor market assigns us? These are reasonable questions, but they may not be yours. The focus on completion rates and starting salaries makes perfect sense if your family feels as though attending college is mostly about getting a job and making a living. If you're on this mobility pathway, where attending college is about finding a stable profession and climbing a few steps up the social-class ladder, the College Scorecard data and the other numbers that Itzkowitz generated are precisely what you need and ought to be a primary source.

No matter what we value, however, we all ought to raise our eyebrows at the fact that we need the government to get us these data and that the schools don't always make it readily available. Though private colleges may not be able to get salary information from alumni, they can certainly share more retention and completion data—and do it more prominently. As for the public universities that may save you a whole lot of money, ask them this: Do the graduates of any given branch of the state system earn more, on average, than bachelor's degree recipients nationally—and more than high school graduates or alumni of the other schools in your state? They ought to know whether their graduates are outperforming others in the labor market, and if they aren't, they ought to be able to provide a very good reason. For what it's worth, Texas does outperform; perhaps that's why it's so free and easy with its data! You can examine it in all sorts of ways at a website called seekUT.

But if anyone in your state university system looks at you cross-eyed when you ask the question and can't produce any data at all, you ought to think very hard about sending it $100,000 and one of your offspring.

CHAPTER 20

How the College of Wooster
Puts It All Together

When I set out to report this book, I knew I couldn't visit every college, grill every president, give every vice president of enrollment management the third degree, and satisfy the considerations of every family in the market for undergraduate education. I chose to focus on what seemed to be one of the key questions: Even if you *can* figure out a way to pay full price for a private college or university, *should* you? And given the amount of discounting that private schools are doing with merit aid, are there schools that offer great value for not much more than what a flagship state school costs in many states?

The willingness to pay full price is on the decline, and the merit aid movement is already entrenched in many institutions. Not surprisingly, the two go hand in hand, since lower prices are necessary when a growing number of people won't pay the sticker price. The schools that offer some merit aid are in a delicate marketplace position where they must fight for every dollar and hope that at least some families will pay in full. I was curious when I began my multiyear reporting binge whether any one of these schools would stand out at the end. I toured them like the parent that I am, imagining my own daughters living and learning on their campuses someday.

I had a couple of other criteria as well. As a stand-in for value-conscious readers, I wanted to know which schools were talking openly about price, cost, and discounting. It quickly became clear that nearly every president was citing, unprompted, the Gallup research on what defines successful undergraduate education: connecting students with professors who care deeply about them, making them feel excited about learning, and encouraging them to pursue their dreams. The school that surprised me the most in this regard was the College of Wooster, one that some people have never even heard of.

Wooster, Ohio, about an hour's drive south of Cleveland, is just big enough to be a city, not a town, and to have an excellent third-wave coffee shop. And if the College of Wooster is known for anything, it is for its Independent Study, or "IS," rendered in capital letters to distinguish it from the undistinguished mass of optional undergraduate senior theses that students churn out at other schools. At Wooster, every senior completes one; some undertake two at once. The school describes IS as a class of one, where you meet weekly with a faculty member with the goal of producing something entirely original: fiction, data from a lab, art that fills an entire wall of a large gallery. Much of the work that undergraduates do in Wooster classrooms during their first three years is to prepare them for this final yearlong intellectual journey. There are fewer upper-level classes than there might be at other colleges because of the demands that the IS places on both seniors and faculty members.

IS has been part of the Wooster undergraduate experience since 1947, but the school hasn't always been so good at selling families on its value. The current vice president for enrollment management and college relations, Scott Friedhoff, discovered this soon after he arrived on campus. "The subject line of an email that was about to go out was 'Are you interested in attending one of the finest colleges in the country for independent study?' or something like that," he recalled. "And it was absolutely accurate. That's what we are. But when you read it like a sixteen-year-old would, they're going to college to be in class, to work with professors and other students. So the idea of studying independently sounded terrible. One of our former presidents described the IS as the worst-named project for the best activity ever. And it is. It is a terrible, terrible name."

Friedhoff didn't get to rename it, but he did get to rebrand it. Eventually he and his colleagues found a new way to incorporate IS into a tagline: "America's premier college for mentored undergraduate research." Princeton University also has a mandatory undergraduate thesis, which Wooster trumpets in banner ads saying "Wooster and Princeton, Together Again" that Wooster runs on websites targeting parents. Part of the point is to note how often Princeton and Wooster are ranked near each other on lists of schools that give undergraduates the best opportunities to do original academic work.

So back to that Gallup research, which reports that having a grown-up invested in your undergraduate work and completing a long-term project are both elemental to satisfaction after college. Let's break the phrase "mentored undergraduate research" into its component parts. First, the research. What are undergraduates really capable of? It's fine to be a bit skeptical. I visited Ohio State, the public flagship school, before visiting Wooster. There a professor sniffed mightily when I asked him what he knew of IS at Wooster. That's play science, he told me, noting that it was Ohio State that got the lion's share of federal research grants around those parts.

I ran those fighting words by former president Sarah R. Bolton at Wooster, who is a physicist by training. Turns out she had once possessed a slightly arched eyebrow about the whole thing, too. When she took the job, she was coming from Williams, among the most selective small liberal arts colleges in all the land. Only a fraction of students did senior theses there. "The people who did have the opportunity tended to be the most self-confident," she said. "They put themselves forward. That has a way of replicating the extraordinary inequity baked into education."

Bolton had never even been to Ohio before interviewing for the job in 2015. On a spring visit before starting it, her soon-to-be colleagues set aside an hour for her to sit down with a dozen or so students who were nearing completion of their IS projects. "I was supposed to be asking them about it all," she said. "I started with the first student, and she started talking about it, and then the rest jumped right in. 'Tell me more about this. How did you figure that out?' I literally said nothing the entire rest of the hour. The other students were so engaged with it. That was different from what I'd seen at other schools."

To that comment from the Ohio State professor, Bolton responded with a point about perspective. If you're at the flagship state university, one way to keep score is in terms of grants received or patents achieved. But at a small liberal arts college, the primary goals may be different.

"What I'm interested in is what students learn," she said. "Sure, the scale and rapidity with which research is done is different if you have twelve postdoctoral fellows and seven lab techs all driving your agenda at a big university. But what is the experience of undergraduates working directly with a professor at a small college? Their experience is one where they have a fair amount of responsibility for actually making research work. If they don't make it go well, it's not going to go well. They are flying that whole spaceship themselves."

It was a major "duh" moment for me. It's about the learning, of course. Sure, most undergraduate work is not ready for publication, government funding, or patent applications. But that is not exactly the point. In his excellent book *The Thinking Student's Guide to College*, Northwestern University associate professor Andrew Roberts's forty-third tip is to write a senior thesis. He describes in visceral terms the process by which students "make sense of a bewildering array of information as they try to reason their way toward the truth." It is a kind of near-drowning experience, where you ultimately find your way to the other end of the swimming pool even if you don't make it to the NCAA championship competition with your school team.

To do even that, however, you often need a lifeguard—and that's where the "mentored" part of the undergraduate research comes in. Bolton had actually won an award for her personal mentorship abilities before arriving at the College of Wooster, so I asked her what good mentors do. "They have expectations for the person they are mentoring that are very high, often higher than students may have for themselves," she replied.

Again, not every student needs or wants this. And plenty of people who do want it manage to milk the lifeblood out of large schools. "Some people believe it is powerful to be among 50,000 people and fight their way forward to be seen," Bolton explained. "They benefit from that struggle." However, she continued, "most don't succeed in doing that. For ones who do, it's a powerful experience. But most people don't, and if you want to have close attention, you need to find a way to make yourself stand out. Whereas in a place like this, every student is guaranteed that experience. It's true about Wooster even more than other colleges our size."

This idea of being seen—truly seen—ought to count for something. "I don't agree that one form of education is better than another for all humans," Bolton said. "But you will not be invisible if you don't want to be invisible here. Faculty will know when you're trying and know when you are not and will push you beyond what you imagined you could do."

All of this takes a lot of faculty time. This is expensive, and the one-on-one work involved means that there are fewer upper-level classes than there might be elsewhere. Yet look at Wooster's financial statistics via the federal College Scorecard website. The average annual cost for people receiving federal aid of any sort is just under $25,000, about what a flagship state university might cost at full price. If your family earns more than $110,000, it rises to a reasonable $32,000 or so. Nearly all students get merit aid, even if they have no demonstrated financial need; the average merit figure for people who have no need is $24,600, subtracted from a total undiscounted cost of attendance of $68,600.

You can pluck these numbers out of the federal College Scorecard website and the common data set, which we'll talk more about in Chapter 31. They are easy enough to find. And the College Scorecard has the same net price calculator for college shoppers that other schools do.

But Wooster also offers a concierge service of sorts to which you can reach out before applying. When you access it, a human being from the enrollment staff sizes up your merit and need-based eligibility and essentially makes you a nonbinding financial offer. This is a far cry from the approach of most other schools, especially some of the more selective merit aid–granting ones, where the size of the discount may well stay a mystery until after you are granted admission. "We need to acknowledge the financial realities that students and parents face," Bolton said in her inaugural address. "And telling someone 'Don't worry' is not a very effective way to keep them from worrying."

This one-to-one service, which Wooster calls the Early Aid Estimator, is quite a radical level of transparency for higher education institutions, the kind a school probably doesn't do unless it feels that it has to. Wooster could stand to improve its 74 percent completion rate over eight years as well. It also just missed making the list of the top 150 U.S. undergraduate institutions that the data-driven authors of *Colleges Worth Your Money: A Guide to What America's Top Schools Can Do for You* assembled, owing to its relatively low overall starting salaries for young alumni.

As for the College of Wooster students who finish their Independent Study in the spring of senior year, the vast majority of them present their work to the Wooster community on one glorious day in April known as Symposium. There are no classes that day, and the campus transforms into a kind of academic Woodstock, with catering from the best local restaurants and bakeries and a schedule jammed with intriguing possibilities. Alumni return, and parents show up slack-jawed, wondering how their children matured so fast and produced such serious work. I could have happily absorbed a week of it.

It's often the double majors who really shine. The day I visited, Jeremy Smucker, who majored in economics and music, presented twice. First he gave a solo vocal performance of three songs he had written incorporating lyrics derived from the work of former U.S. poet laureate Billy Collins. A few hours later, he was in a seminar room lecturing on behavioral economics and end-of-life decisions: Who makes which choices about invasive medical procedures, how does it change things if medical decisions are made under acute stress, and what might happen if we mandated that every American adult complete a living will. Smucker—who did not inherit a jam and jelly fortune, alas—had chosen Wooster over Kenyon because of the merit aid package. It had saved his family over $100,000. "Kenyon was my dream school, but it just wasn't worth $125,000 of debt," he told me.

Perhaps the biggest crowd in Wooster's brand-new science building surrounded Araam Abboud, a double major in classics and biochemistry/molecular biology. She had translated the writings of Hippocrates (he of the oath that doctors take) and Celsus on wound theory. That would have been plenty, but then she had gone into the lab and re-created an ancient wound care formula called barbarum plaster and proved its efficacy. She is now working toward a graduate degree at Georgetown in physiology with a concentration in complementary and alternative medicine. Originally from Cleveland, Abboud was the fifth of six siblings or half siblings to attend Wooster; at one point her father made it clear to her that he felt so strongly about sending his kids to Wooster that even a full ride elsewhere would not be an acceptable choice.

Not long before, I'd met Justine Walker, who'd graduated the previous year as a double major in physics and dance. Her IS was a monthslong experiment using a pulley system to test and measure how varying gravity would alter a specific routine that two dancers performed repeatedly over the months. At one point, she got up to demonstrate in the middle of the *New York Times* cafeteria, albeit without pulleys. Her dancers had preferred the gravitational forces on Mars, it turns out.

She'd found her way to Wooster from the suburbs of New York City when it had offered more merit aid than Oberlin did.

I could go on, but you get the idea. Among academic professionals, Wooster isn't as underrated or underknown. Jennifer Mihalick and her husband, Jonathan Gutow, met as undergraduates at Princeton, and both managed to find work as professors in the chemistry department at the University of Wisconsin Oshkosh. The couple are parents too, and when it came time for their sons to look at colleges, they hoped for an intimate experience similar to the one they'd had at Princeton.

Their first son ended up studying engineering in college. Their second chose not to make a run at schools with tiny odds of admission. Instead, he focused on places where there were ample opportunities for students who were especially curious intellectually.

Mihalick and Gutow had first heard about Wooster when Gutow's brother had considered it while the pair were in graduate school. While Mihalick had been doing a postdoctoral fellowship at Franklin & Marshall College, she had learned more about a consortium of schools called the Council on Undergraduate Research, of which Wooster was a member.

So when their younger son started visiting schools, they finally took a closer look. As professors themselves, there was one thing they observed that other parents might not: Given all of the work that Wooster seniors must do with professors—sometimes carving IS projects off of larger research efforts that professors are engaged in—the professors had more incentive than most to do a terrific job of teaching the students in their first two years of college. After all, the professors were going to be stuck with the same students as juniors and seniors; if they weren't any good, it would make for some long hours advising the various IS projects. The pair were also struck by how many children of college faculty attended. Mihalick and Gutow's son applied early, received some merit aid, and sent in his deposit.

This is the kind of narrative that President Bolton enjoys hearing about, given the subtle way in which she believes that the language around so-called elite schools is changing. To her, inclusiveness is part of what it means to be elite. Wooster was not founded to serve a population of gentlemen's children. It educated pastors' kids and teachers' kids. Average family income is still well below the figures at Oberlin and Kenyon.

"I met a recent alumna who was back visiting from Harvard Medical School, and she had a poetic turn of phrase," Bolton said. "She talked about how, when she was here, she held all of her peers in a kind of awe. You hear that in a different way in a place like Stanford, where everyone knows they are the best before they get there. She was talking about being in awe of what they were doing here and not how they had been selected."

PART IV

Money-Saving Hacks That Will Tempt You

CHAPTER 21

Community College
Will Save You Money, but
What Might You Lose?

Plenty of applicants and their families who approach community college as a money-saving, system-beating strategy figure it will go like so: *Show up, sign up, fulfill some easy general education credits in two years flat, transfer to just about anywhere, and save $30,000 at a minimum.* Most of them learn very quickly that it's not quite that easy to pull this off.

Starting an undergraduate career at a community college can be a terrific hack. But for it to save a large amount of money without sacrificing potentially important parts of the college experience, students need to develop a plan that is close to perfect before they even begin.

To start, let's dispense with the idea that spending two years at a community college before transferring to a four-year school will be a breeze. At the Community College Research Center, part of Columbia University's Teachers College, a 2016 study of more than 700,000 students who had started community college in 2007 found that just 14 percent of them had transferred to a four-year school and graduated within six years. In some states students had done better, but even in those states only 18 percent of enrollees had gotten their bachelor's degrees. People who had transferred to public schools had done better than those who had ended up at private or for-profit colleges, and students who had ended up at very selective schools had earned degrees at the highest rates. It's important to keep these time-to-completion statistics in mind, given that federal financial aid does not last forever. For instance, you can only draw on Pell Grants for lower-income students for 12 terms.

This is no knock on community colleges. One study showed that nearly half of the college graduates who had eventually gotten a degree from a four-year college had spent at least some time at a community college in the previous ten years. Many students choose this option because they don't have the grades or scores to get into a four-year university, which means they need to improve their academic performance enough to transfer and eventually graduate. Other students are barely scraping by financially, trying to cram in one course at a time while working two jobs and caring for a child. Then there are those who can't be far from home for family reasons. Still, there is no denying that a community college freshman who looks to the right and left may very well see two people who will never make it to a four-year college, let alone graduate. There is often not a strong current carrying these students forward, at least not one that propels a significant number of peers in any given class.

Perhaps that doesn't bother you, because you believe that your child is different, maybe more capable or driven than most community college students. Perhaps you have a hunch that your family is more stable economically than the average community college household, and your kid has a plan and is determined to march through quickly and then go on to a four-year school. Even so, the odds remain long. True, just 10 percent of lower-income students who start at community colleges graduate from a four-year institution within six years, according to John Fink, a senior research associate at the Community College Research Center. But the center's estimates put the figure for higher-income people at just 16 percent. Examining the figures by race changes things a bit more: Asian Americans finish within six years 23 percent of the time, whites achieve a 19 percent rate, Hispanics come in at 11 percent, and Black are at 9 percent.

So that plan you have? It had better be ironclad. The low rates of success are a concern to the federal government, given how much money it spends subsidizing student loans and giving out Pell Grants to low-income students. In 2017, the U.S. Government Accountability Office published a report on the overall question of community college transfers and course credits, and it painted an unflattering picture. On the most basic of levels, schools simply do not provide enough information to people who are trying to make a seamless transfer from one school to the next, including from a community college to a four-year institution. You should begin the process of attending a community college first by assuming you're on your own and ask a long list of questions before you make any decision.

Start with these lines of inquiry at any community college you're considering: What percentage of the people who start at this community college end up with a bachelor's degree within four years? What about six years or ten? Where do the majority of the people who do transfer end up? Then, ask for all the details available about the college's articulation agreements. This part is crucial: These agreements are a sort of curricular road map for community college students to help them understand what courses to take in order to transfer seamlessly to a four-year school. So yes, it is important to have in mind a destination four-year school, preferably one that already has an articulation agreement with the community college you're considering. Find out if there are staff members who work full- or part-time helping students who wish to transfer to four-year schools with as little hassle and as few hiccups as possible.

Sometimes the advisers find you. Stephen Harbeck was, by his own admission, an unserious high school student. When he was a senior in high school, he ended up visiting the campus of the four-year Kutztown University only because his girlfriend was checking it out and he decided to tag along on a lark. There he met with Professor Lisa Frye, a last-minute replacement for the person he was actually supposed to talk to. It ended up being the perfect match, though. Harbeck was interested in technology, and she was a computer science professor. And she did not seem put off by his plans to attend community college to save money and buckle down as a student.

To the contrary, she effectively took him on as a sort of project, and Harbeck happily went along with it. "She was all on board with trying to help me," he said. "The second time I met with her, she told me to send her my entire class schedule and she said yea or nay to my courses. I was able to transfer seventy-two credits into Kutztown, and she planned my entire four years in advance even though I wasn't enrolled at the school yet. I knew I wanted to do something with computers, and I think that is the reason she latched on. She saw potential." Harbeck graduated Kutztown under five years after he started community college and transitioned directly into a technology job with a local school district.

Students at community colleges need to find their own Dr. Frye if people like her don't find them. Then they need to make their advisers, preferably one each at community college and the intended destination school, their new best friends. They should talk with them before enrolling in community college and ask them all of the transfer-related questions I posed up above. A few others to keep in mind: If there are eight or twelve or sixteen classes that I must take to finish at community college and transfer out in two years, what quirks might I run into? Are there particular classes that fill up fast? If so, what's the trick to making sure I get registered in time? Are there classes that are offered only in certain semesters or at certain times? If so, should I be registering for those first and building the rest of my schedule around them?

And this is only half of it, according to John Fink, the community college expert at Columbia. That's because any given target transfer school may change its rules at any time. This can have implications for the choice of major, since oftentimes only certain community college courses will fulfill its requirements. Fink explains it this way: Imagine yourself as a community college adviser. You're probably trying to help hundreds of students at once. They may be trying to transfer to at least ten schools. Perhaps you have good working relationships with transfer admissions representatives at those schools, but maybe you don't or your contact is on leave or is new. Oh, and each of those ten schools has dozens of potential majors. And perhaps the math prerequisite for the business major at one of the schools is statistics while at the other one it's calculus. You can't possibly keep up with everything.

Because of all that, any given student has to stay on top of every possible transfer permutation, although many community college advisers are there to help. This will mean figuring out a short list of transfer schools and potential majors. Then it's necessary to develop and maintain relationships from the very beginning of community college with three people: an adviser at the community college, a transfer admissions representative at the intended four-year college, and the faculty member in the major department who can help make sure that all the community college courses taken will qualify for that major. Then it's essential to check in with all of them before every registration period to see if any of the rules has changed.

It's hard to get the credits exactly right. According to Fink, people who start at community college typically earn more credits than they need to by the time they graduate from a four-year institution and end up with more credits than people who started and ended at the same four-year college. Having too many unnecessary credits is a good way to waste a portion of the money you thought you were going to save by opting for community college in the first place.

Outside the classroom, students need to be similarly focused, depending on their goals. For people with little money who have a strong desire for a degree and want to incur as little debt as possible, it is certainly possible to get from community college to a four-year degree even if the odds show that it is not easy for everyone. But splitting the undergraduate experience in two does make it harder to seek out real kinship or have a mentor blow your mind. Instead of having four years in the same place to bond with peers, community college students tend to spend two years (or three or four part-time) with people who are probably commuting instead of living in a small group of dorms. Because of that, connecting with people is harder and may require joining clubs. Community college instructors may teach more classes than professors at four-year institutions do, but it's challenging to forge a mentorship relationship with them in just a couple of years and then have to start all over again somewhere else. Here too, dogged commitment is necessary to be truly seen and known by someone who can help shape a student's future.

The need to be deliberate extends to students once they transfer to a four-year college or university as well. It may be easier to seek out schools that enroll plenty of transfers from community colleges each year. Public universities generally have more slots than private schools do, according to a study by the Jack Kent Cooke Foundation. According to that research, the 35 most selective public schools took in more than four times as many students from community colleges as the 139 most selective private ones. In the prestigious University of California system, 29 percent of graduates began at community colleges.

Other studies show that transfer students from community college do not, on average, avail themselves of the sorts of high-impact activities that tend to help students thrive. One study showed that whereas 62 percent of seniors who had started and ended at the same school had completed at least one internship, only 43 percent of people who came from community colleges had done so. Another study documented the struggles that community college transfer students face when trying to make social connections.

A third study tried to be more prescriptive, or at least diagnostic: Transfer students seemed to do best when they lived on campus, joined a fraternity or sorority, or had some kind of longer-term connection to a member of the faculty. Otherwise they were in danger of feeling isolated and reporting less overall satisfaction with their education. Any struggles like these are not the fault of all or even most community college transfer students; there may be many reasons for the above results, such as having to live off campus and steer clear of time-consuming social obligations to save money or support family members. But all community college transfers ought to be aware of the potential challenges and then actively try to end up on the right side of those percentages.

The larger universities that take in lots of transfer students from community colleges are aware of the research. Many have created support hubs of sorts for these students, and they are encouraged to live on transfer-student floors in residence halls. John Fink, the community college expert at Columbia, said that there isn't good research yet on whether transfer students find mentors less often than people who spend four years at the same undergraduate institution do. And although he acknowledged the potential problem—say, science professors wanting to train freshmen for a year or two to get them up to speed in a lab assistant role and not wanting to invest in new juniors who will be around for only two years—he asked people to consider the advantages that community college students may have at their schools of origin. Instructors at those colleges are under little if any pressure to produce academic research, so they may be more inclined toward mentorship than instructors at larger universities, even if they don't have four years with many students. "Finding mentors is a unique and powerful thing that not enough students have access to regardless of whether they started at a community college or a university," he said.

Fink's research group wrote a free guide called "The Transfer Playbook: Essential Practices for Two- and Four-Year Colleges." For those who are serious about starting in community college, it's well worth finding online. Use it as an additional source to question schools that your family is considering and find out if they're following the practices that experts such as Fink recommend. As for the man himself, he has nothing but confidence in the people who make it from a two-year school to a four-year one. In fact, he met scores of them while working in student affairs at the University of Maryland before he became a researcher. "The ones who do transfer are generally rock stars," he said.

"They blew everyone's minds. They'd often been student leaders at community college and were developing amazing relationships with faculty. They were pros at transition."

These are the survivors, though, the cream of the crop. Mimicking their path requires paying attention to detail and shouldering a fair bit of risk. Maureen McRae Goldberg has assessed that risk from many sides. She was a women's studies major at the private University of Redlands in California, where she received financial aid. Since then she's spent decades handing aid out to others, including the eighteen years she spent at Occidental College in Los Angeles. More recently, she moved to Santa Barbara City College, a two-year school, having worked in one much earlier in her career as well. Personally, she said, she would not trade her four years in one place, given that she graduated with a manageable $15,000 in loans after getting lots of grant money. But now that she's back in a community college with a strong transfer culture, she's less certain about what the advice should be for today's teenagers. Are too many of them blindly presuming that stretching financially to spend four years in the same place will pay off? Shouldn't they at least be investigating alternatives?

"I don't think the mind-set has shifted enough in America," she said of the families that have a four-year-school-or-bust attitude. "People think that the value is still there [at every four-year school]. And I'm not sure that it is."

Honors Colleges and Programs Can Make Bigger Schools Smaller—if You Stick with the Program

Merit aid isn't the only way colleges and universities try to persuade successful applicants to enroll. Sure, throwing discounts at teenagers and calling them scholarships can be persuasive. But other families seek out more challenges for their children—and pats on the back. So it should come as no surprise that several hundred colleges and universities designate scores of matriculants as honors students each year, even before they've taken a single quiz or set foot on campus. Then they cordon them off for special treatment when they do arrive.

The world of undergraduate honors is enticing, and for plenty of students it offers a spectacular experience. But it is also complicated, and the vast majority of families that consider it have no idea how to evaluate this option.

What are we talking about when we talk about undergraduate honors? Perhaps you remember the University of Michigan's offering from when you were an undergraduate or a few other similar programs at large state universities. They began as points of pride (How can we keep the best students here in our state?) and practicality (How can we make our big university seem like the intimate college that many families seem to want?). As with merit aid, once some universities had these programs, lots of others wanted one, too. Plenty of private colleges followed suit, and even some expensive universities such as the University of Southern California and Tulane got into the game, aiming to shed their party school reputations.

In this world there are honors programs and there are honors colleges. Honors programs tend to be smaller and exist at smaller schools. Honors colleges are bigger, although not every flagship state university with an honors offering has turned it into a college. Is it always an upgrade? Honors colleges tend to have more resources of all sorts, but there are generally more students using them, too. We're going to check off the various components of an honors program or college here, so you know what to look for as you visit colleges and get more serious about seeking value in this way.

As always, it's important to start with a refresher on why this may be important to you. If a student is a just-here-for-the-corporate-job type, it's not clear that an honors program or honors college will help. There are not a huge number of special internships specifically for participants: 15 percent of honors programs have them; 44 percent of honors colleges do. Employers may reward the initiative of undergraduates who participate in honors. Enrolling in a program or a college tends to signal in a nonbragging way that the candidate could have attended a more selective school. Still, employers may be more likely to care about résumés and grades in job-related classes.

Undergraduate honors administrators tend to focus their pitch on academics and not postgraduate employment. There are a few things that have come to seem standard. First, the classes: Honors students often get to sign up for courses before other students do. There are usually special seminars, often interdisciplinary, that all honors student must take in their first year at a school. The big idea is to reinforce the notion of entering a small community of scholars who will learn in a different and presumably better way. The University of Minnesota offered a team-taught course on the biggest problems facing humanity in the twenty-first century. Who wouldn't want to spend some time trying to solve those?

At Purdue University, I met Michael Repella, who took a fall-semester class on the human mind and identity and a spring-semester course on the concept of Utopia. He also helped develop an on-campus Utopian learning community, where students from different majors who were passionate about the connections between science and society could live together. One of the concepts the group worked through was the sociological aspect of potentially colonizing Mars. That was catnip for Repella, since his goal is to work as an aerospace engineer someday.

Aside from inquiring about mandatory honors seminars, you'll want to ask about overall curriculum requirements. About half of honors colleges and programs require some sort of "capstone" class, which may be a research-intensive seminar that ends with an undergraduate thesis or some other significant body of work. Along the way, there will probably be other honors requirements, too. They may involve a small honors section that breaks off from a larger lower-level academic course.

With other classes, especially at the larger honors colleges (which may have well over 1,000 students in them), the requirements can get a bit looser. The college may ask students to fill out what are known as honors "contracts." In that instance, the class itself isn't segregated and the content is no different from what everyone else takes. Instead, a student meets with the instructor early in the term to define, via a contract, what the student will do to make his or her participation in the class honors qualified. Some administrators at Purdue once worked at Barrett, the Honors College at Arizona State, which is one of the biggest and best-established programs. They reported that the contracts at Barrett often involved simply writing another paper, a pattern they're trying to avoid at Purdue.

The goal of providing some kind of alternative experience is one that honors administrators share. "Best practice is not more but different," said Richard Badenhausen, an English professor who is dean of the honors college faculty at Westminster College in Salt Lake City and a past president of the National Collegiate Honors Council. "More isn't distinctive." And although having a special section of a class may lead to a better experience than merely signing a contract, professors may not always want to teach a separate section. In many universities, administrators keep careful score of undergraduate demand for their department's offerings. If a professor teaches an honors section of twenty in lieu of another course that could attract one hundred, does that count against his or her department? This can matter a lot later on when, say, a colleague retires and the department wishes to replace that person, according to two professors I talked to who teach at a university that has one of the nation's largest honors colleges.

Here are some questions to ask of any honors college and program: What classes are mandatory? Must you maintain a minimum grade point average of some sort? Do you get to register for classes before non–honors students? What other requirements are part of the program? And when it comes to the basic curricular requirements, what percentage of them do students satisfy through honors sections versus honors contracts? If there are a lot of contracts, how much does the program or the college know about what students are really doing to satisfy them? Writing more papers isn't necessarily bad, but it may not be what you had in mind. Take an inventory of the instructors for honors sections too to see if their classes provide access to more professors in majors that attract hordes of students. "Economics majors almost never see tenured or tenure-track professors until senior year or maybe junior" under normal circumstances at the University of Minnesota, said Matthew Bribitzer-Stull, its honors program director. "And that is not the only department like that."

And of whom will you be asking these questions? The lineup of honors-affiliated staff is worth examining. How many professors are there? Whom does the person in charge report to? I get that these aren't questions you will necessarily be comfortable asking until after admission, but they are fair game. You should be similarly curious about honors advisers.

Are they faculty members or staff? (The question of which category of professional does a better job of advising is a subject of ongoing debate in academia, but you'll want to know why each school does what it does.)

Many schools with honors programs or colleges try to persuade applicants to attend by promoting their honors living communities. Yes, they've set aside their own floors or dorms, in some cases building new residence halls for honors students only. At the University of Southern California, the honors dorm for the first-year students has pride of place in its new USC Village development. Purdue put its new honors dorm smack dab in the middle of campus to make it as convenient as possible for its prized undergraduates. About two-thirds of schools with honors programs have some kind of honors housing, according to the National Collegiate Honors Council's count; 88 percent of honors colleges do. A smaller fraction also have freestanding academic buildings of various sorts for the honors operations.

What could be wrong with that? Well, some schools make honors students live in honors dorms for at least a year. This may smack of elitism. Badenhausen, the national association's past president, wrote a book chapter called "Honors Housing: Castle or Prison?" that made the case for the detractors. Part of the problem is one of perception: Separation doesn't look great, even if late-night honors gabfests may unfold on a higher level. Shining towers for the smart set can set up the wrong sorts of expectations. The former head of the University of Florida's honors program, Kevin Knudson, wrote an article for the *Chronicle of Higher Education* saying that some incoming students and their families made him feel as though they were treating their forthcoming experience as if they were about to fly first class. One mother called and demanded that he hand over the layouts for the honors dorm so she could make sure her son was in a good location.

The honors students I met at Purdue seemed puzzled by this. "They don't keep us locked up in here," Michael Repella noted. Another undergraduate, Lauren MacKenzie, a Massachusetts native, said that she always invited nonhonors friends over on Sundays. In her new honors dorm, which has a great cable television package, they all watch the New England Patriots play football.

If your child is considering an honors program or college and will end up living only with classmates who are in the program, it's worth considering what kinds of people they will be. Chances are they'll be white—overwhelmingly so. According to a recent census by the National Collegiate Honors Council, 86 percent of honors students are white, and that figure includes two-year colleges. The percentage of white students among the overall population of students enrolled in degree-granting institutions is just 57 percent. Honors students are 63 percent female, 7 percentage points higher than women's overall representation in the college population at large. If you are not white and it's important to you to have peers who look like you or share some of your experiences, this ought to suggest some pointed questions to ask. And if you *are* white and it's important to you to learn from people who are different from you, this ought to suggest a similar set of questions.

There are a few more queries that will probably be instructive. Though the federal government requires undergraduate institutions to disclose the percentage of people who graduate within a reasonable period of time, there is no such mandate for honors programs and colleges. The average honors retention rate is not a part of the census mentioned earlier. But Richard Badenhausen, the president of the group that publishes the census, did say in his article about honors dorms that students in larger honors colleges at state universities can have completion rates as low as 20 to 25 percent. Given that, every school ought to disclose its rate, and if it's low, the school should explain why.

Here are a few follow-up questions to ask if a school does have a low retention rate: Are large numbers of students leaving the school altogether for reasons that have nothing to do with the honors program or college? If not, this may suggest that students move back into the regular undergraduate population because they believe their grades are suffering or think that the program is not as strong as the school said it was. Is the average grade point average different for an honors student than for other students? If so, why? If it's lower, will that affect their ability to get into graduate school or find jobs where employers care about grades? Grades could well be higher among honors students, and that's worth knowing, too. Also, are there people in certain majors or undergraduate schools—say, engineering, business, or premed—who find honors work incompatible with their other work for whatever reason?

You may be able to find answers to your questions in an honors program's or college's annual report. About two-thirds of them publish one. It may be available on a website waiting for curious prospective families like yours, but ask for it if it's not online. If a school hasn't published one, ask the director or dean if you can look at its most recent external program review documents: The National Collegiate Honors Council members parachute in every so often to take a look around and make suggestions to a school, so it can't hurt to ask to see a copy of its most recent report to administrators.

Honors administrators try their best to attract, challenge, and retain good students. No institution wants to lose them to some other school, and the students represent a legitimate market with their own needs and demands. But all of this honors activity begs what may be a difficult family conversation: If a school has set up a two-tier system, everyone ought to agree about why it makes sense to pay for the lower one.

CHAPTER 23

Attending College Abroad Is Often Cheaper, but You Won't Get What You Don't Pay For

When families find their way to a college consultant named Jennifer Viemont, it's often for two reasons. First, they think they can save money by sending a teenager to college outside the United States. And second, they are bewildered by the lack of available information for people who are considering that possibility.

Years ago, Viemont started a service called Beyond the States that focuses on English-language undergraduate degree programs at European universities. During her time deciphering the process, she's learned the following: Not everyone will save a big pile of money. But students who study abroad for the entirety of their undergraduate years—the right students, ones who know about both the limitations and the possibilities that going to college outside the United States entails—can end up with a more valuable experience than what they'll find domestically. Her book on the topic is called *College Beyond the States: European Schools That Will Change Your Life Without Breaking the Bank*.

There are not many students who actually have the nerve to try to do this under normal circumstances (let alone during a pandemic or its aftermath), even if the option is something you hear a lot about. There are so few, in fact, that there does not even seem to be a proper census of them. I took a guess at what the most popular programs are: semifamiliar names such as McGill University and the University of Toronto in Canada, the University of St. Andrews in Scotland, and Oxford and Cambridge Universities in England. Those schools were at least somewhat responsive to reportorial inquiries, and there are about 4,000 Americans enrolled in them total, full-time (not on one-semester study-abroad programs). When I moved farther down my list of likely destinations, there were a few schools with a few dozen American students each. Many more would not reply to email inquiries or demanded that I jump through a series of freedom-of-information type legal hoops just to ask a question about these undergraduates.

And therein lies a clue. "These are not student-driven experiences," said Jennie Kent, an independent college counselor who helps many families who live outside the United States and others who want their child to consider a non-American school. Things are not set up for parents of prospective students who have a thousand questions, either. These facts should not be disqualifying, necessarily, but they should give you pause.

Let's start with the supposed savings. Sometimes they just aren't there. At St. Andrews, the all-in annual cost for Americans is about $52,000, including all fees and estimated expenses. At McGill, Americans will likely pay as much as or a bit more than they would at their flagship state university in the United States (though more for certain degree programs). Even at less costly universities in Europe, you may have to prove in advance that you'll be good for the full cost of the school year by demonstrating that you have a five-figure amount at the ready. Whatever costs you see online probably don't include room and board, and the school may not even own a dorm or run a student cafeteria.

Schools often don't award the same number or types of scholarships as they do in the United States, and, depending on the institution, you may not be able to borrow money via the U.S. federal student loan program to attend. Also, if you have money saved in a 529 college savings account, you may not be able to use it for college abroad without paying a penalty and taxes, so you'll want to ask the school well ahead of time whether it is a qualifying institution. Those using GI Bill benefits following military service will want to check on their eligibility as well. One big plus: It may take only three years to complete many undergraduate degree programs outside the United States.

Let's say you do manage to get someone to give you an all-in net cost quote and once you add up the various expenses you decide that the savings are quite pleasing. Then you need to understand what you're buying and what you're not. At many schools outside the United States, students must choose a course of study when applying. If they are applying to a business program, they probably won't have to choose a specialty such as accounting or marketing until a year or so in. But applicants for a scientific field may have to choose one before they commit to attending. And there may not be the possibility of changing their choice once they arrive. Many teenagers claim to have absolute certainty about their field of study and career plan yet change their mind more than once after a year or two of testing it out. Having to start college over again elsewhere because the first field was not a good fit will drive up the cost—in terms of both added years and lost earnings from what hypothetically could have been a year or two of salary.

Then there's what happens outside the classroom. There may not be student housing, so students may have to look for an apartment nearby and furnish it, too. There probably won't be a meal plan, so there will be food shopping involved, perhaps in a grocery store where no one speaks English as a first language, to say nothing of actually cooking meals. That's a lot for a teenager to manage, and although it may add up to a fantastic adventure with dinner parties and potlucks attended by people from all over the globe, it may also be too much of a challenge for some undergraduates. Socially, there are challenges as well. Making friends with at least some local students is ideal, but many of them may leave town on the weekends.

And if there are stumbles along the way? Well, again, this is not the United States, and you will probably not get what you have not paid for. School is cheaper elsewhere for a reason. One reason is that national governments tend to subsidize their universities more than we do in the United States. Another reason is that the schools generally don't provide as much in the way of amenities, extracurricular activities, intercollegiate or intramural sports, and support. So if your child is having trouble, there may not be mental health counselors to talk to or administrators running diversity initiatives and keeping the school in compliance with a variety of laws governing equity and access. Tutors may be scarce, too. "The United Kingdom is probably stronger than other areas, and they love to brag about their pastoral care," Jennie Kent said. "But it's like a joke compared to what kids would get in the States."

Like Kent, Jennifer Viemont has visited scores of schools abroad, and she echoes these observations. "It is absolutely true that you are not spoon-fed," she said. For that reason she does not recommend European universities unless they have some kind of designated office for international students. That way there is someone who can, hopefully, help a student plug into any resources that he or she may need off campus.

None of this should be disqualifying, necessarily. But students who are right for this option need to be able to raise their hand for assistance. Molly de Aguiar and her husband, whose daughter started school in the Netherlands in 2019, spent their daughter's first years abroad talking to her about the power of asking for help. "I think most students don't love to ask," de Aguiar said. "We tell her often that teachers love to be asked for help—that you'll get so much more out of school and college if you do that. But it's her job to ask."

As for seeking kinship, this may not be as much of a struggle for more introverted students as it might be if they were attending school in the United States. Students who are not from the university's country all have something in common, and presumably a big part of the reason they travel to a university abroad is to make as many friends as possible from all over the globe. In English-language programs in non-English-speaking countries especially, American students may have a leg up in making connections in the classroom, given that it's good to have a native English speaker on a team for a group project. And although maintaining the bonds they create may be hard if people scatter back to different parts of the globe after graduation, those who maintain their ties will have a world of couches to crash on and some important connections and friendships that often last a lifetime.

But how employable will American students be if they don't attend college in the United States? Does attending a program abroad create opportunities for the kinds of internships that make it easier to get a job back home? Not only do résumés citing such experiences matter to employers, but they often hire former interns. Some programs outside the United States understand this and have tried to address it. At Anglo-American University in Prague, for example, some degrees include a mandatory internship. In those instances, the schools generally have a pipeline to local companies. Summer internships may also be possible, but ask if they are for credit. If not, do they pay at all? Rules regarding work and residency permits in any given country may not be easy to sort out on your own.

I had very little luck extracting data from schools outside the United States on what happens to American undergraduates after they finish. Viemont did not chalk this up to a lack of transparency. Instead, her advice is to ask the program directors at the school your child will be applying to for any outcomes data. Maybe they'll be more responsive to parents than they are to authors.

Viemont doesn't necessarily dismiss a school if it can't say much about what happens to its graduates. After all, many of the non-American students who attend these schools go straight to graduate school after completing their three-year degrees. Given how few students look for jobs right away, it's somewhat understandable that the schools wouldn't have much data on postgraduate employment. She also makes some good points about the recognizability and reputation of some of the European universities that will serve the graduate well. There are plenty of American schools that have iffy reputations or none whatsoever, and many of their graduates have done just fine regardless. Think about the number of people you know who grew up outside the United States and went to college abroad as well. Have they managed to make careers for themselves in the United States? Do you ever give their alma mater a second thought now that they're in their forties or fifties?

These were not the thoughts that consumed Molly de Aguiar and her family. The price mattered, and neither she nor her husband wanted either of their two kids to graduate with the $30,000 or so in loans that the average college graduate who borrows ends up with.

Something else mattered, too: what de Aguiar described as a deep reluctance to participate in a system that, to their mind, perpetuates inequality and American exceptionalism. The family lives within walking distance of Rutgers, New Jersey's flagship state university, but familiarity had not bred much comfort. Her husband had once worked as a university teaching assistant, and he was no fan of the fact that so many of the actual instructors at big state universities make so little money.

Meanwhile, their daughter felt that nearly everyone she knew was headed to Rutgers and that doing the same wouldn't push her much beyond her comfort zone.

The family ultimately found the rat race around American college admissions exhausting and off-putting. "A major motivating factor of wanting to go abroad is a rejection of this system that our kids are in where the pressure to go to the right schools starts in prekindergarten," de Aguiar said. "One of my daughter's responses was to note that if she went to a school that no one had ever heard of, then no one could judge whether it was a good school or not."

So off her daughter went to Amsterdam University College, the honors operation at the University of Amsterdam, which most people have never heard of. She's studying biology, and she'll finish in three years instead of four (or the five that it takes many people to finish at Rutgers). The all-in cost per year is about the same as the undiscounted rate at most state universities. And her parents will give her any remaining savings for graduate school—not to mention a shot at standing out in a way that students in the United States will not. "Going over there does give her a bit of a creative advantage," Molly said. "I've spent the last eighteen years trying to instill working hard and thinking creatively in her, too—not to be able to make money but to create opportunities for herself, whatever she wants those opportunities to be. Encouraging her to distinguish herself by going abroad is a good example of that—or perhaps the culmination of that."

CHAPTER 24

Athletic Scholarships for the Few (and Probably Not in Full or at Your First-Choice School)

We know that athletic prowess provides an admissions edge. Sometimes it's enormous. Data that sprang loose during litigation over whether Harvard's admissions policies discriminate against Asian Americans laid out the school's 1-to-6 academic ratings for applicants, with 1 being the highest. Athletes with an academic rating of 4 have an acceptance rate nearly 1,000 times as great as nonathletes with that rating.

But what about the financial factor? Here we'll be looking at the fever dream of athletic scholarships, one that drives at least some families to invest thousands of dollars and hundreds of hours per year in travel teams and training. What are your odds of paying less for college or nothing at all due to a child's talent in a sport? There are some data, at least for the very best athletes. The odds are long, the money pot is not that large for most sports, and schools don't necessarily distribute the money quite the way families may think they do.

According to 2020 NCAA data, nearly 7.2 million high school students play sports. Just 499,000, however, play in college. Not bad, right? Well, only a little over 180,000 of those athletes get scholarships, and most of them do not get a full ride. So it's only about 2.5 percent of high school athletes who get any discounts based on their sports skills, and schools don't necessarily guarantee that the scholarship will last until graduation. Moreover, many schools in Division I, the most competitive group of schools that have the most money to offer, are state universities where any partial scholarship merely offsets the higher out-of-state student price tag.

Odds are better in some sports than others. The website Scholarship-Stats.com publishes the numbers (and has an accountant audit them), which show that 16.9 percent of the young women who play ice hockey in high school will also get to play in college, while just 3.6 percent of female high school tennis players will compete at the next level. Among young men, 13.5 percent of high school lacrosse players get to play in college, while just 4.5 percent of wrestlers do. Again, this is only a measure of who gets to play, not who gets a scholarship.

An average Division I scholarship comes in between $18,000 and $19,000 for the men and women who get them, according to ScholarshipStats.com. And whether they get one depends on what sport they play, the NCAA rules for scholarship allotments, and how any given school chooses to use that allotment. Some sports—basketball for both genders, football for men, and gymnastics, tennis, and volleyball for women—are what are known as head-count sports. Schools give out full scholarships for those sports, although there are generally not enough to go around to everyone on the team. All other sports are equivalency sports. In those, teams that get, say, 4.5 full scholarships can divide that money up as they see fit, assuming they use all of it. According to the *Chronicle of Higher Education*, in a magazine-length investigation by Brad Wolverton titled "The Myth of the Sports Scholarship," dozens of Division I programs give out fewer than half of the scholarships that the regulations would allow them to. That's because not every athletic department is flush with the budget to throw lots of discounts around.

All of this plays out in an annual game of chicken in which athletes visit schools, schools size up athletes, and teams dole out scholarship offers piecemeal as they attempt to determine which students are most serious about attending. It is highly unpredictable. And unless playing for the college team that offers the biggest scholarship is the only thing that matters to a given family, any preferences about academics or geography or overall fit will complicate things further. In short, even if you're lucky enough to have lots of options, none of them may be the one you would have picked if a sport hadn't been in the picture.

But perhaps this is not you. Maybe you're pouring money into participation in the travel-team circuit to help your child with a B-plus average eventually get into a selective Division III school where most nonathletes arrive with an A average. The admissions edge is real at these schools too, and they grant that advantage through a so-called tips system that coaches use to boost the number of applications from favored prospects. "Athletic recruiting is the biggest form of affirmative action in American higher education, even at schools such as ours," Philip Smith, Williams College's former dean of admissions told the *New York Times*, speaking from the safety of retirement in 2001. Schools dole out the most help, he said, for "helmet sports" such as football and hockey. "I can name on one finger the number of kids on the Williams hockey team who could make it on their own without hockey."

But the NCAA prohibits Division III schools from offering any athletic scholarships. Students are supposed to apply for need-based aid, and schools can evaluate them for merit aid as well, come what may. As you might imagine, things can get murky. Some financial aid officers may come to know that certain admitted students are also star athletes, especially by the time the students call in the spring seeking more money. At that point they may have better financial aid offers from other schools and will want the one they are calling to do a bit better, given their status as a recruit.

It turns out that a number of Division III schools are offering athletic scholarships outright and getting caught. The engineers at Rose-Hulman Institute of Technology were guilty, as were the aggressive discounters at Denison University in Ohio. At Emmanuel College in

Massachusetts the school got a slap on the wrist because athletes were appealing financial aid awards (successfully) at a rate disproportionate to the rest of the student body. An NCAA memo from 2014 reported that of 207 institutions it had examined, 89 had committed violations. Bending the rules, whether inadvertent or not, seems to be widespread. And that's just the schools where the violations were evident.

It would seem odd if the moral of the story here is that you're better off covering your eyes and hoping for illicit financial aid from a Division III school than a legal discount from a Division I institution. I don't aim to knock sports or the students who play them. Quite the contrary: Gallup's survey data on the topic showed that former student athletes were more likely to be thriving in four out of five main measures of overall well-being than were college graduates who had not played sports in college. They outperformed in measures of purpose and social, community, and physical well-being and did just as well as the nonathletes in financial well-being, too.

But if you're a parent trying to figure out how much money to put into or continue to put into a child's budding athletic talent, try not to think about it in terms of financial returns. Given the costs, it is indeed hard not to consider whether making a team or winning a tournament will justify all the money spent. But perhaps the best measure is your child's answer to this question: Just how happy does all this competition make you?

CHAPTER 25

Gap Years: Great, Sometimes Pricey, Might Help You Get a Better Job Someday

When high school students raise the prospect of taking a gap year or a forward-thinking counselor suggests considering it, parents' minds tend to go to dark places. I should know. In 1996, I coauthored the first book on the topic that was filled with profiles of people who had taken time off between high school and college. Many of the stories featured tales of the parental angst that students had to overcome.

Sometimes the concern is about momentum. Will people who take time off deliberately, with an acceptance letter in hand and a plan to matriculate in a year, actually go to college when the year is over? They will. Two researchers in the United Kingdom, where taking a gap year is more common, found that people there and in Australia who deferred their admission for a year ultimately enrolled at the same rate as people who didn't take a gap year.

Other parents wonder what colleges will think without realizing that with each passing year, more colleges are creating formal programs or processes to persuade more people to spend a year away. They know good and well that leave-takers come back to the classroom with experience, perspective, and drive that make them valuable contributors to most any classroom. At schools like Colorado College, this has become so obvious that Mark Hatch, vice president of enrollment, is practically shouting from the nearby mountaintops that many eighteen-year-olds should stay away. Five years of research have proven to him and his colleagues that people who take a gap year get in less trouble, are more likely to graduate on time, do little if any binge drinking, and have higher GPAs. Young men, in particular, seem to benefit from the extra year. "We decided that we needed to aggressively say that if you are on the fence with our admissions committee, a well-defined gap year concept is probably worth three votes in your favor," he said.

Still, this is a book about money and value. And taking a gap year, it turns out, can also help make college cheaper and enable undergraduates to get more out of their college experience than they might have without a year off. Let's start with the obvious: Students who don't have enough money for college or want to avoid debt can work for a year or two first. The effective minimum wage in the United States —what a median minimum-wage worker earned—is about $12 per hour, though that may vary by a few dollars depending on local or state regulations. That's $480 per week (for 40 hours of work) before taxes and $24,000 if someone works 50 out of 52 weeks in a year. If you are applying for financial aid, a school will likely reduce your aid accordingly, so keep that in mind. But still, if everyone is good with the gap-year taker living and eating at home, there are no room and board costs. And if the parent or parents are able to save a bit more money during that year, all the better.

Now consider financial aid. Let's say you have two kids three years apart. If the elder child takes a gap year and the younger one does not—or doesn't take one until after sophomore year—then they'll be in college at the same time for two years instead of just one. Many schools may continue to offer families more eligibility for need-based assistance when two family members are enrolled in college simultaneously. For many families this could mean well over $10,000 in extra grants per student per year.

Given that level of savings, perhaps there will be less pressure to earn a bunch of money during a gap year. And sure, there are plenty of parents who see a year off as just another expense, with privileged kids flying all over the place to find themselves. It's certainly possible to spend a lot of money on formal courses, although some of the more established ones such as Outward Bound, NOLS (National Outdoor Leadership School), and Global Citizen Year can provide a truly life-changing experience (and their own financial aid). Still, it's possible to break even by working in the AmeriCorps federal national service program for eight months, then traveling on the cheap for a few months, then traveling on the cheap for a few months after that. Many volunteer opportunities outside the United States offer room and board in exchange for work, too.

Then there are the more indirect financial considerations, which have to do with what happens to undergraduates once their gap years are over. One framing device I've found helpful in talking to parents about taking time off from college is this one: What do you actually want your child to get for the money you're spending on college? Do better grades and better jobs sound good to you?

Great! So let's have that conversation, because people who take a gap year get better grades than those who don't and better grades than they might have otherwise, all things being equal. One Berkeley economist found this out when he was trying to prove that Mormon missionaries assigned to a country where they had to learn a new language improved their undergraduate grade point averages more than people who spoke English on their two-year missions. That did not turn out to be true, but the researcher did find that across majors and course loads, those who embarked on a two-year mission during college improved their GPA by an average of 0.11 point for women and 0.24 point for men—enough in many instances to boost, say, a B-plus to an A-minus.

Bob Clagett, the former dean of admissions at Middlebury College in Vermont and a longtime senior admissions officer at Harvard, conducted his own study. He began with a student ratings system he had used at Middlebury that was not unlike what other admissions pros use: one that tracks grades and scores, teacher and counselor recommendations, whether applicants took advantage of all possible offerings in high school, and whether any lust for learning and living emerged in their essays. That score was usually a pretty good predictor of how an applicant would do at Middlebury. Then Clagett looked at the grades students who had taken a gap year had actually achieved in college compared with how the rating predicted that they would perform. He found that people who had taken gap years had almost always overperformed and had done so throughout college. Later, data from the University of North Carolina told a similar story.

So why do better grades matter? First, there's the obvious immediate return on investment: If part of the reason you attend college is to learn, getting excellent grades is an indicator that you've engaged with the material more intensively. This is a good thing all by itself. But then there are all of the things that good grades can get you. Professors hire people with better grades to work as research assistants. They may be more likely to recommend them for other jobs. Better grades can help you get into a better graduate school, which may set you up for better job opportunities later. Some employers look at transcripts, and you can always put a sterling grade point average on your résumé so that hiring managers have no choice but to reckon with your academic prowess.

Aside from better grades, taking a gap year sets college seniors up to tell a great story about themselves when it comes time for the job hunt. Hiring entry-level workers is not easy. You've got a stack of résumés from people with decent grades and a few internships. The good ones have trained and drilled for job interviews within an inch of their lives at their newly rebooted undergraduate career services offices. Imagine being the person confronting that pile of résumés and then finding, next to the pile, a different one. The applicant is twenty-three years old instead of twenty-two, someone who made a deliberate choice to go out into the world and do something entirely different for a year. Everyone else you're considering went to college just like the rest of the lemmings. And now that leave-taker is going to show up with a ripping good yarn about the why of the gap year, the learning along the way, and how it led to absorbing more in the classroom and in relationships with peers and professors. You will have fun talking with this person who has taken these risks. Whom would you rather hire?

Maybe the mistake we make here is in the naming. A gap year is not a break, not dead air, not white space. It is a year on, not a year off. Or, as Abby Falik, the founder of Global Citizen Year, puts it: Gap years are bridge years; a well-engineered connection between one life stage and another; a deliberate pause that is nevertheless not silent or still but filled with something other than what would happen inside a classroom. Students may well find that a gap year will be a bridge to getting so much more per hour, per dollar, out of college than they ever thought possible.

CHAPTER 26

Army, Navy, Air Force, Marines, Coast Guard: Decent Money, Big Responsibility

Joining the military is a serious matter. As we've learned at fairly regular intervals over the last fifty years, we can't always predict what choices our leaders will make about the use of force, nor do we know when our nation will come under attack. Leaders change here, regimes change abroad, terrorists strike seemingly out of nowhere, and then, suddenly, hundreds of thousands of American lives are on the line.

Recruiters don't sugarcoat this reality, either. The branches of the U.S. armed forces decline to publish the relatively low historical odds of experiencing combat or grave danger or even attempt to define those terms as the very definition of war evolves. Instead, the Army, in a FAQ for high school students on its website, answers a query about the chances of being "deployed to support the Global War on Terrorism" like so: "It depends on the Army branch the Cadet chooses and the unit to which he/she is assigned. However, Army missions and challenges are always changing, so there's no way to know in advance which specialties and units will be needed where. All Soldiers in the Army or Army Reserve face the possibility of deployment at some point during their careers. But all Soldiers are fully trained and proficient in the tasks and drills of their units. And Officers are specifically trained to make the right decisions so that missions can be carried out safely and successfully."

Anyone considering enlisting in the armed forces for financial reasons alone should think hard about this uncertainty. That said, our armed forces are not a "volunteer" military in one important respect that many families do not fully appreciate: It is not an unpaid job, and doing it can pay for college—all of it.

The most obvious way in which the federal government rewards its veterans is through the GI Bill. If you serve for three years, you qualify for full benefits under the bill. Those benefits include full tuition and any mandatory fees for four academic years for full-time students at any state university at in-state tuition rates. Students also get a housing allowance (if they're in school more than half-time) and money for books. For those hoping to attend an out-of-state public university, a private college, or a school outside the United States, the costs are capped; as of this writing, it sits at about $25,000 per year, although additional funds may be available through something called the Yellow Ribbon Program.

There are a couple of important financial aid considerations too, both of which work in favor of veterans. First, the money that the federal government spends to pay this tuition is not considered income. As a result, a student doesn't have to report it as such on the FAFSA or other financial aid forms. This can allow applicants to qualify for more financial aid. Moreover, there is no income tax on the amount of the benefit. Another twist: Upon completion of service, the federal government and financial aid administrators consider veterans to be financially independent. That means parental income doesn't figure in when schools determine eligibility for need-based scholarships. That too can mean much more aid for veterans who need money beyond what they would get as a result of the GI Bill.

Although we tend to refer to the foot soldiers of our armed services as an "all-volunteer" force, teenage soldiers do make money. As of this writing, pay starts at $1,800 per month and goes up from there depending on rank and experience. There are opportunities to take classes online while serving full-time, and education benefits may be available then as well, depending on the branch of service.

Finally, for people who want to start college soon after high school but still use military service as a way to pay for college, there's the Reserve Officers Training Corps, or ROTC for short. The Army, Navy, and Air Force all have programs at some but not all colleges and universities. People who want to serve in the Marines can work through the Navy's plan, while those interested in the Coast Guard can apply for an alternative precommissioning program that it runs. Though the plans differ some, the basics are these: Participants start college right after high school (or after a gap year) and enroll in ROTC right away. They take some military courses during the school year, perform certain extracurricular training and activities with their unit, and engage in summer training as well. Then, after graduation, they enlist full-time for several years, depending on the branch of service.

In exchange for that commitment, that branch may pay some or all of participants' college tuition, provide a stipend for living expenses, and pay for books. There may be per year caps on the cost of tuition, and there is sometimes more money available for people majoring in in-demand subjects such as science and engineering, nursing, or certain foreign languages.

Let me repeat: Making a military commitment is serious, and failing to fulfill it means having to repay some or all financial benefits. The rewards can be outsized too, given how much respect veterans command in many industries and parts of the country. The training and leadership skills alone might well be worth actually paying for if they didn't come with the risk of going to war. So consider all of those risks first and foremost. But for those who serve in this manner, college could well be free, or close to it.

CHAPTER 27

Skipping College Is Probably Not a Great Idea

Paying for and attending college is, among other things, an investment. And if you've ever invested money, you know that all investments with even small projected returns come with at least some risk.

So if you're inclined to believe the people who tell you that college is for suckers, the right response is this: What are our children's chances for having the life they want if they do attend and complete college, and how do those odds look if they don't go to college at all?

The best data we have on these questions relate to earnings. Let's start with some estimates that a couple of Federal Reserve Bank of New York researchers worked up. It noted that average college graduates with no graduate degree earned about $78,000 per year—$33,000 more than someone with just a high school diploma. Though you may wonder whether the increasing number of people who finish college may depress this advantage somehow, the opposite has been true in recent years. At that point, the so-called college wage premium was almost the highest it had ever been. The New York Fed researchers estimated the value of that premium over a forty-plus-year career and came to the conclusion that the annual average rate of return on investment in college is about 14 percent. That figure, which is for people who finish their degrees in four years, is double what most people would be happy to earn in the stock market over time.

Now for the throat clearing and caveats, which should give some of you a bit of pause. Averages are just that, and the tidy story they tell can often mask trouble. First, let's repeat the refrain that we have sung before: Finishing what you start and doing so in a timely fashion makes an enormous difference. Other data that the New York Fed published showed that the 14 percent annual return for investing in a college degree falls to 11 percent if you take five years to finish college and 8 percent if you take six years. This happens both because the extra time in school costs money and because of the opportunity cost if you are not in the workforce for that extra year or two.

Much also depends on your major. Douglas Webber, a Temple University associate professor who studies the economics of higher education, crunched some numbers on the topic for a report called "Is College Worth It? Going Beyond Averages" that he wrote for the think tank Third Way. In his projections he excluded people who got graduate degrees, assumed that everyone took five years to graduate, and figured that families pay for one-third of college expenses with debt. His conclusion? Most science, technology, engineering, or math majors are very likely to achieve a positive return on their investment, but arts or humanities majors who attend private colleges with average costs have only a 50 percent or so chance that what's known as the net present value of the money they're putting into the expense of college will be positive. Moreover, the difference in lifetime earnings between the highest- and lowest-earning majors can approach $2 million total over the course of a career, given that people who choose these majors often choose different kinds of jobs afterward. Families probably sense this somewhat vaguely before a child chooses a major, but this puts some numbers to it, even if they are only averages that cannot predict any single English major's experience as a high school teacher or investment banker.

Webber's report, which is a must-read for any doubting family members who want to seek it out online, is quick to remind readers that he examined only earnings—not the value of the friends or contacts students make, the higher household income that might result from a spouse they might meet in college, or the overall feelings of well-being and life satisfaction that may result from higher education. Also, he doesn't necessarily want people who are passionate about particular subjects to switch away from those majors. Researchers, he explained, don't have a good way to know what would happen if students who love literature switched to engineering just because they thought they were supposed to. Would another $2 million come their way? Even if it did, would it be worth it if they were miserable at work?

And then there's this: A full 25 percent of people who graduate from college do not earn much more than those who completed only high school, according to a New York Fed report. Many in that group actually earn less than high school graduates do. Sure, some people earn less because they chose lower-paying professions or prefer part-time work. But two economists for the nonprofit W.E. Upjohn Institute for Employment Research found some surprising patterns. First, college pays off more for people from higher-income families. If family income was above 1.85 times the poverty level in their survey, they estimated that career earnings for college graduates were 136 percent higher than for high school graduates. But people whose family incomes were below that 1.85 mark saw just a 71 percent income premium from graduating college. For white men from families with incomes at 100 to 200 percent of the poverty line, the return to 2 falls to near zero. Women see no such changes in patterns in differing social classes.

Overall, Black people from the poorest family backgrounds earn much more as college graduates over time than poor whites do. But white men from more affluent families seem to have greater access to some of the most highly paid jobs, such as ones in finance. And if that's the ultimate goal, it's worth adding this observation from Webber's Third Way report: College graduates are 177 times more likely to earn $4 million and up during their careers than are high school graduates.

In recent years the Federal Reserve Bank of St. Louis has been examining wealth in addition to income. This is important, since wealth measurements take into account whatever assets younger adults in particular have managed to gather (or have not been able to afford yet) and subtracts whatever debts they have (student loan debt in particular). What St. Louis Fed researchers found was that for people born in the 1980s, there has been an enormous decline in the so-called wealth premium that college graduates once maintained over people who had completed only high school. For some demographic groups, such as young Black people, it has nearly disappeared. This is logical, according to the researchers. As student loan debt and other forms of consumer credit have become easier to access over time, is it any wonder that teenagers without a lot of life experience sometimes borrow more than they should? And once that happens, doesn't it make sense that the money going to debt payment does not end up in retirement accounts or as part of a down payment for a house, the value of which could contribute to overall wealth?

This narrowing of the wealth gap may not be permanent; perhaps people will make up for lost time once they pay off their debts. Some of the gap may have to do with bad luck and their reaction to it, too; putting a lot of money into stocks right before the enormous market declines in 2008 and 2009 might have scared some people away from investing for a while. But at the very least these numbers should give families pause if they're considering maxing out on student and other loans for degrees that tend to lead to lower-paying careers.

If your primary concern is what prospective employers will think about the value of college degrees, they mostly still like them. But there are some signs of change. In 2018, Sean Gallagher, the executive director of Northeastern University's Center for the Future of Higher Education and Talent Strategy, published a report called "Educational Credentials Come of Age: A Survey on the Use and Value of Educational Credentials in Hiring." In it he summarized a survey of 750 human resources managers at U.S. employers across a variety of organizational sizes and industries. Among that group, 48 percent believed that educational credentials are more valuable in hiring than they were five years ago, while 29 percent believed that their value has stayed the same. The rest—23 percent—are the doubters who think degrees and certificates aren't what they once were. That 23 percent figure may give you pause, but remember: This was not a survey about entry-level hiring or employees in their twenties; it was a look at hiring overall. Given that, it probably shouldn't be surprising that 74 percent of the respondents said that years spent in a job can substitute for the lack of a credential, even if the credential is supposedly required.

That said, credential inflation seems to be a real thing. Survey participants reported that their preferred or required education levels have increased 44 percent of the time for the exact same roles compared with five years before. Another 31 percent of jobs required a similar education, while 20 percent had decreased slightly and 5 percent had done so significantly. Though 63 percent of the respondents who said that they had increased requirements reported that they had done so because the candidates for those jobs really did need new and different skills, 51 percent (they could check off numerous explanations for the qualification inflation) admitted that they had increased the requirements simply because there were so many people with degrees in the marketplace.

What we don't know is how these figures will change. Often surveys like this are trailing indicators of whatever is going on in the labor market. And labor markets differ from region to region and industry to industry. Perhaps those 25 percent of respondents who lowered their educational requirements did so because they had to, given how low unemployment rates were when they completed the survey. Beggars can't be choosers when most people who want a job already have one, and things may look very different under different economic conditions.

Is your child tempted by the blue-collar trades and is considering skipping college altogether or just for now? If so, take a look at the U.S. Bureau of Labor Statistics page for any given profession. What do people tend to earn? What about those at the top end of the wage scale in any given industry? If that's less than what you make, does your child understand how that might translate into a different way of living or how economic cycles might affect an electrician in ways that probably wouldn't affect a teacher?

As for those mythical six-figure welders you may hear about from time to time, they are out there in teeny-tiny numbers. Paul Tough did a good job of dismantling the rich welder myth in an excerpt from his book *The Years that Matter Most: How College Makes or Breaks Us* that appeared in the *Atlantic*. First, you have to take many post–high school courses to become a welder; you can't just do it, although you don't have to graduate from a four-year college, either. And even though the salary floor for a welder is higher than minimum wage, the average annual salary is just $41,000 for someone experienced. In the 90th percentile, people make $63,000. Six-figure welders work dangerous jobs, sometimes in remote locations, and may have to move frequently for work.

Tough suggests three reasons why some pundits continue to recommend seeking blue-collar work in lieu of attending college. Some people are simply ignorant of the data and the poor odds of outsized earnings for people who do not attend college. Others point to the six-figure carpenters or plumbers and conclude that anyone who can't get a job like that must be lazy, without accounting for a variety of inequities that may keep someone from finding and learning a trade or becoming an apprentice or a union member. Finally, there's a sort of nostalgia for bygone days when people worked with their hands and lived by their wits and there was much less credentialism, with no gatekeepers collecting tuition tolls and setting curricular standards.

If you are dead set against your child going to college, check your assumptions and see if any of the above applies to you. College is a bet, but so is avoiding it outright—a big one at that. And though all of us are right to wonder if our kids have what it takes not to end up among the college graduates who don't earn more than high school graduates do, the opposite question is necessary, too: If they don't graduate from college, what are the odds that they'll be among the small percentage of people who make it—who start a business or find a trade that will always be in demand? And if they don't outearn the average college graduate—if they never do or never come close—will they be happy about that?

In his book on adjunct professors, *The Adjunct Underclass*, Herb Childress takes a somewhat cynical view of all of this. There is no wage premium for college graduates, he writes; just a wage defense. A college degree is "indispensable employment insurance," nothing more and nothing less, although it may cost somewhat more at private universities. If he's right, we can ask ourselves this: How comfortable are we when we go without insurance in other parts of our lives? Can't bear to leave yourself bare when it comes to your home coverage or your car? Would you never in a million years skip medical insurance altogether? If that sounds like you, urging teenagers to attend college if and when they are ready seems like a pretty good bet with favorable odds, especially for those who approach it with the sort of care and discernment that we've outlined in these pages.

PART V

The Plans

Saving, Talking, Touring,
Bargaining, and Borrowing

CHAPTER 28

How to Make the
Big Financial Plan

If you've landed here with a plan to do some planning, welcome.

Maybe your first child is on the way or on the horizon or still in diapers. As with most financial goals, the earlier you set them, the better off you will be. But if this is not you and you've done less planning than is ideal, not all is lost. You'll need to adjust most of the numbers I mention here according to your family's timeline, but the basic conversational and organizational framework will still be useful if your child or children are already in their teens. You're welcome here, too.

Any discussion of big plans has to begin with a bow to the unknown, and there are so many things that we cannot know about the future in this context. If your children are small, you have no idea what sort of students they may be, with what sort of passions or wanderlust or drive. But we grown-ups don't know as much as we think about ourselves, either. Over five years or certainly fifteen or twenty, we can't predict whether we'll continue to enjoy our careers or how successful we'll be. We know nothing about future economic cycles or even the trajectory of the one we're in as you're reading this. Our investments may do better or worse than we predict, and the irrational feelings resulting from big gains or losses may cause us to buy or sell the wrong assets at the wrong times. Health crises can strike at any point, and not just our own: An adolescent's mental health crisis or an aging parent with a slowly progressing incurable condition can wreak financial havoc along with the emotional kind. And how much do we really know about our own goals? How long do we want to work, if we have any say in the matter? How hard and where?

In the midst of all this uncertainty, it can seem foolish to plan. But here's the thing: It is a very rare family that regrets putting some money away for a child's higher education and an even rarer one that wishes it had saved less than it did.

I am not here to peddle planning clichés. For instance, one common piece of advice in the world of personal finance is to put your own oxygen mask on before making sure your kid can breathe. In practice, that is supposed to suggest that you should make sure you are saving enough for your own retirement before putting any money into college savings for a child. This advice, however, is at odds with our basic emotional instinct to sacrifice ourselves for our children. I'm not going to try to persuade you to defy those feelings and rewire what evolution has programmed. Nor am I going to make the common point that you should favor retirement savings because you can borrow money to pay your child's college tuition bill but you can't borrow for retirement. That isn't true, no matter how often it shows up in articles by journalists who should know better. Plenty of people borrow for retirement via something called a reverse mortgage, and many more will do so in the coming decades. That is a topic for another day and another book, though.

I am also not here to shame or judge you for what you do or do not do. Unlike the federal government and the great expectations it embeds in the figure that springs forth from your completed FAFSA form, I have seen enough to know not to expect anything from any parents no matter how much money they have. Look, it's enough that you're here in these pages with an open mind and a willingness to do something. I'm also keenly aware of something that Caitlin Zaloom described perfectly in her book *Indebted*, an anthropological examination of how and why families take on debt in the pursuit of higher education. Making good plans increases your chance of achieving financial stability and then maintaining it, to be sure. But they are so hard to make and keep. To do that, she wrote, you need stability in order to plan in the first place. Without it, you're constantly making new plans when the previous ones break. And who among us has true financial stability these days?

So this is all pretty hard. And against this backdrop, making any plan to save and pay for college feels a bit like an act of faith. But making a plan and saving some money can pack a surprisingly large emotional punch. There is something about making some kind of a commitment that just feels good. Doing it bit by bit on a regular basis has a calming effect. Doing something, however small, feels better than doing nothing. Saving can become habit forming, and any progress helps bring on a slow-growing feeling of well-being.

Still, coming up with a monthly dollar goal or a round number you should aim for after fifteen or twenty years of saving is difficult. There are simply too many variables, including your own age, the age of your kids, your present assets, and the intentions of any grandparents who may want to chip in. Instead, I'll use the advice that Carl Richards, the former "Sketch Guy" columnist for the *New York Times*, offers up in these sorts of situations: Save as much as you reasonably can. Remind yourself that few among us can save enough to pay for four years of college in full, so that's probably not the goal. Familiarize yourself with a good college savings calculator. (I like the one on the investment firm Vanguard's website.) Play with different projections based on when you start, how much any investments you have might earn, and what you think college might cost or you'll be willing to pay for it.

That last bit will require a serious chat with your spouse if you have one—and a more complicated one, perhaps, with any ex-spouse, especially if you haven't spelled out obligations in a divorce agreement or if your child's desires have outpaced any financial commitment. The sooner you come to an agreement about what you might want to save or pay for college, the sooner you can start making a plan. And the necessity of getting every parent onto the same page applies equally to how you'll convey any plan and its particulars to your child, which we'll talk about more in the next chapter.

The most calming formula for planning is one that Kevin McKinley, a financial planner in Eau Claire, Wisconsin, shared with me many years ago, although I later learned that the financial aid expert Mark Kantrowitz had been suggesting a similar version of it for a while as well. McKinley has three kids, including two in college, so he knows whereof he preaches. He suggests thinking in fractions. Take a family aiming to send one child to a state university or a private one that offers plenty of merit aid. Their all-in cost in today's dollars might be $100,000. McKinley would have them divide that into quarters. The goal would be to save one-quarter of the total, $25,000, through regular deposits as the child grows up. Then they'd pay $25,000 out of their current income during the four years of college, with the undergraduate working part-time during the school year and full-time during the summer. The remaining $50,000 could come from debt, with the student borrowing a bit more than half that total from the federal government and parents borrowing the rest from home equity or through a federal PLUS Loan or a private lender.

Let's break that down a bit more gradually. When setting a savings goal, you have to make some kind of assumption about what kind of interest the money will earn. Some people put all or most of their college money into stocks, while others crave safety and will use only savings accounts or similar low-interest, no-risk accounts. (I'll address the specialized 529 college savings plans in more detail in Chapter 30.) Let's split the difference here and assume a 5 percent annual rate of return over eighteen years of saving. Anyone wanting to get to $25,000 would need to save about $75 per month. In his book *Make Your Kid a Millionaire: 11 Easy Ways Anyone Can Secure a Child's Financial Future*, McKinley suggested a typical budget exercise: Check your debit and credit card statements for things that you want but don't truly need. Then he suggested asking a provocative question: Would you rather help your kid go to college or would you prefer to keep buying or doing those things on the bill that add up to $75? "Most people with kids going to college wish they could go back and change what they spent, because a lot of it was on things that didn't have any value in the long run," he told me when I caught up with him for a 2016 column.

Now, about that $25,000 of spending out of current income during the four undergraduate years . . . let's call it $6,000 per year just to keep the numbers round. It is totally possible for college students to earn all of that themselves. If they can make $4,000 during twelve weeks of full-time work in the summer, that's two-thirds of it right there. The rest can come from part-time work during the school year. If you don't want your child to face that burden, you can pay some portion of it out of your current income if you're able to do so.

Finally, there's borrowing. I'll address the mechanics of doing so in Chapter 34, but just briefly it could go like so: First, the student borrows $25,000 total over four years, staying several thousand dollars short of the maximum amount that the federal government lets one borrow as an undergraduate. Borrowing only from the government leaves any debtor eligible for an income-driven repayment program, which means that during periods of low pay or unemployment, debtors can adjust their payment so that it is affordable. Parents, meanwhile, can borrow against a home if they own one and the interest is reasonable. If not, they can often borrow via the federal government's Direct PLUS Loan program or a private lender if one is offering a better interest rate.

Adjust the fractions any way you wish. When I first talked to McKinley about it more than a decade ago, he suggested that people save one-third of the projected cost during the first eighteen years of a child's life, pay for one-third of it over four years out of current income, and borrow one-third. Mark Kantrowitz isn't fond of the $50,000 in debt that McKinley's current fractions could leave families with, and he suggests that families save more and spend more out of current income while a child is in college. (Indeed, McKinley's eldest child chose to attend a branch of her state school precisely because she intends to move to New York City someday and doesn't want to bring any debt to such a high-cost area.) Boost your monthly savings to $100 or $125, and that's possible. Add parent earnings beyond the $25,000 that a student might earn over four years, and that can reduce the debt load, too.

One problem with introducing a formula that spits out dollar figures is that people who don't hit those goals or can't do so right away can get discouraged. Kevin Mahoney, a financial planner in Washington, D.C., takes a different approach with the fractions that he deploys with clients. He's younger than Kevin McKinley, and his clients tend to be young too, often with piles of their own student loans left to repay even as their kids start to arrive. So Mahoney does not assign them a savings goal, but he does keep an eye on the changes in their lives. After all, the sooner they can start saving, the more time compound interest (when your earnings are themselves earning) has to work its magic. And as soon as Mahoney spots a change—day care costs plummeting as the youngest or only child enters public kindergarten; a raise; a bonus; a paid-off student loan—he asks them to take at least some of the freed-up money and put it toward college. His math suggests that if families can devote a decent chunk of this "new" money toward that goal, they can save as much as or more than they might using the McKinley formula but perhaps feel less burdened by any up-front savings rules.

If your own parents are still alive, still in the picture, and more than merely solvent, perhaps you're hoping that they have their own plan to help. Maybe they've even let slip that they hope to pay for part of their grandchildren's education or have set aside some money already. If so, you're incredibly lucky. You probably know this, and as a result you may be reluctant to ask too many questions about their intentions. And maybe that's fine. If they show up in a decade with a pile of money, perhaps you won't have to borrow or spend money out of your current income. There's no need to ask them for any details just yet, given that their financial situation could change during that time, too.

But waiting to broach the topic with grandparents isn't practical for everyone. Take this scenario: Your parents appear to be in a position to help, now or later, and they have made vague statements that they intend to do so. In the here and now, however, you don't earn enough to repay student loans, save for retirement, assemble a down payment, pay for child care, and save for college. Help in any form would be welcome. You're not ashamed to ask for it, either, but you're worried that even bringing it up could backfire in any number of ways.

If this sounds like you, consider the following script: "Mom, Dad, Moms, Dads, you have raised us right. You put me through all or most of college and taught me to work hard. I've done that and am doing that. Being a parent brings me joy that is second only, perhaps, to the joy you feel in being grandparents and watching me do what you did. But the struggle is real here, with costs that you didn't face or didn't face in such high volume. You've mentioned the possibility of helping, which is so generous. But in the absence of specifics, it's very hard to make a plan and set a strategy that will prevent even more struggle or sacrifice later. So if you do have a plan, it would be great to know about it now. If not, that is okay, too. I don't expect it, but I would be grateful for help if it came, and knowing the details now would help alleviate the stress."

That sort of script is unlikely to lead to blowback. And if you're a grandparent reading this book because you want to help, this next sentence is the most important one: Do what you can right now if possible. If you have $75 per month to spare for an infant grandchild, put it aside and watch it grow to $25,000. If your teenage grandchildren are borrowing for college, see about making the payments for them afterward if that's within the realm of possibility. As Kevin McKinley put it to me when I first spoke to him in 2009, "In most otherwise healthy families, the willingness of grandparents to save generally exceeds the willingness of parents to broach the subject with the grandparents. That's good. It shows that parents aren't money grubbing. But it means it's usually the grandparents' duty to bring the subject up."

Sure, pulling money from investments that could be part of a larger inheritance later does have potential costs. But so do the strain and stress that families experience, sometimes for decades, around saving and paying for college. You as a grandparent may be able to help lower that stress. And it's just as true if you have little money but plenty of time. In that instance you can help bring child care costs down by pitching in with grandchild care to make it easier for your adult children to work longer hours or recover from having done so.

The McKinley plan is admittedly quite linear. Even the Mahoney plan assumes some kind of upward trajectory, with new sources of money making semiregular appearances. At each step along the way, however, there will be competing expenses, perhaps none so powerful as the immediate ones that involve short-term spending on children. Caitlin Zaloom frames this as a choice between planning—putting money away for college—and provisioning. If you're paying for a tutor, spending money on travel team expenses, or laying out four figures each year on summer enrichment activities, that's provisioning. At each step along the way, there will be peer pressure if others around you are doing it. And there will be internalized pressure as well: What do all of the college savings add up to if there's no investment in the here and now in making your kids smarter and faster and shinier specimens to catch the eyes of college admissions officers someday in the future? Plus there is pure fun. Remember that? Passion projects and family vacations and the solo trip to see the former classmate who moved to Spain and that sort of thing? In Zaloom's anthropological study, provisioning seemed to win most often, which is part of what left so many of her subjects short of savings and vulnerable to debt and feelings of guilt when their kids started college.

You will face these questions constantly. Simply naming what they are may help, at least sometimes. But perhaps the greatest financial hazard is how nonlinear your life will likely be, with all that planning set against stock market crashes, periods of unemployment, illness somewhere in the immediate family, or a global pandemic. Hopefully there will be financial surprises on the positive side, too. And in the background are the ever-rising costs of college (and health care and housing) and unpredictability about what sort of higher education system any given five-year-old might be facing a dozen years from now. You'll know for sure only a double-digit number of years from now, and then you'll have a few weeks, if you're lucky, to make an enormously consequential decision.

It's not a pretty picture, and we shouldn't expect it to get more rational, given how long it took to create such a broken system. Just try not to let the complexity of it all paralyze you into doing nothing at all to get ready.

CHAPTER 29

How to Have the College Money Talk with Your Child

Choosing a college isn't merely the biggest financial decision that most families will ever make. It may also be the final big one you make together as a family. Not all young adults come back to their parents for advice after graduation, after all. So you'll want to try as hard as you can to be deliberate about the first conversation.

Getting the college money talk right is a tall order, given how many emotions are involved. So let's break it down into two smaller questions that parents need to answer for themselves and then figure out how to address with a child: How much are you able—and willing—to pay and borrow? And what should you disclose and when about how colleges reward grades with five- and six-figure merit aid discounts?

Talking about college and any money that is available early and often does seem to matter. One piece of research showed that among kids who planned on graduating from college, those who have any kind of savings account in their name are six times more likely to hit their goal than children for whom there is no savings. Other research has shown that it is assets—including family savings—that affect graduation rates even more than income. These studies merely show correlation, and it shouldn't come as much of a surprise that families in which children have savings accounts and parents have their own assets tend to end up with a degree hanging on a wall. Still, they do suggest a course of action: If you are saving, say so. I like getting paper copies of our college savings accounts in the mail, since they serve as a tactile reminder to keep telling my older daughter that we are working toward a goal and we expect her to help us fulfill it.

Sometime during the teenage years and before visiting colleges, you should also let your kids know what they can expect you to contribute. By then, you'll probably have a decent sense of what sort of savings you have and how much more you might be able to put away if there are no financial surprises before college. You can also make some projections, based on your current income, on how much you might be able to contribute from your take-home pay each year. And you can certainly begin to broach the question of how much you might be willing to borrow yourself, if anything—and whether you intend to place any limits on what a child might borrow with loans that you would have to cosign.

Depending on how much you've already talked about money as a parent, your teenager may have no idea what college can cost, no context for a number that large and little idea of what you earn and how you divide your household budget. If you suspect that your teen is in the dark about all of this, it's probably best to give them that education first.

Some parents feel embarrassed about their lack of savings or feel bad that they don't earn enough to allow their kids to choose among all colleges, debt free. Please don't. The chances are very good that you've done the best you could. You don't owe anyone an apology, least of all your child. Don't measure yourself against nearby families, either; nobody really talks about this stuff, and you can't possibly know which families have generous grandparents in the picture or who is pulling six figures from their home equity to pay the bills or is in five figures of credit card debt.

Does the idea of talking about all of this with a younger teenager still feel weird? In her book *Indebted*, Caitlin Zaloom kept asking about this reticence. Parents don't want kids to feel like a burden, even if it is obvious that debt or painful financial choices are going to be necessary. And teens often don't push the issue by demanding answers, either.

Zaloom describes these actions and reactions as "nested silences," where many parents prefer saying nothing to disclosing information that will place their children into some kind of socioeconomic pecking order. This is somewhat delusional, given that most kids have a keenly honed sense of social class by the time they've finished middle school. But it's also understandable. In attempting to break the silence, it may help to frame the conversation around opportunity—the excitement that you have about whatever this money can actually buy.

Now to the question about what to say about the merit aid system that links price in part to high school grades. Logic would suggest that rules are rules and everyone who is playing the game ought to know how the scorekeepers operate. The obvious hypothesis, then, is that all parents ought to sit down and explain the system to their kids right before they begin to make a permanent record for themselves, after eighth grade ends. I asked all the enrollment management professionals who use merit aid that I could round up whether they thought it was inappropriate for parents to have this part of the talk before high school started. Nobody quite forbid parents from disclosing all. "A grade point average of 3.6 versus 3.8 could matter a great deal to the final price point," said Jeff Allen, vice president for admissions and financial aid at Macalester. Those are, after all, the facts.

As a parent, however, how much more pressure do you want to put on your child? Many high school students are self-motivated enough, so heaping financial stakes on top of whatever admissions odds they may encounter probably won't light that much more of a fire under them. For students who are less inclined to apply themselves in the classroom, however, earlier disclosure might make a difference.

No matter how much money you make or have, you probably don't want your child to feel that leaving home—or perhaps leaving the state and your state's public university system—is some kind of entitlement. And if merit aid is going to be a literal requirement for them to matriculate anywhere except at one of your state schools because you are unable or unwilling to pay the full price elsewhere, shouldn't a child learn that at the beginning of high school?

After all, the math on grade point averages is quite vicious. If you start off with a 3.4 average and realize only in the middle of sophomore year that your grades count for dollars, getting straight A's for the next four semesters can pull your overall average up only so much. Now imagine a high school senior discovering the merit aid system for the first time and then coming to you, demanding to know why you didn't explain it sooner. By then, college choices may be limited to ones that are much less selective. Will high school seniors accept the explanation that you thought it best to protect them from pressure? Or will they hold it against you?

It is possible that all of this hand-wringing over when to talk about merit aid is entirely moot. With each passing year, more and more families encounter the system earlier and actually learn how it works (two vastly different things, as we've already seen). Some members of the previous class of college applicants tell the younger students about the acceptance letters and, perhaps, the discount negotiations that follow. And in some parts of the country, the money story is out, whether counselors and parents want to keep students from hearing about it or not. At the University of Oregon, a 3.85 grade point average gets in-state residents the biggest scholarship. In Georgia, earning a 3.0 GPA in high school can be worth $16,000 or so over four years in college. Florida has a range of similar discounts. "You learn this in sixth grade," said Ashley Darcy-Mahoney, who grew up in Florida, taught at Emory and Georgia Tech, and is now an associate professor and director of infant research at the George Washington University School of Nursing. You certainly learn it in Texas, where all students in the top 6 percent of their high school graduating classes are automatically admitted to the University of Texas at Austin. Some parents even try to game the system by sending their kids to less competitive high schools.

Darcy-Mahoney, who reviews the packages of high school applicants when she helps with admissions at George Washington, played Division I soccer at Georgetown on a partial scholarship. In the realm of serious youth sports, middle school students are well aware of the financial stakes that exist as they advance through the travel-team circuits as a young athlete while hoping that colleges will reward them with athletic scholarships. "In seventh grade, you knew which teams you had to make," she said. "You just knew."

How should parents communicate this information? What do middle school kids actually pick up on in what is said or what is left unsaid? This felt like a particularly urgent question for Darcy-Mahoney, because she lived it herself. Had her parents told her that they were measuring the return on the untold thousands of dollars they had invested on travel-team soccer in terms of the number and amount of athletic scholarships she won? No, she said. But she and her husband, Kevin Mahoney, the financial planner from the previous chapter, told me that they would have no problem talking honestly about the financial stakes of athletics with their own kids someday, as long as there were no mental health or other challenges involved. "Most teenagers want to be treated like adults," she said. "And treating them that way in giving them information about adulthood and adult decisions is also what they want."

College counselors in high schools are a bit more wary, especially when it's parents who are pressing them. "I get a lot of pressure to start the college process before the time that we do," said Kelly Richards, who advises students at St. George's School in Middletown, Rhode Island, and is the mother of three children herself.

She is all for financial literacy, and she wants every student and all three of her own kids to enter high school with a thorough grounding in the basics of personal finance. Although her school does work from the beginning of ninth grade to set each student up to become an interesting college applicant, her version of starting the college money discussion isn't to begin by being explicit about merit aid or the discounts that might be on the line. She and her colleagues focus on engagement and effort, knowing that students who participate in after-school activities and around campus tend to get more A's than B's. "As parents we are too outcome focused and not process focused enough," she said. "To tell people that more A's equals more money could put too much pressure on kids."

College administrators try to thread the needle of this delicate balance as well as they can. "Merit aid is a tactic used by colleges to influence a student's enrollment decision," Bob Massa, a longtime admissions, financial aid, and communications administrator, told me when he was working at Drew University in New Jersey before he became a consultant. "So the better the student—and this includes curricular choice as well as grades—the more money it will take to change a student's enrollment choice."

When I pointed out that the process of curricular choice begins before ninth grade, he winced a little. "Take a strong course load because you want to," he said. "Not because you think I want you to."

This is all hard enough to explain to a teenager, but there's one other thing to consider emphasizing, too: Though you intend to share all of this adult information about money with a teen, you may not be ceding decision-making authority. On the one hand, it certainly seems reasonable to say to eighth graders that if they get the maximum merit aid at, say, the University of Georgia, they should go there since they earned the highest discount. But perhaps you have a hunch that a smaller school would be a better fit, even if it costs more. Or maybe you are certain that a particular teenager belongs somewhere very far from home. In other words, money may not be the only thing that matters, and perhaps you even want to reserve the right to decide later how much it actually does matter. "When they go to the mall, the question of how much they can spend is usually not at their total discretion," said Kevin McKinley, the financial planner and father of three, whose twenty-year paying-for-college game plan appeared in the last chapter. "So why would we let ourselves give an eighteen-year-old overriding decision-making authority on something that could cost over a quarter million dollars?"

While you're in the middle of this dialogue, you should probably add the following agenda item, too: The way everyone around you talks about the college decision, including school counselors, may be extremely confusing. In communities where some people, or even the majority, do not need to worry about paying for college, much of the public conversation may be just about getting in. Ever notice how so many of those college matriculation lists that high schools publish don't say anything about the amount of merit aid students qualified for, as if people are simply choosing the most selective school they can get into? It can be tricky to talk about money in any given community—whether with counselors who don't want to ask families too many personal questions or teenage peers who simply don't know that financial constraints around college are in their immediate future.

So let your kid know that many families will not in fact have honest conversations about money until senior year and others may not face any financial limits at all. The kids from families in which money is no object may not understand what you're going through and be blissfully unaware of their own privilege. The conversations that are happening around college during high school in your circles may not resemble the conversation you want or need to have at home. Try, if you can, to present your transparency as a virtue, without necessarily criticizing the choices other reticent or oblivious families make. After all, we can't really know what anyone else is saying or going through, but we can be sure that our own kids know the facts of our own family's situation and how or if that will affect their college choices.

If this all sounds rather fraught, please be advised that the experts in the field haven't quite figured out what they're going to say to their own kids, either. Maureen McRae Goldberg, the former executive director of financial aid at Occidental who now has a similar role at Santa Barbara City College, seemed both resigned and exasperated when I asked her what she intended to say to her nine year-old daughter when the time comes. Would telling her that her high school performance could be worth a six-figure discount be an absurd amount of pressure? Is it even fair to bring it up when many schools—private colleges especially—don't reveal what mark a teen will need to hit to get merit aid at all? "I am dreading it," she said. "These are the same questions I've been asking for twenty years, and in my naiveté I thought we'd have some of this fixed by now. I thought that our need analysis would be repaired, that it would be a measuring device and not a rationing device. I thought that the state and federal governments would step up and contribute more. I have zero confidence in that now."

CHAPTER 30

All Your Questions About Saving for College and 529 Plans

So you're new at this, or you've needed to wait a bit until the day care bills were done, or you've procrastinated. Now you'd like to get started with putting money away for college. And you've got some questions. I know, because I've spent a fair amount of time over the last fifteen years debating the finer points of college saving strategy with fellow finance writers and financial planners who are themselves trying to puzzle it all out.

Many of the questions are about mechanics and rules and facts. But others are about feelings—about predicting the future or trying to. What you'll find below are the questions that I've found myself trying to answer most often, both for readers and for myself.

What is a 529 plan?

The federal government wants us to save money. Take retirement: With an individual retirement account (IRA) or a 401(k), 403(b), or 457 plan, we get tax breaks that are meant to encourage us to save for our postworking years. Why? To be blunt, the more people save, the fewer people the federal government will need to bail out if they run out of money in their old age. At that point, there would be a need for increased Social Security payments or Medicaid budgets to care for low-income people in nursing homes.

529 college savings plans and other accounts that you earmark for college are like that: If people save money, there is less pressure on the government to subsidize tuition or loan payments later. When you put money away in a 529 plan, the money grows free of any federal and state income taxes and federal taxes on the earnings in the account over time. When you take the money out, you don't pay taxes, either, as long as you use the money for legitimate educational expenses. Even better, many states have gotten into the act, too; a majority of them offer immediate income tax breaks of various sorts in the year when people first deposit money. In many states, you can use a 529 plan to pay for tuition-charging elementary and secondary education as well.

Are there different kinds of 529 plans?

Yes, there are two basic kinds—and then, confusingly, most states have their own versions of the two kinds (which, even more confusingly, can present as three different plans, not two). Let's break them down in the simplest terms possible.

First, the two plans. The first one is known as a prepaid plan. Some states—though not all—have plans that allow you to pay for chunks of future college tuition at a set price for any given year. There are catches. Different states do the math differently in terms of how much they discount future tuition for you to pay for in today's dollars. Some states set these discounts in such an inopportune way a decade or more ago that they've had to close entry to their plans; they hadn't anticipated how much tuition would go up and had given away deals that were just too good.

The other catch to the state prepaid plans is that they generally cover only state schools in that state. Many people who start to save when their first child is very young have no idea whether the kid will want to go to a state school. If your high school senior ends up with different aspirations, you can still get the money out and use it for a different school, but it generally won't have grown very much during the years it was in the plan; it's usually some preset tiny interest rate. That's a real big catch. Often, because of this uncertainty, families don't start using prepaid plans until late middle school or early high school, when it may be clearer what kind of trajectory any given child is on.

The second main kind of 529 plan is an investment plan, although states may use slightly different descriptions for it. This plan looks a lot like a workplace retirement plan. There is an account administrator who offers up a menu of investments, such as stock and bond mutual funds. Then you deposit money into the plan and decide how to divide it up among the choices. There are some administrative fees—and fees for each mutual fund or other investment you select—although these are much lower than they once were.

An additional source of confusion here: Some 529 accounts are for people investing money on their own without help from a professional. Other ones exist only for financial advisers to sell to their clients. (Separate entities are necessary because fees are higher in the adviser accounts so that the advisers can receive compensation.) This is how you can end up with three choices of 529 plans in a single state: a prepaid plan, an investment plan for individuals, and an investment plan sold by advisers.

A word about all the choices: Though it may not be their fault exactly—the history of how 529 plans emerged is a bit complicated—states made this intensely confusing years ago by all going off and starting their own plans. As I explained above, prepaid plans are generally good only for state residents who want to attend that state's schools. When it comes to investment plans, you may need to invest in your own state's plan to take advantage of any state income tax break that exists in your state. So why would you go outside your state? If your state has no 529 tax break at all—such as California and New Jersey—you should pick the 529 plan that has the investment options you want and the lowest fees. For you, the best choice may be elsewhere. Even if you do have a tax break in your state, if the state's plan has high fees—which can be the case in smaller states—that may offset any tax break, especially if it's a small one.

I've seen ads for another kind of 529 plan, one for private colleges. What is that about?

It's called the Private College 529 plan, and it's a strange beast. Like the prepaid state plans, it allows you to buy chunks of future tuition at a price the plan sets based on how many years away your child is from entering college. The exact discount depends on the school. And here's the weird thing: Over three hundred private colleges and universities participate. And then . . . lots of others don't. I've reported on it sporadically for years, and it's never been clear why the rest of the schools don't just get with the program—literally. Because that's the big catch: If your child ends up wanting to go to a college that isn't in the plan, you do get your money back. But all the benefits of prepaying at a discount go away, and you get credit for no more than a very low annual interest rate for the years you had the money invested. Get the downside there? If your kid goes to a nonparticipating school, you almost certainly would have done better putting your money into a normal 529 investment plan. But we generally can't predict where our kids will get in or want to attend so far in advance.

If I save for college in a 529, won't that hurt me when it comes time to prove that I'm eligible for need-based financial aid?

This is a totally reasonable question, and the appropriate response is both to define "hurt" and then imagine alternative scenarios in which you save nothing in an attempt to appear as needy as possible.

There is actually a technical definition of how much saving "hurts" in this instance. When it comes to the federal financial aid formula for determining your expected family contribution or student aid index, the answer is quite specific: The government expects your family to contribute 5.64 percent of your nonretirement savings each year to the cost of college. That includes money in a 529 plan. So if you have $10,000 saved, the formula will put you on the hook for $564 the first year of college. (The expecters who make the family contribution formula leave your retirement savings alone.)

But wait, you must be thinking. *That's it? I won't have to use the rest of the money in my 529 plan?* Well, no. In some ways this is about optics and marketing. The formula doesn't demand all of the college money, because that might disincentivize even more people from using 529s. And there is an unspoken recognition that of course you're going to use most or all of the money in the account; that is what it's there for. And yes, individual colleges that ask for supplementary information will indeed see your fat six-figure 529 balance if you've been lucky or persistent enough to save that much.

So could saving hurt you so much more than 5.64 percent per year worth of pain? I don't see it that way. Instead, I imagine the opposite: no savings at all. Unless your household income is relatively low and has been so for a long time, some financial aid administrators may wonder about your priorities if you've saved nothing and then expect everything in the way of a significant financial aid package from them. And because so much of what schools (and the federal formula) will ask you to pay depends on income, you'll need an awful lot of it to pay for college if you have no savings.

But let's say you own a small business or are retired and can somehow manipulate your low-savings financial portrait to include a very low income for four years. That's great—clever, even. But remember: This is an application. Your child needs to be accepted to college and then want to attend a school that can afford and is willing (two different things) to give a large amount of grant aid to a family with a low income and no savings. Many schools will do this. Many more won't have the resources or will use them only for the students that they value most highly. And many of those that offer lots of grant aid look very carefully at the assets and background of the families who present themselves as needing a lot of help.

With all of this as a backdrop, I'd rather be saving. Having some money in reserve gives me more options, and more options mean less stress. You may feel differently, but I'd think very, very hard before declining to save as some kind of strategy for getting more grant money.

How will my income and savings affect merit aid calculations?

They usually won't. In most instances, you don't have to apply for merit aid. Instead, the admissions office (not the financial aid office) uses your child's application materials (but not your financial information, if you did apply for need-based aid) to make an offer. Sometimes, there are separate merit aid applications for particularly generous awards. And sometimes, those separate applications may ask for a FAFSA or other financial information. But this is relatively rare.

Okay, I'm convinced that I should cast my lot with my state's investment 529. What exactly should I invest in?

I can't say for sure, and that truly is not a cop-out.

A few basic facts of investing: No one can predict the future. There have been fifteen-year periods when, if you had invested your money entirely in the stock market, it would have gone up threefold or more. That can pay for a lot of college. There have been other fifteen-year periods when stocks did not rise at all or didn't rise very much.

Saving for college is also different from saving for retirement in one crucial respect: When it's time for your kid to go to college, you need the money right away, or at least over a short period of time. Retirement often lasts thirty years, which means that if you stop working at a time when stocks have fallen, it isn't the end of the world. After all, you probably have at least a decade or two of life left to allow some of the money in stocks to rise in value again. College isn't like that.

So as with any investing exercise, you have to figure out how much tolerance you have for risk. How much financial pain would it cause if your college savings didn't grow much or lost a lot of value when your child was a senior in high school? Do you have other resources to draw on? Are you comfortable with borrowing to make up the difference? Too much risk aversion is dangerous, too. If all of your college money is in a savings account that earns 1 percent in interest annually and not in a stock fund, you're going to need an awful lot of savings, since that account won't gain very much over time. In fact, net college costs will probably rise more on a percentage basis each year than your savings balance will.

You may not be much of an investing expert, and perhaps you don't want to become one, either. You wouldn't be the first or the millionth or the ten millionth person who resents being put in this spot. For you, I suggest something called a target-date fund, which is part of many 529 plans these days.

Target-date funds work this way: Each fund is a collection of other funds, with a title that reflects the date your child will likely start college. So you might buy a 2030 fund for a kid who will turn eighteen that year. It might contain a stock fund, a bond fund, and a money market fund. The beauty of a target-date fund is that the proportions change automatically over time, going from more risky and aggressive (with more money in stocks) to less risky and aggressive as the start of college grows near (with more money in lower-risk bonds or no-risk cash to shield you from stock market declines right when you need the money to pay the college bills).

Seems like a no-brainer, right? The only problem with target-date funds is that the fund manager's definition of "prudent risk" might not match yours. You have to check how the division of assets will change over time. Or perhaps you have some stock or savings bonds outside of a 529 account that you've earmarked for college, so the balanced approach that the target-date fund takes may not be right for you. One other crucial thing: Not every target-date fund moves all of the money into cash at the start of college. Back in 2008, when the stock market fell dramatically, some target-date funds for people starting college imminently fell by a fair bit. Investors were shocked, but if they'd read the prospectus of the target-date fund, they could have predicted that a massive market meltdown would lead to a big drop in their target-date fund. Few people prepare for a market disruption like that one, but at least now you know that it can happen.

What's the best 529 plan in all the land?

Again, it's hard to say. Any analysis has to begin with an assessment of whatever tax breaks your state offers on contributions. Then look at the fees and investment choices in your plan. A website called Savingforcollege.com provides an encyclopedic guide to 529 plans, and a company called Morningstar ranks 529 plans as well. Don't get caught in "analysis paralysis," though. These days most plans have decent fees and reasonably good investment choices. Get started, and you can make different choices later without too much hassle if you feel that you've made a bad choice.

What if we put money away and then need it before college for an emergency?

You can get the money out, but it will cost you. First, you'll need to pay taxes on whatever your contributions earned—any growth in the stock or bond or other funds or investments, including dividends and interest. You may owe money to your state too, depending on its tax rules. Plus there's a 10 percent federal penalty on those earnings, just to make you think twice about using the money for something else before college.

Okay, but can I borrow against my 529 balance the same way I can with my 401(k) retirement plan at work?

No.

What if my kid goes to one of the military academies for free or gets a full ride? Or what if there is a big merit aid award? Do we get the money back?

Yes, and you won't have to pay that 10 percent penalty. But you will have to pay taxes on the gains. And it is only the amount of the scholarship that gets the waiver on that 10 percent.

What if my kid chooses not to go to college or dies? Can I get the money out?

Yes. If it's a choice, you pay both the taxes and the penalty. If a child dies, there is no penalty but you still have to pay the taxes.

What if college is no longer appropriate because my child has become disabled?

You can take savings out without paying the penalty, although you'll still have to pay the taxes. Or you may be able to transfer the money in a 529 plan to a relatively new savings vehicle called an ABLE account. There, money grows free of taxes and you can withdraw it without paying taxes, either, as long as the money goes toward expenses related to the disability. The transfer is subject to an annual cap on the amount.

What other options do I have if I have excess money in a 529 plan for any reason, especially if I'm trying to avoid taxes and penalties?

If your child gets a big scholarship or you saved private school dollars for a child who goes to a cheaper state school, you could simply keep the money in the account for graduate school. You could also change the name of the beneficiary and use the money for a younger sibling or a niece or nephew. You could even use it for yourself to take classes for credit, even in retirement.

One particularly generous option: Just let the money ride for a few decades more in the hope that grandchildren will appear on the scene. It would take a lot of pressure off your adult child or children, and the magic of compound interest would have that much longer left to work. Also keep in mind that the 529 plan rules changed in 2017 to allow people to use some money from the accounts each year for K–12 tuition in most states.

I'm old-fashioned and risk averse. Can I just use savings bonds for college?

Sure. Your money will be 100 percent safe, although the interest may be so low that it won't even keep up with tuition inflation. There is a tax benefit here, too: You don't pay federal taxes on the interest as long as you follow a few basic rules and fall within certain income limits. This last part is a hard thing to plan for, because if you start investing in savings bonds when your first child is, say, five years old, there is no telling what your income might be fifteen years later.

What about pulling money out of my retirement accounts for college?

I'd think twice about this unless you're certain you have more than enough saved for retirement or don't have some other, better way to help pay for college.

That said, some people actually plan to do this by using the retirement savings vehicle known as a Roth IRA. Unlike with a workplace savings account such as a 401(k), the Roth rules allow you to withdraw, without penalty or taxes, any of the original contributions (but not any earnings) to use for educational expenses, since you paid taxes on the income before it went into the account. Roth accounts have lower fees and a wider array of investment choices than 529s do, and some people favor them for college saving and planning because any money that is left over (for whatever reason) can just keep growing for retirement.

Roths have drawbacks, though. There are income limits that can make using them complicated. There are annual contribution limits under many circumstances. They don't come with state tax breaks the way that many 529 plan contributions do each year. Plus, if you pull money from your Roth for college, that withdrawal will count as income for financial aid calculation purposes, and income is the thing that financial aid officers examine most carefully when determining eligibility for need-based aid.

Why not just save money for college in a basic brokerage account?

You could do this. If you are more affluent than most people—and have really good discipline about not touching the money—it might even net you more savings in the long run. The explanation gets a bit wonky, but let me try to outline it for you briefly.

There are three big advantages to 529 plans. The first two have to do with taxes: First, you pay no federal taxes—neither income taxes nor capital gains taxes—if you use the savings for education expenses. Second, there are often state income tax deductions or credits for putting money into a 529 in the first place. If you save in a regular brokerage account, you'll not only pay taxes on capital gains but those gains will count as income when the financial aid administrators examine your ability to pay. The third big advantage is psychological: There is something calming about having the 529 money there, knowing that you've set it aside for this specific purpose. I personally find this helpful; my favorite mail of all is the 529 account statement each quarter.

But there are disadvantages, too. The 529 plan administrators may charge fees that are higher than what you'd pay if you were saving in a basic brokerage account. The menu of investments is limited. Given that the money in a 529 plan is for one specific use—education—only the most risk-tolerant person would not move the 529 money out of stock funds as the beginning of college approaches. Moving money to safer investments, however, often means getting lower returns for the rest of the college years. And then there is the fact that your child may not go to college at all or may get a big scholarship.

Financial planners who discourage 529 plans do have a bias, because some of them can make more money if you don't keep your savings in a 529 plan. But they are genuine in pointing out the following: If you have lots of kids and they're all young, there is just no telling what will happen to the higher education industry in fifteen years. There is a decent chance that at least one child won't go to college or will train in a way that we cannot yet imagine and that may not cost much.

And then there's this: If you put all of your money into a brokerage account and put that money mostly into stocks throughout your kids' childhood, you will probably earn higher returns. Worried about having to pay taxes when you sell the stocks to pay for college? If your tax bill is likely to be high, it's probably because you earn enough money to have saved a lot during your child's first eighteen years. If that's the case, you may well earn enough to be able to pay for a fair bit of college out of your current income. This is important, since if you keep your college savings in stocks and the market falls as a child approaches college, you may not want to lock in losses by selling then. If you have a decent amount of income, maybe you won't have to; you can wait to sell until the market recovers. In the worst-case scenario—you lose your job and the market is down—you can deduct the losses on your investments. Also, if you're in that tough spot, you might want to use your savings for other things besides college, such as basic living expenses, but if you have lots of money in a 529 plan, you'll pay a penalty for accessing it.

Because we can't predict the future when our children are young, I can't tell you which move will be right for you. If you find the brokerage option equally compelling, perhaps you should split your college savings 50-50. If nothing else, I'd consult a financial planner on the matter just to bat these ideas around. I'll explain how to find a good candidate in Chapter 32.

My parents keep insisting that I'm doing it wrong and that I should be putting all the college money into something called an UTMA. What are they talking about?

This is kind of old school stuff, as it's a way of saving that was popular before 529 plans came onto the scene in the 1990s. "UTMA" stands for "Uniform Transfers to Minors Act," and it allows people to create what are known as custodial accounts for children or grandchildren and manage them until they are at least eighteen. There is a similar account called UGMA, which stands for "Uniform Gifts to Minors Act." The especially affluent like UTMAs because they can put real estate and other fancy alternative investments into them, whereas UGMAs are more limited.

These accounts don't shield most investment gains from taxes, so that is a big disadvantage. Here's another: Financial aid administrators will want you to use a lot of the assets before awarding you any need-based aid. And a third downside: The beneficiary gets control of the money upon turning eighteen or not that long afterward, depending on state law. (Parents and grandparents can easily maintain control of 529 plans.) At that point recipients don't have to use the money for college if they don't want to. A troubled or stubborn teenager could suddenly have more freedom to wreak more havoc or decide to avoid higher education entirely—although, again, for a compliant young adult engaged in a thoughtful planning process, the fact that you don't have to use the money in these accounts for college, as you do with a 529 plan, may be advantageous. That flexibility can be useful, depending on the circumstances. But do note: The flexibility does not extend to the "giver" of the money being able to change the beneficiary and hand the money to, say, a more compliant minor's sibling.

Can grandparents set up their own 529 accounts and name the grandkids as beneficiaries?

Yes. Some grandparents like having control of the money, for a variety of reasons. That's fine, although it may create some planning uncertainty for the parents about the circumstances under which the grandparents would not, in fact, use the money for their grandchildren's college expenses.

This is a lot of technical stuff. Is there anything here that is, like, fun? Hacks? Tricks?

For the last fifteen years I've been enrolled in a service called Upromise. You shop online through its portal—I use it for sites I would be shopping at anyway—and the service rebates a portion of your purchase price into an account. Then you can tell Upromise to automatically move the money to your 529 account. I've picked up about $1,500 this way for doing something I was already doing anyway.

Like playing the credit card rewards game? Once upon a time, earning frequent-flier miles through card use could get you first-class travel to overseas destinations that would otherwise cost you $10,000 or more. That was, in my view at least, the highest and best use of any credit card rebate. But those deals became much harder to come by at the end of the 2010s, especially for people who are trying to find scarce available seats to travel with children when school is not in session. Instead of using miles-earning cards, you might check out the Fidelity Rewards Visa Signature Card. There is no annual fee, and it rebates 2 percent of all charges into a rewards account that you can then move into a 529 plan with the investment company. There are other 2 percent cash-back credit cards out there too, and you could use them in a similar way, albeit without the direct connection to a 529 plan that the Fidelity plan has. (This is not a paid endorsement, by the way. I don't even have the card myself, but it might be just the thing for others.)

If you average $25,000 in annual credit card spending, that's $500 per year that comes back to you for college. But you'll have to go cold turkey on chasing free travel with credit card rewards, something I have had trouble doing. And it shouldn't go without saying: If you don't pay your balance in full each month, the interest will wipe out any rebate and then some. The card companies genuinely hope you will carry a balance—or at least spend more than you might if you used a debit card.

Finally, here's a neat trick that works in many states that offer tax breaks for deposits into 529 plans: There may not be a minimum time limit on how long you have to leave the money in an account before qualifying. So even while your child is in college, it makes sense to drop money into the 529 to pick up the tax break that year. Then you can move the money right back out again to pay tuition. Just check with your plan to make sure it hasn't cracked down on this yet; some have, and I imagine more will in future years.

CHAPTER 31

How to Shop for College (and Where to Find the Juicy Merit Aid Data)

Throughout this book, I've tried to give parents and applicants a framework for defining success and figuring out what features of an undergraduate education are so important that they might be worth paying extra for. You now know that before you go looking for any college for your child, everyone in the family needs to be clear on the point of pursuing higher education in the first place. Is having an intellectual adventure paramount, or is finding your people or getting a great job most important? If you care about all three, how do they weigh against one another? And once you have that figured out, you need to consider the questions I laid out in each of the chapters in Part Three. Which ones most apply to you?

Then, at some point during high school, families usually start visiting some colleges in person and try to extract all of this information. This chapter will help you figure out exactly where to do research to get the answers you need about schools you're considering, including data on merit aid that are often hiding in plain sight.

As I reported this book and visited dozens of colleges, I developed a routine of my own. There was a list of things I did to prepare for my meetings with presidents and enrollment management officials, and then there were other items on a reportorial to-do list that I tried to check off when I was on campus. This is just basic journalism—the things you do to educate yourself on any given subject. But when I tagged along on campus tours and chatted up families that I met, I realized that few of them had done the same homework I had. Many of them just hadn't known where to look beforehand or even what to ask on campus.

So here's how to prepare for the visit.

The search begins online, with a school's website. I have two places I like to look to get a sense of how a school views itself. The first is the president or chancellor's page. There you often find a collection of speeches, blog posts, and other writings. For leaders who are relatively new in the job, their inaugural address will be there, too. Read it all, or at least skim it. You're looking for evidence of what the board of trustees and the college community have asked of these leaders and how they have responded. This is particularly useful at smaller colleges, where the president is focused almost entirely on the undergraduate experience.

The second resource is the college or university's strategic plan; the best way to find this is to do a general web search using the school's name and "strategic plan." These are often no-holds-barred documents declaring what the school is good at and all the ways it hopes to improve. Not every school has one or posts it, but I've never failed to learn a lot from the ones I've found.

Now to their financial aid pages. They range wildly in clarity and transparency. When you first visit them, you're probably trying to establish some basic facts: Is the school need-blind, i.e., does it admit students regardless of how much financial aid they need? If not, then people without any demonstrated financial need may have at least some advantage in admissions, and it's okay to ask how much.

If the school is need-blind, does it meet the full demonstrated need of the family? If not, there's a chance you'll be "gapped." Here's how that works. There are two numbers at play: There is the amount that FAFSA or the CSS Profile says you can afford. Then there is whatever financial aid the school is willing to offer you. The difference between them is the gap, and if you want to attend the school, you may have to fill it yourself.

As for merit aid, you never know what you'll find on these pages. One recent wrinkle has to do with the increasing number of colleges that are temporarily test-optional, permanently so or entirely blind to tests (as in, they don't want them and won't look even if you send in a 1600). How are schools evaluating people for merit aid if they don't have test scores to input into their algorithms? Ask them. Your grades are likely to matter that much more. And do people who do not submit scores decrease their chances of getting the biggest merit aid awards? Again, ask. I did in a 2020 *New York Times* column where I basically told the College of Wooster that I didn't think families would believe the school when it insisted that there would be no merit aid disadvantage to not submitting a score. "They should believe me," said its enrollment chief at the time, Scott Friedhoff. "We are test-blind when it comes to merit." Ask other schools whether they feel the same way.

In the no-surprises category, some schools will tell you straight up what combination of grades and scores you need to get what level of discount. Wabash College publishes a grid, with grade point average on the *y*-axis and SAT or ACT scores on the *x*-axis. Your discount, from $17,000 to $32,000, lies at the intersection of your marks. Oglethorpe University in Atlanta doesn't even need a grid; it just promises to match the tuition at your flagship state institution as long as you have a 3.8 grade point average and at least 1400 on your SAT or 30 on your ACT. Even at the grid schools, however, it isn't always clear what you'll need to do to keep getting the same (or increased) amount of merit aid each year if you attend. If it isn't clear, ask before applying and then get it in writing if you become serious about matriculating.

The College of Wooster takes a more personal touch to helping prospective families do research on the net price. Starting a bit more than a year before students start college, it takes in their information and estimates their need-based and merit aid before they even apply. It's like the net price calculator that every school has, except that human beings do it and you can talk to them afterward. It's something smaller schools can do that big ones can't—or just don't if they don't feel they need to in order to compete in the marketplace. After I heard about what Wooster was doing, I kept showing its offer to other vice presidents of enrollment management whom I met, asking them to match or better Wooster's level of service to curious (and freaked-out) parents. Nobody took me up on it. "I could imagine my dean of financial aid seizing up and dying at the whole notion of that," said Katharine Harrington, the former chief enrollment officer at the University of Southern California.

In 2020, Whitman College in Washington State announced a similar service that came with an actual guarantee on the price quote. And while the school doesn't say so on its website, Connecticut College will also do a kind of merit aid pre-read upon request. The dean of admission and financial aid told me that he does it himself.

You'd think those net price calculators could help some. Sometimes they do. But as we've discussed, at many schools the calculators don't even try to determine how much merit aid the institution might give you. Quite often, schools that have calculators that decline to predict merit aid also have financial aid websites that don't offer much additional detail. I wish more schools offered plain-English explainers on who gets it, what those people's qualifications are, how many people get it each year, and what you have to do to keep it for your entire time as an undergraduate. This last part is especially crucial if you'll lose thousands in discounts if your grades drop below a certain level.

At the end of 2021, I noticed something strange on the merit aid section of Northeastern University's website. The phrase read, "Students who are in the top 10–15% of our applicant pool are considered for competitive merit awards." Note that it tells you nothing about what percentage of the people who enroll actually get the awards, or what percentage of people who have no demonstrated need still get them. But if you read it quickly enough, you might think that only 10 to 15 percent of people get merit aid at all—and you wouldn't be inclined to complain if you didn't get any. When I pointed the odd language out to the school, it changed it to say that "typically about one-third of freshmen admitted" get merit aid, which *still* doesn't tell you what percentage of the people who attend actually get. That figure, for people who have no demonstrated need, turned out to be 59 percent.

In other words, Northeastern has to offer a hefty discount to the majority of well-off first-year students to get them to matriculate. Not long after I asked why it didn't just say that, the school changed the site again and removed any such data at all; it simply said that "select students" get merit aid. Why did the school make that change, I wondered? The data and the language the school had used to describe it, a spokesman told me, was "not adding clarity or helping anyone." In other words, the school took away the very information that many people seek and tried to suggest with a straight face that everyone would be better off because of it.

The schools insist that much of this lack of predictability is because the process is "holistic" and what any school needs in its student population—and is willing to pay for—may change from year to year. "It's a buzzword I don't particularly like," said Vince Cuseo, the vice president of enrollment management at Occidental College. "But families understand that we're not formulaic in the way we make an admission decision, and we're not formulaic in the way we provide merit money."

If you want to learn more about merit aid than what the school posts on its financial aid web pages, the best place to look is at the common data set. The CDS is a standardized form that schools use to collect all of the data that various college guides and rankings publications request. It is a treasure trove of information, but it's a rare college that encourages applicants to check it out. To my mind it's required reading. You can find it by doing an internet search for the school's name and the phrase "common data set," and the right landing page should just pop up. All sorts of information are available in the CDS, and you should read every bit of it if you are even remotely interested in applying. For instance, the form discloses information about retention: What percentage of any given first-year class departs within twelve months? And how many students stay on until graduation? It bears repeating: If you don't finish college, that's the worst financial outcome of all. Transferring may mean that you won't be able to finish in four years, raising the total cost significantly.

As for the merit aid data, you can find it this way: In section H2, you'll see basic information about the number of new first-year students who applied for need-based financial aid, who actually got it, and what the average amount was that they received. Right below that you'll see line H2A, "Number of Enrolled Students Awarded Non-need-based Scholarships and Grants." That's the number of people who got merit aid, even though they didn't have any financial need. Skip back up ten lines or so, and you can figure out how many people in total had no financial need by subtracting the total number of people who qualified for need-based aid from the total number of first-year students. At that point you have a pretty good sense of where the school sits in the marketplace: how many affluent families are willing to pay in full and how many end up getting some kind of discount because the school assumes that a student won't come without one. You'll also learn the average amount that those affluent families received.

Though the CDS won't tell you point-blank what sort of grades or scores were required to get that money, you can look elsewhere on the form to make a reasonable guess. Up in Section C, you can see the range of test scores for admitted students. If you're in the top quartile, your odds are pretty good unless the school offers merit aid to a tiny percentage of students. Again, the schools claim their award-giving process is holistic, and this may well be true. Test scores are not the only criterion, particularly if a school does not require tests at all for admission and extends that policy to merit aid qualification. But often an algorithm does the first sorting of admitted students to suggest eligible students and even award amounts. The chances are good that the machine is using test scores to do so, at least in part.

Once you've learned all you can learn from a school's website, it's time to consider secondary sources. There are a few specialist sites that focus on the financial side of applying that are well worth your time. Tuition-Fit uses real data from actual students' financial aid award letters to help you compare college costs. It also allows schools you might not have considered to pay a fee to TuitionFit in exchange for the ability to make you offers. Edmit takes in your financial and academic data to try to predict the price any given school will offer, using some of the same data I've cited above. It also warns families away from the kind of debt it thinks you might have to take on to afford that price. MeritMore and College Raptor are also worth a visit.

The single place where I've learned the most during my reporting is in the Paying for College 101 Facebook group. It's a private group, but anyone can join by putting in a request with the group's moderators. It is a community of parents, mostly, who are in the thick of things and swap notes on all aspects of researching, applying to, and paying for college. You'll see conversation threads on nearly every major topic we've covered in this book. Though it can be a bit unwieldy to navigate and not every participant posts good information, the stories people tell are inspiring and informative. I found it indispensable in my first years of doing research for this book. There is also a related service called College Insights that offers helpful merit aid and other data.

Now for more general information that may help as you consider what students might learn at college, whom they might meet, and what kind of job they might get afterward ...

The U.S. Department of Education maintains the College Scorecard, which we've examined in previous chapters. It has good, basic data on debt and average salary, but in 2019 it quietly added something else: average first-year earnings by field of study. Colleges have resisted this for years, as they are concerned that students will steer clear of the humanities if it becomes evident that people who study them don't earn very much, at least right out of the gate. As you navigate the site, look for a tab or drop-down menu for majors or fields of study, and you may be able to see just how much more a math major is earning than a geography grad is. There aren't data for every major at every school, but the site is still useful, especially if you plan to borrow money and hope to be able to pay it back quickly. If you see something alarming, mention it to the school; given how new these data are, it is likely that there are errors.

As a journalist, I'm also inclined to trust reporters, even the youngest ones, to ask good questions and shine light into dark corners. College newspapers have websites, so read them and follow their social media accounts during the application process. There are two trade publications that cover higher education, both of which are excellent. The *Chronicle of Higher Education* is the more established one, and applicants' families would be a lot better informed if they bought a subscription and read it. The upstart is the online-only Inside Higher Ed, and it does not require a paid subscription. Even if you don't become a regular reader, search for stories about the schools you're interested in to see what you can learn. The *Wall Street Journal*'s coverage of higher education is outstanding, and those of us who write about the topic at the *New York Times* like to think we're at least as good. Read them both. And definitely set a Google News alert to feed you stories of all sorts about the schools on your list.

Now to the rankings. Plenty of people believe that the *U.S. News & World Report* lists are the worst thing ever to happen to higher education. In 2018, I attended the annual conference of people who work in the institutional research offices of colleges and universities. They're often the ones who produce a school's common data set. Just about every higher education conference has a hand-wringing, garment-rending session on rankings; often, Bob Morse, the longtime impresario of the

U.S. News lists, presides himself or sits in the audience. Most everyone knows who he is. At the session I attended, the moderator asked the assembled masses for a show of hands of people who had a positive view of college rankings. Not a single person raised a hand.

Even so, plenty of schools have made it their mission to take a giant leap up the rankings. Some, such as Northeastern, have succeeded beyond almost all imagination. In the space of a generation, it transformed itself from a commuter school to one with an acceptance rate in the teens, in no small part through a sharp-elbowed gaming of the *U.S. News* criteria. There is a classic *Boston* magazine story about how it happened that's well worth your time if that school is on your list or you just want to geek out on the topic.

I'm with the realists on rankings: *U.S. News & World Report* exists, and it's not going away, so we might as well reckon with it. I wouldn't place an outsized importance on a school's ranking. After all, the magazine's lists never specify just exactly whom its "best" lists are for. There is no universal applicant, and part of what we're trying to do here is figure out exactly what kind of school is best for our own kids and then make our own ranking order based at least in part on value. But bless its editors and reporters' hearts for having smoked so much information out over the decades and made the raw data easy enough to find and use for a reasonable subscription fee. You'll learn a lot from the data it has gathered, even if you ignore the rankings altogether.

I'd still at least glance at every other ranking you can find, from every major publication or service, for the schools that interest you. The first thing you should do is figure out what criteria any given ranking is using; that's how you'll figure out whether its lists are for people like you. *Forbes* tilts hard in its equation toward alumni salaries and whether lots of its graduates make various *Forbes* leadership lists. *Money* magazine (sadly, just a website nowadays) focuses on quality and affordability; its list doesn't look much like the others, with a number of state schools in the top ten. The list that *Washington Monthly* publishes focuses on social mobility, opportunities for public service, and research. As a former *Princeton Review* customer and author, I always look at the books and lists it publishes too, especially the quirkier ones such as its best party school list. And the *Wall Street Journal* list is noteworthy for feeding student survey results into its formula, along with more standard data.

My personal favorite, however, is the list published by a little-known operation called the Alumni Factor. Its ranking, the most recent of which came out during the 2013–14 school year, is rooted in a large web-based survey it conducted with people who had actually attended the schools in question. The age of the data is an obvious flaw, although Alumni Factor has been working on updates for a couple of years, and I hope they'll eventually publish them. Its value comes from the fact that it is the only college survey based entirely on customer satisfaction. In the corporate world, there is something called a net promoter score: companies ask customers to rank them on the likelihood that they would use a product or service again. The Alumni Factor's rankings are a cousin of that.

The overall Alumni Factor top ten is a fascinating document. Sure, some usual Ivy League suspects are there, such as Princeton and Yale. But Columbia is way down at number 106. Other selective schools that draw plenty of eager applicants and rank even lower than Columbia include Tufts (133), the University of Chicago (136), Emory (151), Tulane (162), Northeastern (169), the University of Vermont (212), and New York University (218). In every case it's worth drilling down into the data to find out why. If only more people knew about this list and asked tough questions of the schools that didn't do so well. If you haven't heard of Centre College in Kentucky, you have now; it landed at number 8 on the list. The four major military academies are all in the top twenty as well.

How much should the opinions of alumni matter? In case the value of polling customers themselves isn't self-evidently obvious, a Gallup economist recently did a study of the matter. He found that as long as you have a mean of the ratings of at least twenty other alumni—which is a lot fewer than the minimum that Alumni Factor gathered—their past ratings will provide a better prediction of the satisfaction of current individuals than any other media ranking system does. Neither net tuition nor the total cost of attendance predicts ratings better, either, so alumni do seem to be grading on value more than on price. Though Gallup has so far chosen not to issue its own full set of college rankings based on all its survey work, the appendix of this study included some intriguing findings, with the University of Maryland, Baltimore County, and a Christian school, Wheaton College, appearing in its top twenty-five.

Eventually you'll want to see the schools for yourself. This is expensive, although so is dropping out or transferring because you and your applicant didn't know enough about how a place really felt in person until after enrollment. You might try spreading the expense of visiting over a few years, starting in tenth grade. Another possibility, depending on how long the pandemic remains a risk, is to research like mad via virtual means and then visit only schools where your child is admitted and the price seems right.

How best to tour? I'd try to avoid visiting more than one school per weekday if possible. The tour, plus the group information session, plus a possible interview, plus sitting in on a class or meeting with a faculty member, won't leave time for a thorough second visit. You do know you can meet with faculty members, right? Kids who are passionate about a particular subject can drop an email to a professor who teaches it and ask for a meeting or an invitation to sit in on a class. If the professor doesn't write back, that should tell you something. But most of them will. An overnight stay with a student is also worthwhile. Some admissions offices can arrange this, but if they can't, you or your child should try to find a friend or a friend of a friend who can accommodate a guest for one night. That way your child can get a sense of what a place is like at midnight and at breakfast.

A few things to keep in mind about the tour: At some schools, being a guide is still a volunteer job in which there are minimal filters and maximum exposure to real information. But at an increasing number of schools the tour guides are paid and undergo extensive training, often by outside consultants who parachute in to spiff up a school's overall visitor experience. These tours may be great in their own way, but they are also . . . different.

I find that some of the best information I glean from tours comes from the walls of the buildings that we visit. Posters, fliers, protest notices—it's all grist for the observational mill. Pick up a copy of the student newspaper and other publications, or check them out online. Take visual notes with your phone's camera so you can remember specifics later. And consider what the tours don't take you to see; I doubt I'll ever forget that the golf cart tours at High Point University didn't bother with the library, while the one at Bowdoin came complete with a stop at the counseling center and a heartfelt discussion of mental health awareness. If there's something you want to see that isn't on the tour, walk into the building anyway or ask someone to let you in.

How many schools should you visit—and ultimately apply to? It is hard to say. But I wouldn't be doing my job unless I made you aware of the existence of a growing number of families who take some extreme measures. They earn too much to qualify for a lot of need-based aid but are unable or unwilling to pay private college retail prices or anything close to them. Their children, meanwhile, want to take a shot at the smaller, more expensive private colleges and universities. A generation ago, the University of Southern California, Northeastern, and Tulane were safety schools for great students. Now their acceptance rates hover between ten and twenty percent or so. Combine that with a fair bit of uncertainty about merit awards at the more selective private colleges that offer them, and is it any wonder that some students are applying to ten or fifteen schools or more in the hopes of hitting the discount jackpot?

When Lara Mordenti Perrault's first child got ready to apply, she did not yet see a tidal wave of applications in her daughter's future. But she and her husband had set some strict parameters; they have four kids, and they figure they'll be able to pay $100,000 each for them to go to college. Add on incidentals and touring and whatever else, and she figures they will be on the hook for half a million dollars total. She and her husband were not going to feel guilty about not spending more, nor were they going to sign on to a pile of loans if their children wanted to pay full price at a private college and shoulder the debt themselves when they got out.

But then that first kid came along with Ivy League–level SAT scores and grades. Duke was among her top choices, but it was offering merit aid to only a tiny number of students. Her list was going to need to grow, and Perrault found her way to the Paying for College 101 Facebook group. There among the conversation threads she read about another member who had made a list of private colleges that offer full-tuition merit scholarships to at least some students. Eventually she got that list, and although it was outdated, it gave her a place to start her research. Not long afterward, it became clear how competitive those scholarships were going to be. "If a full-tuition scholarship is your goal, that is more selective than getting into the Ivy League," she said. "So you need to cast a wide net and apply to a lot of schools and hope there are one or two who want your kid. That was kind of startling."

How wide was the net? The Bel Air, Maryland, family visited over twenty-five schools, spending $8,000 or $9,000 total to do so, plus some money for someone to conduct mock interviews and give feedback. There were over sixty essays that were ultimately necessary to apply to all of those schools and then some, including Clemson University in South Carolina, Loyola University (both Maryland and New Orleans), Penn State, and the Universities of Alabama, Georgia, Delaware, North Carolina, and Maryland, Baltimore County. "It turned into a full-time job for me," said Perrault, who works part-time in a family-owned camper rental business while her husband works for the student lending giant Sallie Mae.

When all was said and done, after several follow-up visits for finalist weekends for some of the more prestigious awards, Perrault's daughter got her full-tuition scholarship, to Tulane. Over $2 million in merit discount offers came her way from 25 colleges and universities.

Here are a few more technical details Perrault learned along the way. First and perhaps most important, much of the best merit money is tied to the application channel known as early action. Some preliminary deadlines came as early as October. If you're going to play the game as Perrault's family did, you basically have to be done with your research by late spring of your child's junior year. You've got to have the test scores in hand and some essays written that can be quickly reworked for various supplementary applications. You should be prepared with a giant spreadsheet and a nearly empty schedule just to grind out applications. If offers do come in, see if they last for only four years. If they are capped, consider that your child may not be able to finish the intended major in that time. Try to find out what the odds are by asking a department chair what percentage of kids persist in a major and finish in four years. Also, check to see whether the scholarship will evaporate if the student's grade point average falls below a certain point.

On the Paying for College 101 Facebook group, Perrault is a hero, and each year there are others like her and her family. But she understands that everyone else might think she's nuts even though her family essentially won a tax-free lottery of over $200,000 after her daughter did the work to earn a ticket to the drawing. She said she'll probably refine the process somewhat when her next child applies, but it didn't sound to me as though the plan was to decrease the number of applications that much. And the irony is not lost on her that her research skills, free time, and relative affluence are a big part of what helped her work the system with her daughter.

"If you have money, you can get money," she said.

CHAPTER 32

When (and How)
to Hire an Independent
College Counselor or
Financial Planner

I am a big believer in paying for the right kind of financial advice. And chances are your family would benefit a great deal from meeting with a financial planner to talk about your overall financial health before making any big decisions about college. Moreover, you should probably at least consider an independent college counselor if money is going to be a factor in your college search.

Think about it this way: There are two kinds of people or families that can benefit from paying for help when applying for college. First, there are people who lack knowledge. Though I've given you enough information in these pages to ask good general questions, a book can't give you granular information on what it's like to repeatedly seek merit or need-based aid from any given school. Some experienced independent counselors will have that knowledge or the network to find it.

And the second kind of person who should consider hiring help? People who lack time. If the adult or adults in your household work full-time (or more) outside the home, are busy parenting other kids in the family, or feel overwhelmed for whatever reason, a good counselor can help you short-circuit the process.

Why an independent counselor and not the people at your high school who are in charge of college advising? It's not that they are not good at their jobs; I've met countless numbers of people in those roles who are amazing. But consider what they are up against. The average American high school has one school counselor for every 430 students. They may not be dedicated college counselors, either, since they may have other guidance or academic duties.

At better-resourced public schools, the ratio falls pretty quickly, and at private schools it falls further still. But the more affluent the community, the less specialized knowledge the counselor may have about the financial side of the process, given that many applicants weren't all that focused on cost until recently. Counselors are also under pressure in a world where so many prestigious schools are ever harder to gain admission to, simply to ensure a good fit and matriculation someplace that will make a family happy. At private schools the counselors may also have board members and others looking over their shoulders, hoping to produce a spiffy list of destination colleges that the high school can market to prospective families. Those lists don't come with asterisks explaining that a recent graduate from a high school in Colorado chose the University of Alabama over Northwestern because of the giant pile of merit aid money he or she received.

Perhaps you feel that you have the college research under control. What about your financial plan? Are you on track with your retirement savings? Is your plan to borrow heavily for college going to cause problems later? Would it help to speak to someone neutral just to assess your situation?

You're probably wondering what this sort of thing costs. Some of the best financial planners charge you an annual fee based on how much money they manage for you. Let's say they are managing $300,000 of retirement accounts. Often, they'll charge 1 percent of that, or $3,000 per year. That's a lot of money. The question you have to ask yourself is this: Each year, what kind of mistakes would you make—or what kind of benefits or strategies would you never find out about—without professional help, and does that add up to $3,000 of value?

That's the knowledge part of financial planning. Then there is the time element: Even if you know what to do and where to find answers to your questions, will you manage the details of your affairs promptly, in a stress-free fashion, without needing to spend lots of time away from your family? Will you do it at all? That's the other case for paying for financial help.

If you're not convinced yet, that's fine. It may still be worthwhile to meet with professionals just to see what they ask you and how they respond to your questions. Most of the people we're talking about here will get on the phone or meet with you once for a free introductory session. So let's talk about how to find ones who may be good and what to ask them once you are in the meeting.

First, financial planners. If you've never hired one before, they are a different breed from the old-fashioned stockbrokers that your parents might have worked with. Though financial planners do help people with investments, the good ones also advise on every other aspect of your financial life, from insurance to housing to student loans to retirement. You will want to hire someone who is a certified financial planner (CFP), a designation that isn't easy to get. (There is a long exam involved.)

Financial planners—or people who hold themselves out as "financial advisers" but never got the CFP designation or couldn't pass the exam—have many ways to make a living. Many of them do so through commissions. They sell you financial products of various sorts, such as insurance, and describe the advice that they give you along with that product as "free." The worry here is that they might be most likely to sell you the product that makes them money, even if it's not what you need or is not optimal for your situation.

Ideally, you would pay financial planners directly for their time or advice. Sure, there are planners who charge on the basis of the assets they manage for you. That's all well and good, but many of the better ones aren't interested in clients with less than $1 million to manage, and you may not have that or anything close to it. But there are CFPs who charge by the hour. They are part of something called the Garrett Planning Network. That might be a good first stop for finding a planner near you, although there are plenty who work remotely with faraway clients, too. Another source for planners is something called the XY Planning Network, where people should be willing to work by the hour or by the project. Many of these planners are younger. Though they may have less experience than other professionals, lots of them are wrestling with making a long-term family financial plan themselves. They are worth considering.

What should you ask them? I'd start by seeing what they ask you. They'll want to know why you approached them, and you might open with something like this: "It's hard to know how much to save or spend for college when you don't know what your goal should be." Then see where the conversation goes. Within ten minutes you should be fielding questions about feelings and not just the facts of your financial life. What do you need, and what do you want? What would happiness and success feel like to you two decades from now? Rather than imposing their own round-number goals and inserting you into products that can get you there, they should slowly pull back the layers of your financial uncertainty and confusion to reveal the complex emotions that always lie just below the surface.

Then it's your turn to ask questions: What are two ways that similar clients have handled similar issues in the recent past? How did you help them find their way to a plan? What emotions do you see most often in this general area of personal finance that are most and least helpful? And then the nitty-gritty: What are all of the ways that you make money? What would you charge directly for helping us in this instance? And finally: Would you always be working in our best interest? That last one is to check to see if they would be willing to work as a fiduciary, a legal standard that has at least some heft in the regulatory world.

Ideally you'd be able to hire someone who is something of a hybrid— say, an independent college counselor who specializes in need-based aid, merit aid, and helping families navigate questions about ability and willingness to pay. Unfortunately, finding a good counselor like this is a bit harder than finding a financial planner. Some of this has to do with history: Traditionally, many independent counselors have made their living mostly from people for whom money is no object. Yes, plenty of them take on pro bono cases, but those families are often seeking need-based aid and a lot of it, not merit aid. The need-based process is a bit more straightforward.

There are at least four membership organizations that independent college counselors belong to: the Independent Educational Consultants Association (IECA), the Higher Education Consultants Association (HECA), the National College Advocacy Group (NCAG), and the American Institute of Certified Educational Planners (AICEP). You could do worse than looking up people near you at each of them and seeking them out. What would be a lot simpler, however, is if those organizations created better sorting mechanisms. Then it would be easier to find someone anywhere in the country with a specialty in merit aid and paying for college.

Before you start quizzing the consultants, you'll probably want to have worked through many of the questions that I've raised both in this chapter and in some of the previous ones. After all, consultants can't help you if you haven't really reckoned with what you're able to pay and what you're willing to pay. When you talk to them, try to feel out their method for helping a family make a list of target schools. What data do they use, aside from the student's own, to figure out which colleges are likely to offer the most aid? Do they have favorite sources from the colleges, the government, or other third parties? Do they have a handy list of schools that offer no or limited merit aid, just so you can keep them in mind or cross them off your list entirely? If you don't see any evidence of systematic thinking—and if they haven't worked with a double-digit number of families like yours before—you might want to look elsewhere. Referrals from other families in your community can help too, although do consider the fact that clients often don't know what they don't know, let alone what their consultant hasn't figured out. Ask a lot of questions.

Again, you can absolutely sort out your financial goals and do all of the college homework on your own. But you will need to acquire a lot of knowledge over a lot of time to get it right. If spending a few thousand dollars can yield twice or five or fifty times that—or just double your peace of mind—it's well worth considering.

CHAPTER 33

How to Appeal Your Financial Aid Award

Why not ask for a better deal?

It's not a rhetorical question, and it's puzzling that given how much all of this will cost, more families don't inquire. We don't pay the full list price for a house unless we absolutely have to, and the same thing is true of an automobile. College shouldn't be any different, so why don't more families ask for a discount or a bigger one? Some people don't realize that it's even possible. Others are embarrassed. Still more worry that, having groveled for admission, haggling a bit on the price might have some negative consequences for their child if they do attend. (It doesn't, as long as you aren't overwhelmingly obnoxious about it.)

Then there are people who say that colleges don't actually negotiate. As I was writing this chapter, one expert on the subject sent me a thread from a private Facebook group where a bunch of college counselors were dismissing expert advice on getting bigger discounts. Perhaps they don't want to sully their own or their high school's relationships with college admissions officers by advocating on behalf of their clients after the admissions letters arrive? Or they think bargaining a bit is beneath them? In any event, new legislation literally forbids financial aid departments from having a policy that they deny all of a certain kind of appeal for more need-based aid.

It's hard to say, but it is indisputable that appealing your financial aid award can pay off big time. Let's be clear about what we're talking about.

You can appeal your need-based aid, and you can appeal your merit aid, but the processes tend to be different. You'll usually appeal need-based aid to a financial aid department, while it's an admissions officer who will often handle your request for more merit aid. With need-based aid, your best chance of getting a better package will come if you can prove that your financial circumstances have changed recently. Then again, at some schools, if you have a more generous offer from a similar school, that may help move the needle, too. That is especially true when it comes to merit aid.

What are the odds of getting a better package and hopefully more grant money that you don't have to pay back? Unfortunately, there isn't anyone who systematically tracks the percentage of families who appeal and end up getting a better deal. In general, however, private colleges have more flexibility than public ones do. For one *New York Times* column, I called up a couple of dozen of the most expensive private colleges and universities in the United States to ask them what percentage of appeals were successful. Some schools treated me as though I was somehow problematic for asking. At the University of Chicago, a spokesperson archly informed me that the answers to my questions were not public information. Maybe they don't want the phone ringing any more than it already does each April? I'm not sure.

Other schools were more forthcoming. At Occidental College, one-third of the entering class had appealed successfully—and that number includes people who had not applied for aid in the first place. At the New School's Eugene Lang College of Liberal Arts in New York City, 57 percent of people who appealed did so successfully. Dartmouth wouldn't give an exact number but confirmed that it too granted more than half of all aid appeals. At Sarah Lawrence, about half of admitted students succeeded. Cornell reported similar figures and takes an interesting approach to the process now; on its website it says the following point-blank: "Want to attend Cornell, but received a better financial aid package from another Ivy League institution, MIT, Duke or Stanford? Cornell will strive to calculate the same eligibility based on the information provided." It is quick to add, however, that it will do no such striving for any other schools, including ones such as Williams, Pomona, Vanderbilt, or Notre Dame that are evidently not quite in Cornell's league.

Before you can think about appealing, you need to be sure how much a school has actually offered you. You get your financial aid package via something called an award letter. It's a misleading name, given that many of them don't arrive by mail anymore. Also, it may suggest that the student take a work-study job or apply for loans, neither of which is an award in any normal sense of the term.

But this is mere annoyance; the real trouble is that these letters are notoriously, almost comically confusing. One journalist, Kim Clark, helped set up a website at FinancialAidLetter.com to try to demystify these communications. And in 2018, New America (formerly the New America Foundation) and a nonprofit called uAspire examined hundreds of award letters and found the following: Among the 455 colleges that offered an unsubsidized student loan, there were 136 different terms for it in the letters, including 24 that did not include the word "loan." It gets worse. Among 515 letters, more than one-third never bothered to place the figures into context by telling the student what the total cost of attendance actually was. Almost 15 percent of the letters referred to the parent PLUS loan line item as an "award." (Congratulations, here's some debt!) Proposed federal legislation to standardize these letters appears periodically, but it has not yet passed.

So expect to be confused. To decode the letter, begin with the school's overall cost of attendance, which usually appears somewhere on its website even if it's not in the award letter. If you can't find it, do an internet search for the name of the school and "cost of attendance" in the search box. Then look at the letter for any "grants" or "scholarships" or any other award that is indeed subtracted from the cost—money you do not have to pay back. Next, see if the school is giving you access to a work-study job on campus with money that comes from the federal government (which is why the college refers to it as "aid"). Note: You don't have to take the job, but if you don't, the school will expect your family to come up with the money some other way. Finally, look for loans: You may see a subsidized student loan (for which the government pays the interest while you are in school and you yourself don't have to make payments toward the principal on the loan during that time) or an unsubsidized loan. There may be a line for PLUS loans, too.

Now add up the grants and scholarships and work-study. Subtract the total from the cost of attendance, and then you'll know what the college is expecting you to pay, whether through debt (federal student loans, parent loans, or some other kind of borrowing) or through your own earnings and savings. If that amount is much higher than whatever total the college has said you can afford, you have been "gapped." What that means is that the college is unable or unwilling to meet your demonstrated financial need. If you want to attend the school, you'll have to fill the gap yourself, with more work or savings or by taking on more debt in some way, shape, or form.

Sometimes this will all be perfectly clear from the letter. At other times it will seem like a foreign language. If you don't understand it—if you're anything less than 100 percent certain about what the college is offering you—send an email to a financial aid officer there and ask. Keep asking until you achieve 100 percent clarity. Get it in writing, in plain English. And while you're at it, be sure to tell the people there when their language in the award letter makes no sense.

Eventually you'll understand what it is they're asking you to pay and what sort of discounts they are offering to you. If it's not enough, then it's time to write your appeal letter. It should be short, and it should take a long time to write. Short because admissions and financial aid officers are under tons of pressure after the award letters go out. Not only is there a high volume of communication coming back at them, but they don't have much time to respond. The college administrators want to get back to you just as fast as you'd like to receive an answer.

Still, you should put care and time into the note. After all, making a convincing case could net you well into five figures over four years. Tone is crucial. Make no accusations. Outlandish statements or outright lies will get you nowhere. As Mark Kantrowitz put it in his book *How to Appeal for More College Financial Aid*, financial aid administrators have been sniffing out cheaters for a lot longer than you've been trying to put one over on them. Two online services, Edmit and Swift Student, can help with appeal letters, too. Be advised too that there are moments each season when financial aid officers simply get fed up. Jennifer Delahunty, who was running Kenyon's admissions and financial aid operation at the time, said this to a reporter for *Washington Monthly*: "You know how there was the age of the enlightenment? Well, this is the age of entitlement."

Given how intense the competition was and is for students among the small liberal arts colleges in Ohio, Delahunty knew that it was the colleges themselves that had inspired the grabbiness by dangling merit aid offers in front of affluent families. Still, be sensitive to the optics and the social class subtleties. Perhaps your family has a household income of $150,000 and feels that it can't possibly pay full price or close to it at Kenyon. Or maybe you earn three times that and expect Kenyon to pay up—or down, as the case may be—to pry your child away from Cornell or Northwestern with a merit aid offer. Go ahead and make your case, but consider the salaries of the people you're appealing to. Private colleges don't disclose them, but they probably aren't too much more than what people make at large flagship state universities. At the University of Wisconsin–Madison, senior advisers in financial aid make $55,000 to $60,000 per year. The associate director there hasn't yet cleared $100,000. See how they might think that you seem a bit entitled if your words come out wrong?

Let's begin with the kind of note you should write if you are seeking more need-based financial aid. Spare the financial aid officers flowery details about how wonderful your child is. This isn't the place for that, as they're generally working with a fairly rigid formula that tells them how much you can afford. Hopefully you can show the person reading your letter that you have experienced—and this is a key phrase—a "change in circumstances" and that the reader might use "professional judgment" to consider your appeal. Given that financial aid officers use financial information that can be two years old, it's certainly possible that your circumstances have changed.

Ideally those circumstances are beyond your control; having overspent accidentally on purpose during the months leading up to your appeal isn't going to win you any friends in the financial aid office. And you'll want to focus on factors that have drawn on your income, since the financial formulas depend more on that than on your assets. In his book on financial aid appeals, Mark Kantrowitz provided a lengthy list of possibilities that might apply, although there could be others, too. He mentioned medical costs, dental costs, nursing home or other dependent care expenses if you're paying for a parent or other relatives, costs for a special-needs child, unemployment, a parent in school or retraining, disability, foreclosure, high legal fees, and a natural disaster or fire. Short- and long-term disability belongs on that list too, given how many Americans fell ill during the pandemic. Again, document everything.

If you live in an area with an especially high cost of living or your rent has gone to the moon and you didn't want to move in the midst of your child's junior or senior year and force a school change, say so. If your credit score has fallen enough because of any of the above circumstances that borrowing may be difficult, expensive, or impossible, say so. If you're repaying debt from an older kid's college expenses, bring that up if you haven't already. And it's fair game to mention K–12 private school costs for younger kids. If you feel as though the only way your eldest could have gotten into the private college you're appealing to is due to the tuition you paid (and are still paying for a younger child) at a private secondary school, it's fine to make that clear, too.

If there are similar schools—ones that compete for students with the one to which you are making your appeal—that were more generous with you, it is fine to say so—politely. Suggest, perhaps, that it was your error; these forms and applications are complicated enough that maybe you slipped up. Or begin with the assumption that the more generous school made an error and suggest that you're just inquiring about that possibility to make sure. The school you're making the appeal to won't call up the other school to compare notes or urge it to reduce your award. As we learned above, many schools outright invite these appeals; others will also respond to them, even if they don't say so publicly. And if a school says that it does not negotiate, remember that what you're doing is making an appeal, not bargaining. There is a code here, and some financial aid officers do not see themselves as used-car salespeople even if they do quite frequently adjust award amounts.

There are other tactics to consider that may involve a bit more risk. One former director of financial aid at a school that many of your kids will want to attend, who asked me not to reveal his identity because this anecdote is so specific, laid out the following set of facts: A family in the San Francisco Bay Area bought a house two decades ago, and, through no fault of their own, housing values quintupled. The aid formula suggested that they should tap their home equity to pay for a large chunk of college. But both parents worked at nonprofits that did a lot of good in the world, and they made a point of saying so—politely. The aid director found a way to cut them a fair bit of slack. Would that have happened if one parent had chosen not to work and the other had had some pedestrian job at a corporation? I could practically hear the former aid director winking over the telephone line. So if you think you're a borderline case like this, let that be known subtly and politely and cross your fingers. You certainly won't be punished for doing so.

Another tip for establishing a baseline of sympathy is to be aware that come appeal time, it is not a good look to dwell on the fact that you have no or little savings, particularly if there is evidence that you've earned a decent amount of money over the years. Maureen McRae Goldberg, the former Occidental financial aid director, is typical. "I see so many well-to-do families appeal because of a job loss, and then you ask about assets and they have none," she said. "How can you have no assets when you've been making six figures for more than a decade?"

In other words, aid formulas may take you only so far in some circumstances. When it comes time for real human beings to make judgment calls, you'll want to have established some sort of baseline of responsible financial behavior. And if you haven't been able to save much—whether it's because your income was low for a long time or you were repaying your own student loan debt or for some other reason—say so. It may help head off at the pass any such thoughts in the financial aid officer's mind and tip things in your favor.

Now to the question of who should do the asking and how. In theory, if it's a teenager asking for more money, it could make more of a sympathetic case. Deborah Fox, a veteran financial adviser with a specialty in financial aid, explained it like so: "Colleges have to deal with pushy parents all the time." Her clients have had a higher success rate when the child has led the appeal.

Having your child lead can work well if it's a written appeal and it doesn't appear to have been ghostwritten by a parent. Some families decide to make the appeal in person—say, if the need to ask for more money coincides with an admitted students weekend or open house. Indeed, financial aid officers are often on standby at those events, with twenty-minute interview slots at the ready. Mark Kantrowitz isn't a fan of making an appeal there, as he believes that there is too big a chance of slipping up and saying something you shouldn't. This can be doubly true if your child is leading the conversation or having it alone. If you do go this route, make sure that your child has a fair bit of knowledge of the family finances in order to respond to questions. But it might be better, in that event, to make it a family conversation with the financial aid office.

Merit aid appeals are more complicated. If you have no demonstrated financial need, there's a good chance that your household income is higher than what most financial aid officers make. That can be uncomfortable, so consider your tone. After all, this isn't a conversation about needs; it's a conversation about wants: about what you think your child deserves in the marketplace for undergraduates. And here you're at a disadvantage when it comes to the information at your disposal. Sure, you can use what you have learned from the school's common data set to make your case that your child is at least in the top quartile of students when it comes to grade point average and test scores. But you don't know what priorities any given school has in any given year. Perhaps no members of the orchestra graduated, and your first violinist won't help the school much. Maybe that year's collection of religious leaders or political aces is particularly strong, so your youth group organizer or campaign volunteer just doesn't measure up. You have little way of knowing.

The good news is that if you have competing merit aid offers from similar schools—and be realistic about what that means in terms of colleges that admit students with similar academic credentials—a school will generally hear you out. This is doubly so if the college to which you're appealing is your first choice. And it's triply so if that school has fallen behind in terms of the number of students who have said yes so far that season—something that you generally won't know but that a good college counselor may be able to pry out of the college before you make your appeal. Because of that, it's always worthwhile to keep your counselor in the loop if you're considering asking for more money. All but the most selective colleges do need to keep their pipelines of applicants flowing, and if they aren't willing to communicate with high school seniors trying to make a decision, counselors may discourage future students from applying. As they should.

"I tell families that if they can't write a check for the full cost of college, they should apply for financial aid," said Maureen McRae Goldberg. "If, after they receive their award letter they can't write a check for the remainder, they should appeal. The worst thing an aid office can do is say no."

CHAPTER 34

All the Student Loan Basics in One Tidy Place

Too many of the conversations about student loans begin and end with one question: How much? It's important, but there is a bigger, broader question that is more elemental: How? In other words, which of the many borrowing options will be best for a family, and who ought to do the borrowing?

First, you're likely coming to this chapter having heard and read a lot about paying and borrowing for college, but you probably haven't tackled the topic in any kind of systematic or strategic way. For starters, you should know that your family and your child are unwitting parties to one of the most profound experiments in personal finance that our country has seen in many decades. It took a long time for American adults to go from zero to $1 trillion in credit card debt, with average balances in the four figures. With student loans, balances tripled to $1.5 trillion in about a decade, except we did it with teenagers and young adults doing a lot of the borrowing and balances that can be many multiples of the average credit card debt.

Yes, your average college graduate should be able to repay the average student loan debt without too much trouble. But it's taking a while to get from "should" to "will," because the loan system is so complicated and the borrowers are so inexperienced at dealing with personal finance. Moreover, now that aggregate total student loan debts are well beyond total credit card and auto debts, we're talking about big enough totals that they may begin to affect the way some people make decisions. We don't yet know exactly how student loan debt will change the way people pick careers or when (if ever) some of the debtors will buy homes or have children (or how many).

So we are guinea pigs, and there is really no telling how our particular offspring will behave once the implications of the decisions they make at age seventeen or eighteen become clear. To become debtors, we need to get comfortable with that reality.

Those are the feelings. The facts are these: A reasonable amount of student debt isn't going to ruin people's lives if they finish college. If debt gets undergraduates to a school where they learn a lot, they find kinship in abundance, and they stand a decent chance of getting a job in the field they think suits them, they should by all means borrow. But do not—please, do not—begin the process without taking some time to understand how the student loan system works.

When people talk about student loans, they're usually referring to three different things at once, often without realizing it. First, there is the money that undergraduates, themselves and alone, borrow from the federal government. Many people in the financial aid field refer to this as a direct loan. The second kind of student loan is money that students borrow from a financial institution such as Sallie Mae or a bank or credit union. This is often called a private loan. Nowadays it's nearly impossible to get one without a parent or other adult cosigning the loan, in effect promising that they'll make good on the debt if the teenage applicant doesn't and agreeing to have their credit score marred if the student cosigner does not pay or pay on time and in full. Finally, there are parent loans; the ones that the federal government offers are called Direct PLUS Loans, although private entities have their own version, too.

Let's start with federal student loans. Depending upon a family's level of financial need, a school will offer the applicant two types, subsidized or unsubsidized. Though the student doesn't have to start repaying the debt while he or she is in school, interest will begin to accrue right away.

With subsidized debt, the federal government covers interest payments while the student is still enrolled. If a loan is unsubsidized, the interest starts adding up immediately. (You can make interest and other payments during college if you want to.) People can qualify for a federal unsubsidized student loan no matter how much money their parents make or have. They just have to fill out the FAFSA to get access to the program.

The federal government will allow undergraduates to borrow only a certain amount of money. At this writing, it's $27,000 during their first four years of college and $31,000 total. Independent students, who are generally older or have no parents in the picture, can borrow up to $57,500. That number also applies to students whose parent or parents do not qualify for PLUS loans due to poor credit. Interest rates change periodically, but they are generally quite reasonable, given that the borrowers have little or no credit history and the loans have no collateral.

Repayment generally begins six months after graduation or leaving school, and the standard repayment term is 120 payments over ten years. There are other options, however, that can both help and complicate things rather quickly. There are deferment and forbearance for people who are in graduate school or have run into financial trouble. And there is a variety of income-driven repayment programs as well. This means that if students are unemployed or end up in a low-paying job, the servicer who manages their loan will adjust payments according to what they can afford to pay. That way they shouldn't end up missing payments or defaulting on their loan altogether.

So how do people get into trouble? As we've discussed before, the quickest way is to borrow money and then not finish school. At that point they have the debt but not the boost in income that is supposed to come with higher education. It's the worst of both worlds. If you think there's a chance that your child might not finish—if he or she is just trying college on for size—do not borrow if you can possibly avoid it.

Oddly, the data on student loan delinquencies (when people are very late with at least one payment) and defaults (when they haven't paid in so long that the federal government turns them over to debt collectors and may try to garnish their wages) suggest that it's not people with large amounts of debt who end up in the most trouble in this regard. More likely, they are dropouts or have attended a for-profit school that hasn't delivered on its promise of gainful employment. It's also the case that once students leave school, they lose easy access to financial aid officers and others who can explain the repayment process.

Then there are people who are disorganized or uninterested. These debtors bear some blame, but as a country we're also signing teenagers up for a complicated system and not properly educating them about its ins and outs. The disorganized often lose track of their loans—literally. They do not know how many they have taken out or where to check. They move from home to school, from dorm to apartment, and they don't bother telling the federal government or the servicer that the government assigns to manage the loan and collect payments what their new address is. The uninterested may not move much, but they don't open their mail or emails warning them that the first payment is coming due. Or they put off paying, figuring what's a few months' delay? Turns out that a few months' delay could put their loan into default, and missing all those payments will mar their credit report for years.

Survey research bears some of this out. One study that the Financial Industry Regulatory Authority (FINRA) did of Americans' financial capability found that among people with at least some higher education, 51 percent hadn't tried to figure out ahead of time what size monthly student loan payments they might face when they were done with school. Another 48 percent were worried that they wouldn't be able to repay their loans.

What's a prudent family to do? Most students should not borrow any more than the federal student loan limits. That debt isn't likely to add up to much more than $300 a month or so in payments after graduation, which shouldn't stretch most young adults' budgets to the breaking point. Those who are having trouble can enter one of the income-driven payment programs. As for parental oversight, you could offer—or insist, as a condition of your own cash payments toward tuition—to help track the debt and set up a system for repaying it once it begins to come due. Doing so automatically each month, via direct debit of a checking account, can make things easier on young adults who have a regular source of income.

It would be nice if things were always as simple as I've made them seem so far, and for many families—and young adults who ease right into the workforce and stay there—it can be. But when federal loans are not enough for a school you're considering, it's tempting to turn to that second kind of debt—the private loan with an adult cosigner—to borrow even more. Their interest rates are often higher, or can be, since the rates tend to be variable and thus unpredictable over the life of the loan, moving as they do with underlying benchmarks that themselves follow macroeconomic indicators. There is added complexity, given that the debtor may be making multiple payments each month, on the federal loans and the private ones. A private loan has harsher terms; there is no income-driven repayment for the most part. And anyone with both types will be on the hook for more money in total each month.

A private loan is not always bad. If it's the only way to pay for engineering school or you need another $3,000 per year to put yourself that much closer to becoming a registered nurse, taking one out may be a good idea. But if a private loan is under consideration, students ought to be certain—as a teenager, which is hard—that they know exactly what they want to do and that it is in a field that is not all that subject to economic swings. As a parent, you also need to try to figure out whether the lender will actually underwrite the loan for all four years—ask ahead of time about whether it might cut you off midstream.

Then there is the cosigning part. If you as a parent are the cosigner, you have to assume that it's your loan or could be someday. You'll want to be even stricter here about how your young adult child repays the debt lest your credit get trashed if the payments don't arrive on time. It is possible to get a lender to release you from cosignatory status a few years into repayment, but you shouldn't count on it.

Gallup research has shown that almost half of recent graduates who had any debt at all had postponed additional training or graduate school. About a third had delayed purchasing a car or house due to the debt, and just under 20 percent had delayed starting a business. The numbers get much bigger as the debt burden from undergraduate education grows higher than $25,000—a figure not far off the federal student loan limit.

We want our kids to be on the right side of those numbers if at all possible so their next big life choices won't have anything to do with how much money they owe. And thus we come to parent-only loans, which colleges sometimes propose as a solution to the fact that they are unable or unwilling to commit their own resources to meet your family's demonstrated need. Here the numbers really do tell a story. Consider the study that Ruffalo Noel Levitz, one of the consulting firms that helps colleges decide which students get what discounts, did with client data in 2019. Remember the gapping we talked about up above, where colleges offer a financial aid package that, in total, doesn't meet your actual need? In the 2007–08 school year, the average size of the gap at private schools that had one was $3,779 per year. By 2018–2019, it was $11,177, with schools meeting 76 percent of families' need.

So there is a formula problem, with the aid algorithms assuming that many families can pay more than they actually can. Then there is a resource problem, in that schools don't have enough grant money for all of the people that the federal government and the schools themselves have defined as having need. And so we get the gaps. The schools feel bad, sure; the optics are not great, after all. But they also know that with a gap comes the guilt many families feel for not having saved enough or having done enough to be as financially ready as the schools say they are supposed to be at this point in their children's lives.

And so more and more of us borrow in ever larger amounts. Why wouldn't we? Many colleges tell us to do so explicitly in their award letters; others do so implicitly by leaving that gap. Some do both. And although the federal government caps the amount of money that an undergraduate student can borrow, there is no such limit for the parent PLUS loan. The message is clear: We've left you that leeway because we expect you to do this. The family contribution in the federal expected family contribution formula is, after all, expected, and that expectation is great and becomes greater with each passing year. At the very least, the lawmakers and regulators who oversee the program figure that many of us will want to borrow and that it's not such a great idea to try to stop us. Indeed, nobody checks your income when you apply for a PLUS loan, and the only people who don't qualify for one are those with serious negative marks on their credit reports.

According to a 2019 study that the Urban Institute did to try to raise an alarm and propose some reasonable limits, there are some eyebrow-raising trends. During the 2017–18 school year, parents borrowed $12.8 billion via PLUS loans, a 42 percent increase over the school year a decade earlier. Of all first-year students who were not independent and borrowed all they could under the federal student loan program during the 2015–16 school year, 28 percent had parents who also felt the need to borrow through the PLUS loan program. The prevalence of PLUS borrowing seems to be strongest at private colleges and universities, where 18 percent of parents of new students used them in 2015–2016, compared with 4 percent of parents of kids at public schools. Thirty percent of families with household incomes over $100,000 took out a PLUS loan that year versus 16 percent of families with incomes below $20,000. And remember, this is just one category of parent borrowing; we're not even talking about the people who borrow from private lenders, workplace retirement plans, or home equity lenders. That probably amounts to a fair bit more money.

Given the volume, it should come as no surprise that entire swaths of the higher education industry have come to depend on the fact that you will borrow if you feel you must—or at least that borrowing is what the federal government, the school that has accepted your child, and your kids themselves expect. The U.S. Department of Education, under President Obama, conducted an accidental experiment in proving this in 2011. Middle managers tightened credit standards on PLUS loans a bit in what they thought was a routine move; the effect was to leave scores of families at historically Black colleges, among others, with no good way to make their tuition payments. The volume of loans at those schools fell by 36 percent, while the number of borrowers fell by 47 percent. Within a couple of years the administration had to reverse course lest they threaten the ability of those colleges to remain solvent.

Why do parents borrow? In late 2015, as I was writing a column trying to dispense with the myth that not saving for college might benefit you come application season, I thought to look at the financial disclosures of the presidential candidates at the time. Martin O'Malley, the former governor of Maryland who was running as a Democrat, is the father of four. I did a double take when I saw his and his wife's PLUS loan total: $340,000. Their two oldest kids had attended private universities, not the University of Maryland. Again, that was for just two kids. Were they going to borrow that much for the next two as well? I wondered. O'Malley told me that he and his wife continued to hope "against cruel experience" that the younger two might attend a state school. Fascinating, isn't it, that even when the family was $340,000 in the hole, he and his wife were still going to leave the decision up to the two younger children?

Again, why? "For us, this is what the American dream is all about, working hard and making sacrifices so our kids can pursue bigger opportunities and do better than we did," he explained. Notice in the language the "dream" to "mak[e] sacrifices." "Bigger opportunities" to "do better than" . . . *becoming governor*? "Cruel experience."

The O'Malleys are not alone in not saying no and in framing the issue in this fashion. Parents continue to line up to say yes. They persist even though there is no formal income-driven repayment plan for the parent loans (although there is a loophole that allows some parents to slip in and enroll in such a plan). They do it even though 25 percent of people holding an education loan for a child or grandchild are sixty years of age or older, according to the Urban Institute study.

And now you are thinking about it too, right? Maybe just a little? Look, you wouldn't be doing your job as a parent unless you considered all available options. But here you need a clear-eyed view of what you'd be signing up for. How much do you really know about what kind of work you're going to be willing and able to do over the term of the loan—and how little control you may have over any of it? If you lose your job, how easy will it be to get another one even if you're willing? And if you get hurt or need to take care of someone who is sick, you might not be able to work much if at all. Do you have disability or long-term care insurance coverage to provide a backstop while the PLUS loan payments continue? Can you even get it if you already have a chronic condition?

Ann Garcia, a financial planner in Portland, Oregon, who specializes in planning for college, put it this way: Maybe you talk yourself into a $7,000 loan when your oldest child is in the first year of college. You can afford that. But do you plan to do it for each year? For each child? Pretty soon you've signed up for something between a monthly car payment and one for a mortgage. And even if your employment prospects take a turn for the worse before the last child starts college, won't you feel compelled to offer the same deal to that child, too?

So we should ask ourselves this: This debt we feel compelled to take on—is it the only way that our kids can get the education that they *need*? Or is this school, the one putting PLUS loans into the "award," something they merely want more than anything else they have ever desired, because even if the classroom experience or the income outcomes at the chosen school clearly aren't superior, the quality of the lived experience on campus will be for sure. So does school represent a necessary degree or just an upgrade in lifestyle? Somewhere in your subconscious, do you consider this future debt your legacy—something you'll take on because you know there is no trust fund for this future twenty-five-year-old and perhaps there will be not much of an estate to leave him or her when you die? Is it your solemn duty, the most profound obligation a parent can have? Or is it just so much guilt?

Let's be careful out there.

CHAPTER 35

One More Feeling: Hope

What is the definition of success? And how much is enough?

When answering the first question, I always think back to one of my own mentors, the eighth-grade basketball coach who taught us the way the late UCLA coach John Wooden defined the term in all its mangled run-on-sentence glory: "Success is peace of mind which is a direct result of self-satisfaction in knowing you made the effort to become the best you are capable of becoming."

However much you have saved, however much you can pay, pat yourself on the back for having done your best as a parent until this big college turning point. Try to remind yourself that whatever failings you perceive—or that your ex-spouse does—may not look like lack of effort to your children. Even if you haven't always done your best at every point in your child's first eighteen years, reading this book is one large step toward making it right.

Success here means knowing how the system works and who pays what and why. It is about figuring out what is worth paying extra for—and what kind of child needs what sort of extra investment. Success is also about paying close attention to what your child is doing and feeling in high school, looking for signs that any given kid might achieve more—and your family might spend less—if he or she takes an alternative path to a degree, whether it means attending school outside the United States or taking a gap year. And success is about planning as best you can and understanding the logistical details of the saving, spending, and borrowing that are part of this process.

But more than anything, successfully figuring out what to pay for college is about acknowledging your feelings, airing them, and then bringing them to heel. There are no wrong feelings other than the ones you fail to confront. Fear is natural, and anxiety is part of what gets us out of bed in the morning. There would be something wrong if there wasn't a voice inside of you at least questioning whether harm might come to your child if you were to spend as little as possible on an undergraduate education. Ditto the guilt, for who among us does not feel bad that we can't spend more—more money, more time, more energy—on or with our children. And if you couldn't care less about the snobs and elitists and are not inclined toward the kind of tribalism that exists among many alumni networks, great. But your children might care about how the world of high finance might side-eye their résumés five years from now or might be drawn to some storied collegiate tradition. There is no sin in that.

So how to grapple with these feelings? Take them seriously enough to motivate—but not sway us into spending more than we should or is necessary to achieve the goals we have for our children? How much *college* is enough?

Well, what *is* college? This is not an existential question. In fact, it's a practical one. "We have one word for a million different things," the author Christopher G. Takacs told me. In his book *How College Works*, he and his coauthor, Danial F. Chambliss, made the case that undergraduate institutions work best when they operate much like small liberal arts schools do.

That's a reasonable thesis. But there are lots of colleges that are happy to take your money and provide a different kind of service. There are college as vocational training ground; college as lifestyle choice, where you pay for the party; college as social network, where everyone finishes with a lot of Instagram followers and connections on LinkedIn but not much new in the brain. Then there is college as an ancillary service that a university happens to offer when its real mission is collecting hospital revenue, competing in football, attracting federal research dollars, and maximizing prestige. All of that is in the service of attracting starry-eyed undergraduates whose parents or loans will continue to pay tuition and fill the seats at the stadium while providing graduate students with human guinea pigs on which to hone their teaching skills.

Our journey together ends here, but your own research ought to begin with this question: What kind of college do you want? In all of my attempts at information gathering on campuses or on college websites, not once did I find a pamphlet that read "This is why this place is worth $50,000 extra each year." Trust me, I looked far and wide. Most colleges and universities, no matter the type, don't seem to want to address this in a qualitative way, let alone a quantitative one.

But in their defense there is indeed no algorithm that can tell you how to measure value, even (or especially) when a school's price tag for the four years is $200,000 or $300,000 or more. Just as every teenager is different, all schools are too, even if they aren't always so good at articulating why.

It is tempting to allow this state of affairs to create a sort of low-grade, years-long state of anxiety. In the absence of an equation that can dictate the right choice, how can you be sure that you're picking the right school and spending the right amount? Many experts on college planning encourage families to go by feel—that you'll just know when you visit. This is both partly true and wildly insufficient, given that a short visit doesn't give you any information about how a large amount of debt will feel or the good feeling that having $50,000 of savings left over for graduate school will give you.

So let me suggest one more feeling that ought to hang over this process. It's hope. Hope comes from knowing what to ask. Hope comes from knowing how the schools pull financial levers behind the scenes and how you might get onto the right side of all that at a school that really wants you there. Hope comes from the fact that there are so many more colleges in the United States than there are in other countries. Every one of them has plenty of people on staff who do what they do because they relish serving as mentors and molding young lives. These are institutions that make their students smarter, help them find the people they could not otherwise imagine existing in the world, and send alumni out into the working world with real skills that employers value. And, yes, if we keep asking penetrating questions, we should also feel hope that the administrators in charge will focus on generating better proof that they can do what they say for families like ours.

With hope comes confidence. The thing that families need in this process and that all too many lack is a reportorial mind-set and a consumerist approach. Where is the information that I need that may not be easy to find? And how can I think about this as a skeptical consumer seeking an institutional partner to build a product—a thinking, sociable, working adult—and less as a dutiful, supplicant family?

After several years of reporting, I have real hope that the schools are slowly hearing the growing cry for more demonstrative proof of value. They are coming to understand that they don't get to just say so or wave their arms around and cry "Reputation!" and "Look over here at our famous alumni!" Instead, they have to explain what makes them different from other schools and where the value of their institutions lies.

I have confidence in all of you reading this book to press them further. There is a system at work here. Why not treat the process of trying to beat it—to gain admission against what can be long odds, to get a good deal, to figure out how to maximize every minute of every year on campus, to end up somewhere where you can get every dollar's worth and then some—as a family project that is actually fun? This process need not be confrontational. Instead, you and your child can become satisfied customers, with your child being the product that every under-graduate institution hopes to create: a young adult who goes off into the world and tells others how good the college experience was.

I hope you feel as lucky as I do that all of this is still in front of us. And I hope you'll look back on it someday and know that the price you paid was worth it.

ACKNOWLEDGMENTS

This all started with readers, so I should thank them first.

To all of you who called, emailed, and stopped by my desk in the newsroom to wonder aloud at how you had arrived at your children's senior year knowing so little and paying so much, thank you for trusting me. The last three words of the previous sentence were almost "and fessing up," but that language isn't right. No parents should feel as though they are admitting wrongdoing when professing ignorance of a process that is so utterly confounding.

The *New York Times* has the smartest subscribers of any publication on the planet, and I'm lucky to learn from them via online comments and the notes they send. *New York Times* editors are damn good as well: Bill Brink, Phyllis Messenger, and Randy Pennell have all repeatedly reined me in and straightened me out in recent years. Numerous second readers on the Bizday desk have saved me from careless errors and clunky prose. Ellen Joan Pollock granted me leave to put all of this together and didn't flinch when it took so long. And praise be to the Sulzberger family members who have kept the *New York Times* independent and blessed the business decisions that have helped it thrive. Our chief executives, Mark Thompson and Meredith Kopit Levien, have worked near miracles and made it look easy.

My colleagues at the *Times* never cease to amaze me. Newspaper people used to refer to the print product as the Daily Miracle, and I still marvel at their ability to produce so much that is so good so quickly. I'm lucky to work among them. But I'm most fortunate to be entering year fourteen sitting next to or across from or in a Zoom room with Tara Siegel Bernard, who has never once complained about my blurting out my half-baked ideas and has never failed to make a good suggestion when reading my columns before publication. I don't get to sit next to Carl Richards, a *Times* contributor who wrote the Sketch Guy column for years, but he's in my ear anyhow. He has taught me so much about how to seek out and reckon with the feelings that get in the way of clearheaded thinking about money. Greetings, Carl!

Personal finance Twitter is the best Twitter; higher education Twitter is nearly as good. There are too many pithy geniuses to name, but I have sucked up wisdom from dozens of them. The members of the Paying for College 101 Facebook group have been unfailingly generous, and ringmaster Debbie Schwartz and I vented to each other over shared frustrations many times when I was puzzling this book out.

There are a lot of media outlets that do terrific reporting on higher education, so I tip my cap to so many reporters at the *Wall Street Journal*, the *Washington Post*, the *Atlantic*, National Public Radio, CNBC, MarketWatch, *Money*, the *Hechinger Report*, and the investigative powerhouse ProPublica. But like most reporters who write about a lot of things and then need to get up to speed in just one area really quickly, I probably lean hardest on the writers at industry publications. If you're applying to college in the next couple of years and not reading the *Chronicle of Higher Education* (subscription required, and it's worth it) or Inside Higher Ed (free online), you're doing it wrong.

About halfway through my reporting, it became clear that I just could not track everything down on my own while trying to visit dozens of places and talk to hundreds of people. At that point, two researchers, Maggie Hughes and Seoyeon Kim, parachuted in to help. Maggie began the process smarter than I was and then educated me quite efficiently before colleges started paying her for her consulting. I hired Seoyeon after reading her undergraduate writing about higher education, and it was a joy to watch her work and see what she'd notice in texts and stories that I would never have found without her help.

Enormous thanks to Christine Bader, Zac Bissonnette, Heidie Joo Burwell, Seoyeon Kim, Julie Lythcott-Haims, Brian Page, Andrea Petersen, Karen Phillips, Lynn Rosenstrach Zerbib, Catherine Saint Louis, Ramit Sethi, and Tara Siegel Bernard, who read some or all of this book and provided positive reinforcement and a long list of things that needed to get better. As ever, the Invisible Institute shall stay just out of sight and positively stuffed with badass confidants of the highest possible order.

Gail Winston, my editor at Harper, remains in possession of some of the best hands in the business. But her ears are where she really shines, both for mangled phrases and for tone, as in off key, as in you-don't-really-know-what-you-think-so-instead-you're-being-sarcastic. I swear, I live for her comment bubbles that simply say "Reword." Her associate Alicia Tan was quick on the draw and answered many of my addled questions repeatedly.

Heather Drucker was a willing publicity coconspirator, even though I'm a book launch know-it-all prone to fits of ranting and raving. Designer Leah Carlson-Stanisic, marketing director Katie O'Callaghan, production supervisor Diana Meunier, production editor Nathaniel Knaebel, and copy editors David Chesanow and Lynn Anderson all provided incredibly valuable assistance. And hey, you, Doug Jones: Your first-class ticket to Seattle awaits yet again in case we need to go out there and beat up some robots.

I wouldn't show up to a robot fight or *any* fight without my agent, Christy Fletcher. We're old enough now to measure our time together in decades, and this is one of those relationships that I just never question. She's that good.

Personal finance is more personal than it is finance, as the money guru Tim Maurer once wrote. And this work is personal. To John McClintock, my college counselor at Francis W. Parker School in Chicago; to Roger Koester, the financial aid consultant John sent us to who helped my family crack the code as applicants; and to Saint Joe Paul Case, who heard our appeals every year I was at Amherst and replied with a calm smile and another bucket of money: As time passes, I grow more and more grateful for what you did to help me get to and through college.

The last eighteen months of work on this project, up to and including the first six months of the pandemic, were easily the toughest professional period of my career. We had two books cooking in our household and two parents cooking them who could not do it all. Donna Mitchell is a rock who loves our children as though they were her own and somehow never gets sick or complains about anything. Our teenage deputies, Laila O'Neal and Isaac Wilson, pulled weekend duty when we needed it, which was often during some rough stretches. Felicia Stewart helped with about a thousand tasks large and small as we attempted to maintain some kind of order. And everyone involved with my father's care is a saint; all caregivers are.

I learned a fair bit in college, and I've worked for a few Amherst graduates along the way and others who approved of the credential I earned there. But I'm a kinship guy in the end; it's the friends I made who matter most now that I'm more than twenty-five years out. So much love to the Class of 1993. Whatever college ultimately did cost in inflation-adjusted, financial aid–discounted terms, knowing all of you has turned out to be worth it. Ditto to all you Parker kids who continue to show up everywhere, always, to lift me onto your shoulders and carry me through life.

Mom, Dad, we did it, again. Stephanie, David, Amy, Harry, Wendy, Stefanie, Andrew, Jonathan, Kayla, Alex and Sara, your love and loyalty (and pitching in on toddler care) seem to know no bounds. I am grateful, but most of all I am damned lucky.

Talia, this is a little weird. This book will come out during your first year of high school. I hope it will serve as a kind of manual for Ima and me lest we lose our shit entirely, as parents often do at some point during this process. But it's not meant to make you a poster child for anything. And besides, you seem to have yourself very well figured out. Your passion gives me strength and makes me proud. I can't wait to watch what you do, and wherever you go, whatever it costs, I'll be there cheering way too loudly while whispering snide asides in your ear.

Hi, Vi. Happy kindergarten! Can you read this yet? College is fun.

Mommy and Daddy are saving money for it. But first take a gap year. Ask your sister about it when she is done with hers. I love you.

Ah, Jodi. We survived. (I think. Were we still standing when this thing finally rolled off the printing presses?) Your belief in this book and your pride in me and what I do make all the hard work worth it.

Mostly. Let 2021 and the years that follow mean making up for lost time, all of us, all of it and then some. I look forward to Kantlieb picnics in Prospect Park, vaccine shots in every limb, breakfast with Disney princesses, music festivals across the land, and one twentieth-anniversary trip to rule them all.

And then, after that? We'll hit the road with Tali to tour some colleges.

NOTES

Many quotes or phrases in this book come with notes in this section. If they do, that means that I used a secondary source for that passage. If there is no note here, that quote comes from an interview that I conducted myself with the person I quoted.

Every name and detail in this book is real and true to the best of my knowledge, with one exception. Anabel Mydland is a real person, and her quotes are real. But I changed her name so that she could speak freely about a difficult time in her life.

Introduction

4   one guidance counselor for every 430 students: This figure comes from an American School Counselor Association analysis in 2020 of federal National Center for Education Statistics data. https://www.schoolcounselor.org/asca /media/asca/Press%20releases/PR_18-19Student-to-SC-Ratios.pdf.

5   "bought and sold," *Journal of Economic Perspectives*, 13, no. 1 (1999): 13-36, http:// unionstats.gsu.edu/4960/Winston_1999.pdf.

5   To make sense of it all: The two-question construction, as best as I can recall, goes back to my time writing for *Fast Company* magazine, and it seems to have started with a story in the October 1993 issue by Mark B. Fuller called "Business as War."

6   "Most online instruction": "Remote Learning Is Unequal. Coronavirus Changed That—for Now," *Philadelphia Inquirer*, April 8, 2020.

6   "In May 2020, about 60 percent": "Did the Scramble to Remote Learning Work?," *Chronicle of Higher Education*, August 21, 2020.

6   remote learning: This point was first made by the venture capitalist and author Ryan Craig in his email newsletter, *Gap Letter*, in September, 2020. http://www .gapletter.com/letter_46.php.

6   "Overnight, our small": Mary Schmidt Campbell, "Spelman College Faces a Redefined Reality," *New York Times*, April 23, 2020, https://www.nytimes.com/2020 /04/23/education/learning/coronavirus-spelman-college.html.

7   Robert Kelchen, an associate professor: Robert Kelchen, Twitter, July 6, 2020.

11   blatant institutional adultism: A hat tip to Jacob Swindell-Sakoor, a high school sophomore who coined this phrase in a 2013 speech, as I reported in *The Opposite of Spoiled*, 9.

Chapter 1: Who Pays What and Why the Price Is So High

16   52.6 percent off: All the numbers in this section come from "2020 Tuition Dis-
      counting Study," NACUBO, https://www.nacubo.org/Press-Releases/2020
      /Before-COVID-19-Private-College-Tuition-Discount-Rates-Reached-Record-Highs.

16    $23,952: Ruffalo Noel Levitz, "2019 Discounting Report for Four-Year Private and
      Public Institutions," 3, 6, 7, 18.

17    $15,400 in 2019–20: College Board, "Trends in College Pricing 2019," https://
      research.collegeboard.org/pdf/trends-college-pricing-2019-full-report.pdf, 18.

17   average net price was $27,400: Ibid., 19.

17    $40,000 in the 2015–16 school year: Ibid., 21.

18   "the dysfunctionality narrative": Archibald and Feldman, *Why Does College Cost
      So Much?*, 93.

18   contributed just 6 percent: Robert Hiltonsmith, "Pulling Up the Higher-Ed
      Ladder: Myth and Reality in the Crisis of College Affordability," Demos, May
      15, 2015, https://www.demos.org/sites/default/files/publications/Robbie%20
      admin-bloat.pdf.

18   "The symbolism of this": Kellie Woodhouse, "Lazy Rivers and Student Debt,"
      Inside Higher Ed, June 15, 2015, https://www.insidehighered.com
      /news/2015/06/15/are-lazy-rivers-and-climbing-walls-driving-cost-college.

19   "The most common complaint": Brian Rosenberg, "Are You in a 'BS Job'? Thank
      You for Your Work. No, Really," *Chronicle of Higher Education*, May 29, 2018.

20   80 percent of the price hike: Hiltonsmith, "Pulling Up the Higher-Ed Ladder,"
      4–5.

Chapter 2: FAFSA and Its Confounding Calculations Will Probably Make You Furious; Blame the Federal Government's Great Expectations

23   a piece I wrote in 2015: "Why It Makes Good Sense to Save for College Now,"
      New York Times, October 23, 2015, https://www.nytimes.com/2015/10/24
      /your-money/why-it-makes-good-sense-to-save-for-college-now.html

24   average parental income of FAFSA filers: Ruffalo Noel Levitz, "2019 Discounting
      Report," 9, 19.

29   "moral tensions": Zaloom, *Indebted*, 13.

29   "moral technology": Ibid., 97.

30   "social speculation": Ibid., 15.

Chapter 3: How (and Why) Merit Aid Became Mainstream

38   *Crafting a Class*: Duffy and Goldberg, *Crafting a Class*, 38.

38   "a good sharp contest": Ibid., 171.

38   "outright buying or bribing": Ibid., 62.

39   39 percent: Ibid., 214.

39   fallen 220 points: Ibid., 90.

40   "The message was": Duffy and Goldberg, *Crafting a Class*, 217.

40   Smith and Mount Holyoke tested: Ibid., 216–17.

41 "There are some kids there": Matthew Quirk, "The Best Class Money Can Buy," *Atlantic*, November 2005, https://www.theatlantic.com/magazine/archive/2005/11/the-best-class-money-can-buy/304307/.

41 The University of Alabama now spends: Laura Pappano, "How the University of Alabama Became a National Player," *New York Times*, November 3, 2016, https://www.nytimes.com/2016/11/06/education/edlife/survival-strategies-for-public-universities.html.

41 "For the newspaper." Growing Brain Drain: University of Alabama's Gain in Drawing Illinois Students is a Loss for Illinois, *Chicago Tribune*, April 6, 2018.

41 "Price is the most malleable": McGee, *Breakpoint*, 27.

42 "It's a zero-sum game": Quirk, "The Best Class Money Can Buy."

Chapter 4: The Billion-Dollar Consultants Who Are Wooing You

43 Merit aid puts achievement before disadvantage: Davin Sweeney, "Jon Burdick on Money and College," *The Crush*, Episode 10.1, May 25, 2016, https://www.crushpodcast.com/jon-burdick-part1/.

45 "financial aid optimization": Hardwick Day, LinkedIn, https://www.linkedin.com/company/hardwick-day.

45 using the word "leverage": Ruffalo Noel Levitz, https://www.ruffalonl.com/complete-enrollment-management/optimizing-yield/advanced-financial-aid-management-leveraging-solutions/.

47 demanded to know: Duffy and Goldberg, *Crafting a Class*, 193.

47 At the College of the Holy Cross: Ibid., 193.

48 "false dichotomy": NACUBO, "2015 Tuition Discounting Study," May 1, 2016.

49 one paper: National Bureau of Economic Research Working Paper Series, "Do and Should Financial Aid Packages Affect Students' College Choices?" Christopher Avery and Caroline M. Hoxby. Working paper 9482, February, 2003. https://www.nber.org/papers/w9482.pdf.

53 Mount Holyoke College had success: Duffy and Goldberg, *Crafting a Class*, 195.

54 a front-page story: Steve Stecklow, "Expensive Lesson: Colleges Manipulate Financial Aid Offers, Shortchanging Many," *Wall Street Journal*, April 1, 1996, https://msu.edu/~conlinmi/teaching/PIM821/pricediscriminationuniversity2.pdf.

56 a fair bit of research: See New America's series of reports titled "Undermining Pell." There are now four volumes, all available online; the first one gives a good overview of the equity argument.

57 "Colleges actually": Gaby Dunn, *Bad with Money with Gaby Dunn*, Season 4, Episode 14, July 24, 2019.

57 "We had a sticker price": Nick Anderson, "Attention, College Shoppers. These Schools Are Slashing Their Prices," *Washington Post*, January 21, 2019, https://www.washingtonpost.com/local/education/attention-college-shoppers-these-schools-are-slashing-their-prices/2019/01/21/e384eca0-12bc-11e9-90a8-136fa44b80ba_story.html.

Chapter 5: But Wait, Isn't Tuition a Bubble, and All of Higher Education Is Going to Come Apart at the Seams?

58   "saturation point": Quoted in Duffy and Goldberg, *Crafting a Class*, 185.

58   The next year: Ibid., 187.

58   "border on the ridiculous": Ibid., 187.

58   By 1984, insiders were: Ibid., 26.

58   In 1986, others became: Ibid., 228.

59   That prediction arrived: Abigail Hess, "Harvard Business School Professor: Half of American Colleges Will Be Bankrupt in 10 to 15 Years," November 15, 2017, https://www.cnbc.com/2017/11/15/hbs-professor-half-of-us-colleges-will-be -bankrupt-in-10-to-15-years.html.

59   There he forecasted: Grawe, *Demographics and the Demand for Higher Education*, 69.

59   20,000 *more* students: Ibid., 72.

60   As a result: Ibid., 92–94.

65   "university of everywhere," Carey, *The End of College*, 4.

65   "immersive digital learning environments": Ibid., 232.

65   "different but not solitary": Ibid., 235.

65   "brutal unmasking": Ibid., 249.

65   within the lifetimes: Ibid., 231.

67   transactional instead of utterly transformational: McGee, *Breakpoint*, 5.

Chapter 6: Fear

71   narrative of downward mobility: Seoyeon Kim, "The Fallacy of Meritocracy," *Amherst Student*, March 27, 2019, https://www.amherststudent.com/article/the -fallacy-of-meritocracy.

72   58 percent of Americans: Bruce Stokes, "Public Divided on Prospects for the Next Generation," Pew Research Center, June 5, 2017, https://www.pewresearch.org /global/2017/06/05/2-public-divided-on-prospects-for-the-next-generation/.

73   "The Fading American Dream": Raj Chetty et al., "The Fading American Dream: Trends in Absolute Income Mobility since 1940," National Bureau of Economic Research, March 2017, https://www.nber.org/papers/w22910.pdf.

73   "Make Your Own": "Income Mobility Charts for Girls, Asian-Americans and Other Groups. Or Make Your Own," *New York Times*, March 27, 2018. https:// www.nytimes.com/interactive/2018/03/27/upshot/make-your-own-mobility -animation.html

74   Gallup asks: Megan Brenan, "Americans More Optimistic About Future of Next Generation," Gallup, April 3, 2018, https://news.gallup.com/poll/232076 /americans-optimistic-future-next-generation.aspx.

Chapter 7: Guilt

77   Potential, as Caitlin Zaloom wrote: Zaloom, *Indebted*, 200.

77   "Loans may be expensive": Ibid., 241.

77   blamed themselves: Quart, *Squeezed*, 9.

81   "Don't I work": I used part of this quote in "As College Deadlines Near, Families Wonder What They Can Pay," *New York Times*, April 28, 2017, https://www .nytimes.com/2017/04/28/your-money/paying-for-college/as-college-deadlines -near-families-wonder-what-they-can-pay.html.

83   Their work became known: Stacy Berg Dale and Alan B. Krueger, "Estimating the Payoff to Attending a More Selective College: An Application of Selection on Observables and Unobservables," National Bureau of Economic Research, August 1999, https://www.nber.org/papers/w7322.pdf.

83   two different papers: The second paper was "Estimating the Return to College Selectivity over the Career Using Administrative Earnings Data," National Bureau of Economic Research, June 2011, https://www.nber.org/papers/w17159 .pdf.

83   a different trio of researchers: Suqin Ge, Elliott Isaac, and Amalia Miller, "Elite Schools and Opting In: Effects of College Selectivity on Career and Family Options," National Bureau of Economic Research, November 2018, https://www .nber.org/papers/w25315.pdf.

Chapter 8: The Pull of Snobbery and Elitism

86   He defined "snobs": Epstein, *Snobbery*, 15.

86   extensive jockeying for position: Ibid., 16.

86   "The true snob": Ibid., 16.

86   swan around: Ibid., 25–27.

86   "The number of hopes blasted": Fussell, *Class*, 141.

89   "Many evaluators believed'": Rivera, *Pedigree*, 88.

89   lack of foresight: Ibid., 89.

90   "formally reserved for graduates": Ibid., 275.

90   "Many evaluators were more forceful": Ibid., 207.

91   In the boardroom: Jonathan Wai, "Investigating The World's Rich and Powerful: Education, Cognitive Ability, and Sex Differences," *Intelligence*, 46 (September 2014): 54–72. Change per https://www.sciencedirect.com/science/article/abs/pii /S0160289614000749.

92   the benefit of the doubt: Bruni, *Where You Go Is Not Who You'll Be*, 122.

93   according to one study: Jonathan Wai and Kaja Perina, "Expertise in Journalism: Factors Shaping a Cognitive and Culturally Elite Profession," *Journal of Expertise*, 1, no. 1 (2018): 57–78, https://www.journalofexpertise.org/articles/volume1_issue1 /JoE_2018_1_1_Wai_Perina.pdf.

94   Gallup found: Valerie J. Calderon and Preety Sidhu, "Business Leaders Say Knowledge Trumps College Pedigree," Gallup, February 25, 2014, https://news .gallup.com/poll/167546/business-leaders-say-knowledge-trumps-college-pedigree .aspx.

94   snobbery often takes deepest root: Epstein, *Snobbery*, 132.

Chapter 9: Classrooms Where Experienced Instructors Have Time to Teach (and Actually Want To)

97   some of the best research: Leo M. Lambert, "The Importance of Helping Students Find Mentors in College," Gallup, November 29, 2018, https://news.gallup.com /opinion/gallup/245048/importance-helping-students-find-mentors-college.aspx.

98   "If universities truly compete": Bok, *Universities in the Marketplace*, 160.

98   "Professors are chosen": Anthony Grafton, "The Enclosure of the American Mind," *New York Times*, August 22, 2014, https://www.nytimes.com/2014/08/24/books /review/excellent-sheep-by-william-deresiewicz.html.

98   "Somewhere along the way": Berlinerblau, *Campus Confidential*, 190.

98   "The profession's whole incentive structure": Deresiewicz, *Excellent Sheep*, 81.

99   "Most of the rewards": Roberts, *The Thinking Student's Guide to College*, 15.

99   uses federal data; "Data Snapshot: Contingent Faculty in US Higher Ed," American Association of University Professors, October 11, 2018, https://www .aaup.org/sites/default/files/10112018%20Data%20Snapshot%20Tenure.pdf.

100   A 2015 report: Ken Jacobs, Ian Perry, and Jenifer MacGillvary, "The High Public Cost of Low Wages," UC Berkeley Center for Labor Research and Education, April 2015, https://laborcenter.berkeley.edu/pdf/2015/the-high-public-cost-of-low -wages.pdf.

101   "The working conditions of the teachers": "Background Facts on Contingent Faculty Positions," American Association of University Professors, https://www.aaup .org/issues/contingency/background-facts.

102   One intriguing study: David N. Figlio, Morton O. Schapiro, and Kevin B. Soter, "Are Tenure Track Professors Better Teachers?," National Bureau of Economic Research, September 2013, https://www.nber.org/papers/w19406.pdf.

102   One showed that: Ronald G. Ehrenberg and Liang Zhang, "Do Tenured and Tenure-Track Faculty Matter?," National Bureau of Economic Research, August 2004.

102   Another study: Roger G. Baldwin and Matthew R. Wawrzynski, "Contingent Faculty as Teachers: What We Know; What We Need to Know," *American Behavioral Scientist*, 55, no. 11 (November 2011): 1485–509.

103   reported the following: "The 2014 Gallup-Purdue Index Report," 2014, https:// www.gallup.com/services/176768/2014-gallup-purdue-index-report.aspx.

104   "the pleasures and richness": Childress, *The Adjunct Underclass*, 41.

104   challenge and care: Deresiewicz, *Excellent Sheep*, 177.

104   "You have to assign": Ibid., 182.

105   people with arts and humanities degrees: Andrew Dugan and Stephanie Marken, "U.S. Business Majors Least Likely to Get Support in College," Gallup, November 6, 2014, https://news.gallup.com/poll/179138/business-majors-least-likely-support -college.aspx.

105   In 2019, Gallup published: Steve Crabtree, "Student Support from Faculty, Mentors Varies by Major," Gallup, January 24, 2019, https://news.gallup.com/poll /246017/student-support-faculty-mentors-varies-major.aspx.

105 "perhaps the biggest blown opportunity": Brandon Busteed, "The Blown Opportunity," Inside Higher Ed, September 25, 2014, https://www.insidehighered.com/views/2014/09/25/essay-about-importance-mentors-college-students.

106 "We all believe": Scott Carlson, "A Caring Professor May Be Key in How a Graduate Thrives," *Chronicle of Higher Education*, May 6, 2014, https://www.chronicle.com/article/a-caring-professor-may-be-key-in-how-a-graduate-thrives/.

108 he sees no reason: Berlinerblau, *Campus Confidential*, 94.

108 "Time and again": Chambliss and Takacs, *How College Works*, 3.

108 "It seemed almost magical": Ibid., 57.

108 the dinners mattered more statistically: Ibid., 58.

109 "Finding great teachers," David Coleman, "There's More to College than Getting into College," *Atlantic*, May 22, 2019, https://www.theatlantic.com/ideas/archive/2019/05/david-coleman-stop-college-admissions-madness/589918/.

Chapter 10: Schools Where Students Learn (Because Many of Them Don't)

110 "How much are students": Arum and Roksa, *Academically Adrift*, 34.

110 "Parents and students have no": "A Test of Leadership: Charting the Future of U.S Higher Education," U.S. Department of Education, September 2006, https://www2.ed.gov/about/bdscomm/list/hiedfuture/reports/final-report.pdf, 14.

111 For at least 45 percent: Arum and Roksa, *Academically Adrift*, 36.

111 just one-sixth: Ibid., 39.

111 About one-third: Arum and Roksa, *Aspiring Adults Adrift*, 38.

111 This is much less: Ibid., 35.

112 The researchers asked: Arum and Roksa, *Academically Adrift*, 71.

112 "disengagement compact": Ibid., 45.

112 Georgetown's Jacques Berlinerblau: Berlinerblau, *Campus Confidential*, 140.

112 "No actors in the system": Arum and Roksa, *Academically Adrift*, 125.

112 they would have improved: Ibid., 56.

113 was much wider on average: Arum and Roksa, *Aspiring Adults Adrift*, 42.

113 research does suggest: Arum and Roksa, *Academically Adrift*, 93.

113 68 percent: Ibid., 73.

113 labeled their gains "modest": Arum and Roksa, *Aspiring Adults Adrift*, 44.

113 Students in more traditional liberal arts fields: Ibid., 45.

113 One other more recent bit of data: Berlinerblau, *Campus Confidential*, 109–10.

114 "The measurement and understanding": Arum and Roksa, *Academically Adrift*, 140.

114 Purdue president Mitch Daniels: Stephen J. Dubner, "The $1.5 Trillion Dollar Question: How to Fix Student-Loan Debt?," *Freakonomics* podcast, Episode 377, May 8, 2019, https://freakonomics.com/podcast/student-debt/.

Chapter 11: Undergraduate Mental Health Centers That Are Not in Crisis

116 the *Wall Street Journal* published it: Douglas Belkin, "Colleges Bend the Rules for More Students, Give Them Extra Help," *Wall Street Journal*, May 24, 2018,

https://www.wsj.com/articles/colleges-bend-the-rules-for-more-students-give
-them-extra-help-1527154200.

117 "Many times parents": Kathleen Baker, "Colleges Are Hard Put to Help Students
     in Crisis," *Chronicle of Higher Education,* August 31, 2015, https://www.chronicle
     .com/article/colleges-are-hard-put-to-help-students-in-crisis/.

118 provides a visceral sense: Center for Collegiate Mental Health, Penn State Univer-
     sity, "2018 Annual Report," January 2019, https://sites.psu.edu/ccmh/files/2019
     /01/2018-Annual-Report-1-15-2018-12mzsn0.pdf. Utilization statistics, 15; rapid
     access, 4; shedding, 7.

118 "to prioritize rapid access": Ibid., 7.

118 "our findings suggest": Ibid., 8.

119 There are six pages: AUCCCD, "The Association for University and Counseling
     Center Directors Annual Survey—Public Version 2018," https://www.aucccd.org
     /assets/documents/Survey/2018%20AUCCCD%20Survey-Public-June%2012
     -FINAL.pdf, 44–49.

119 Ohio State's wait time: Holly Zachariah, "Ohio State Students Call for More
     Mental-Health Services," *Columbus Dispatch*, April 13, 2018, https://www.dispatch
     .com/news/20180413/ohio-state-students-call-for-more-mental-health-services.

119 The smaller the school: AUCCCD, "The Association for University and Counsel-
     ing Center Directors Annual Survey—Public Version 2018," 13.

119 At schools with more than 2,500 students: Ibid., 26.

119 The larger the school: Ibid., 37.

119 The clinical load index: Ibid., 20.

119 the student-to-counselor ratio: Ibid., 18.

120 One notable protest: Jeremy Bauer-Wold, "Ground to a Halt," Inside Higher Ed,
     April 18, 2017.

120 Harvey Mudd's president lamented: "A College President on Her School's
     Worst Year Ever," NPR, August 2, 2017, https://www.npr.org/sections/
     ed/2017/08/02/540603927/a-college-president-on-her-schools-worst-year-ever.

121 Tulane responded: Emma Discher, "Students Take Charge of Mental Health Con-
     versation on Campus," *Tulane Hullabaloo*, December 4, 2014, https://
     tulanehullabaloo.com/2518/news/students-take-charge-of-mental-health
     -conversation-on-campus/.

Chapter 12: Peers Worth Friending (or Marrying)

127 By 2017, nearly half: Jeremy Bauer-Wolf, "Duke's Random Roommates," Inside
     Higher Ed, December 19, 2018, https://www.insidehighered.com/news/2018
     /12/19/little-drama-dukes-random-roommate-policy.

127 In early 2018, Duke stopped allowing: Jeremy Bauer-Wolf, "Random Roommates
     Only," Inside Higher Ed, March 2, 2018, https://www.insidehighered.com
     /news/2018/03/02/duke-university-blocks-students-picking-their-roommates
     -freshman-year.

127 By December 2018, it had data: Bauer-Wolf, "Duke's Random Roommates."

128 People stayed friends: McCabe, *Connecting in College*, 171.

128 a 2008 study: Natalie J. Shook and Russell H. Fazio, "Roommate Relationships: A Comparison of Interracial and Same-Race Living Situations," *Group Processes & Intergroup Relations* 11, no. 4 (October 2008): 425–37.

128 A 2009 examination: Thomas E. Trail, J. Nicole Shelton, and Tessa V. West, "Interracial Roommate Relationships: Negotiating Daily Interactions," *Personality and Social Psychology Bulletin*, 35, no. 6 (June 2009): 671–84.

128 according to press reports: Jeremy Bauer-Wolf, "Random Roommates Only."

129 so-called party pathway: Armstrong and Hamilton, *Paying for the Party*, xi.

130 As Laura T. Hamilton, one of the authors, Tamar Lewin, "Class Warfare Along Partygoer Lines," *New York Times*, August 2, 2013, https://www.nytimes.com /2013/08/04/education/edlife/elizabeth-a-armstrong-on-her-book-paying-for-the -party.html.

130 "Prospective college students": Allie Grasgreen, "Paying for the Party," Inside Higher Ed, April 1, 2013, https://www.insidehighered.com/news/2013/04/01 /colleges-party-emphasis-maintain-economic-social-inequality-new-research -suggests.

131 One 2018 study: Scott E. Carrell, Richard L. Fullerton, and James E. West, "Does Your Cohort Matter? Measuring Peer Effects in College Achievement," *Journal of Labor Economics*, 2009.

131 "Smart women can't": Quoted in Maureen O'Connor, "Princeton Mom to All Female Students: 'Find a Husband,'" *New York*, March 29, 2013, https://www.thecut .com/2013/03/princeton-mom-to-all-students-find-a-husband.html.

132 "I've overheard plenty": Eveline Chao, "An Alumna's Advice for the Young Women of Princeton: Marry My Son," Daily Beast, March 30, 2013, updated July 12, 2017.

132 "protective" function: Arum and Roksa, *Aspiring Adults Adrift*, 97.

132 Facebook published: "From Classmates to Soulmates," Facebook, October 7, 2013, https://www.facebook.com/notes/facebook-data-science/from-classmates-to -soulmates/10151779448773859/.

133 "high-contact dorms": Chambliss and Takacs, *How College Works*, 99.

Chapter 13: The Special Power of Historically Women's Colleges

137 all of the data below: Susan Lennon and Jim Day, "What Matters in College After College: A Comparative Alumnae Research Study," Women's College Coalition, February 24 and March 7, 2012, https://www.womenscolleges.org/sites/default /files/report/files/main/2012hardwickdaycomparativealumnaesurveymarch2012 _0.pdf.

137 84 percent answered affirmatively: Ibid., Slide 71.

137 61.4 percent: Linda J. Sax, "Who Teaches at Women's Colleges?: A Comparative Profile of Women's College Faculty," Women's College Coalition, September 2014, https://www.womenscolleges.org/sites/default/files/report/files/main/wcc_faculty _report_final.pdf, 10.

137 flipped around entirely: Linda J. Sax, "Who Attends a Women's College?: Identifying

Unique Characteristics and Patterns of Change, 1971–2011," Women's College Coalition, September 2014, updated April 2015, viii.

138 higher percentages: Ibid., 52.

138 A higher percentage of these women: Ibid., ix.

138 the schools helped them become: Lennon and Day, "What Matters in College After College," Slide 58.

138 "In terms of gains": Paul D. Umbach et al., "Women Students at Coeducational and Women's Colleges: How Do Their Experiences Compare?," Indiana University Center for Postsecondary Research, n.d., https://citeseerx.ist.psu.edu/viewdoc /download?doi=10.1.1.508.4864&rep=rep1&type=pdf, 7, 9.

139 more likely to find their social lives wanting: Sax, "Who Attends a Women's College?," 2.

139 less likely to be on a varsity sports team: Ibid.

Chapter 14: Diversity in All Its Forms

141 There is the meta-study: Smith, *Diversity Works*.

141 according to another study: Eugene T. Parker III and Ernest T. Pascarella, "Effects of Diversity Experiences on Socially Responsible Leadership over Four Years of College," *Journal of Diversity in Higher Education*, 6, no. 4 (December 2013): 219–30.

141 And Gallup found: Stephanie Marken, "Graduates Exposed to Diversity Believe Degree More Valuable," Gallup, October 28, 2015, https://news.gallup.com /poll/186257/graduates-exposed-diversity-believe-degree-valuable.aspx.

142 2019 Discounting Report: Ruffalo Noel Levitz, "2019 Discounting Report for Four-Year Private and Public Institutions," 10.

142 a proprietary college access index: David Leonhardt, "Top Colleges That Enroll Rich, Middle Class, and Poor," *New York Times*, September 8, 2014, https://www .nytimes.com/2014/09/09/upshot/top-colleges-that-enroll-rich-middle-class-and -poor.html.

142 the *Times* published yet another, "Some Colleges Have More Students from the Top 1 Percent Than the Bottom 60. Find Yours," *New York Times*, January 18, 2017, https://www.nytimes.com/interactive/2017/01/18/upshot/some-colleges -have-more-students-from-the-top-1-percent-than-the-bottom-60.html.

143 "As long as they're in the range": Beckie Supiano and Dan Bauman, "For the Wealthiest Colleges, How Many Low-Income Students Are Enough?," *Chronicle of Higher Education*, August 11, 2016, https://www.chronicle.com/article/for-the -wealthiest-colleges-how-many-low-income-students-are-enough/.

147 "I can attest to the fact": Ronald G. Shaiko, "Admissions Is Just Part of the Diversity Puzzle," *Chronicle of Higher Education*, June 9, 2013, https://www.chronicle .com/article/admissions-is-just-part-of-the-diversity-puzzle/.

Chapter 15: How and When Small School Size Matters

150 *U.S. News* pointedly added: Robert Morse and Eric Brooks, "A More Detailed Look at the Ranking Factors," *U.S. News & World Report*, September 13, 2020,

https://www.usnews.com/education/best-colleges/articles/ranking-criteria-and
-weights.

150 In a blog post in 2017: Mark Salisbury, "Ideals, Metrics and Myths (Oh No!)," Delicious Ambiguity, November 27, 2017, https://markhsalisbury.org/2017/11/. This is a website, not a publication.

151 IDEA concluded: Stephen L. Benton and Willima H. Pallett, "Class Size Matters," Inside Higher Ed, January 29, 2013, https://www.insidehighered.com/views/2013/01/29/essay-importance-class-size-higher-education.

151 One look into the records: Eric P. Bettinger and Bridget Terry Long, "Mass Instruction or Higher Learning? The Impact of College Class Size on Student Retention and Graduation," Education Finance and Policy 13, no. 1 (Winter 2018): 97–118.

151 Another study looked at: Cissy J. Ballen et al., "Do Small Classes in Higher Education Reduce Performance Gaps in STEM?," BioScience 68, no. 8 (August 2018): 593–600, https://academic.oup.com/bioscience/article/68/8/593/5039567.

151 Other researchers: Cissy J. Ballen et al., "Smaller Classes Promote Equitable Student Participation in STEM," BioScience 69, no. 8 (August 2019): 669–80.

152 One eye-opening essay: Chad Orzel, "Why Small Colleges Are Great for Science Students," Forbes, April 10, 2015, https://www.forbes.com/sites/chadorzel/2015/04/10/why-small-colleges-are-great-for-science-students/#2de471307b9a.

152 a manuscript by the same title: Mark Umbricht and Kevin Stange, "Perception Isn't Everything: The Reality of Class Size," Association for Institutional Research, May 21, 2018, https://files.eric.ed.gov/fulltext/ED602444.pdf.

152 "Therefore," he and Stange noted: Ibid., 9.

153 "a bullshit statistic": Berlinerblau, Campus Confidential, 79.

153 56 percent: Marc Parry, "'Supersizing' the College Classroom: How One Instructor Teachers 2,670 Students," Chronicle of Higher Education, April 29, 2012, https://www.chronicle.com/article/supersizing-the-college-classroom-how-one-instructor-teaches-2-670-students/.

154 one extraordinary difference: "Strengthening the STEM Pipeline: The Contributions of Small and Mid-Sized Independent Colleges," The Council of Independent Colleges, March 2014, https://files.eric.ed.gov/fulltext/ED561080.pdf.

155 just 9 percent said: Zac Auter and Stephanie Marken, "Alumni Networks Less Helpful than Advertised," Gallup, January 15, 2019, https://news.gallup.com/opinion/gallup/245822/alumni-networks-less-helpful-advertised.aspx.

156 they published their results: John Siegfried and Malcolm Getz, "Where Do the Children of Professors Attend College?," Economics of Education Review 25, no. 2 (April 2006): 201–10.

158 I particularly like two: Irene Starygina, "Does Class Size Matter?," Unigo, June 1, 2015, https://www.unigo.com/get-to-college/college-search/does-class-size-matter.

159 Arizona State is one leader: Douglas Belkin: "At Arizona State, Big Lectures Are History," Wall Street Journal, February 27, 2019, https://www.wsj.com/articles/at-arizona-state-big-lectures-are-history-11551283201.

Chapter 16: Amenities (but Is a Lazy River a Plus?)

160   attempted to quantify how well: Brian Jacob, Brian McCall, and Kevin M. Stange, "College as Country Club: Do Colleges Cater to Students' Preferences for Consumption?," National Bureau of Economic Research, January 2013, https://www.nber.org/papers/w18745.pdf.

160   "In the way they decide": Paul Fain, "The End of College?," Inside Higher Ed, March 23, 2015.

162   not a "luxury" facility: Ali Breland, "If the Tuition Doesn't Get You, the Cost of Student Housing Will," Bloomberg Businessweek, August 14, 2019, https://www.bloomberg.com/news/features/2019-08-13/if-the-tuition-doesn-t-get-you-the-cost-of-student-housing-will.

163   tour guides note: Courtney Rubin, "Making a Splash on Campus," *New York Times*, September 19, 2014, https://www.nytimes.com/2014/09/21/fashion/college-recreation-now-includes-pool-parties-and-river-rides.html.

163   "There is nothing lazy": Chelsea Brasted, "Sure, LSU's Library Might Fall Apart, but at Least It Has a Lazy River," *Times-Picayune*, October 17, 2017, https://www.nola.com/news/education/article_b3c49345-9eb2-50e3-a8ed-9cf3a9d4ca2a.html.

163   "Quite frankly": Jack Stripling, "The Lure of the Lazy River," *Chronicle of Higher Education*, October 15, 2017, https://www.chronicle.com/article/the-lure-of-the-lazy-river/.

164   Malcolm Gladwell podcast: "Food Fight," *Revisionist History*, Season 1, Episode 5, http://revisionisthistory.com/episodes/05-food-fight.

164   Robert Kelchen: Scott Jaschik, "Food Fight," Inside Higher Ed, July 18, 2016, https://www.insidehighered.com/news/2016/07/18/malcolm-gladwell-sets-debate-over-whether-good-campus-food-prevents-more-aid-low.

164   an average school charges: Tara García Mathewson, "A Tough-to-Swallow Reason College Keeps Costing More: The Price of Meal Plans," *The Hechinger Report*, January 18, 2017, https://hechingerreport.org/tough-swallow-reason-college-keeps-costing-price-meal-plans/.

165   "provid[ing] parking for faculty": "Former UC President Clark Kerr, a National Leader in Higher Education, Dies at 92," UC Berkeley Public Affairs, December 2, 2003, https://www.berkeley.edu/news/media/releases/2003/12/02_kerr.shtml.

166   "wealthier students much more willing": Jacob, McCall, and Stange, "College as Country Club," 4.

166   "have a much greater incentive": Ibid., 37.

167   "They're *cheap*, compared to": Kevin Carey, "College Consumerism Run Amok?," *Chronicle of Higher Education*, June 24, 2009.

Chapter 17: Genuinely Reinvented Career Counseling Offices

168   A feature article: Susan Dominus, "How to Get a Job with a Philosophy Degree," *New York Times Magazine*, September 13, 2013, https://www.nytimes.com/2013/09/15/magazine/how-to-get-a-job-with-a-philosophy-degree.html.

168 "Can you hear it?": Andy Chan, "'Career Services' Must Die," TedXLawrenceU, May 3, 2013, https://www.youtube.com/watch?v=6Tc6GHWPdMU.

169 "very public commitment": "St. Olaf Publishes New Data on Activities of Recent Graduates," St. Olaf College, May 2, 2014, https://wp.stolaf.edu/news/st-olaf -publishes-new-data-on-activities-of-recent-graduates.

170 Only 6 percent: "Forging Pathways to Purposeful Work: The Role of Higher Education," Bates College–Gallup, April 4, 2019, https://www.bates.edu/purposeful -work/files/2019/05/Bates_PurposefulWork_FINAL_REPORT.pdf, 33.

170 80 percent: Ibid., 11.

170 And just 23 percent: Ibid., 14.

172 "We spent 18 months": "A Story of Acceptance," *Denison Magazine,* September, 2017, https://denisonmagazine.com/feature/a-story-of-acceptance/.

Chapter 19: Better Salaries When You Finish—*if* You Finish

181 "falsely equates a quality education": Bill Destler, "The President's New Higher Education Agenda," HuffPost, November 3, 2013, https://www.huffpost.com /entry/the-presidents-new-higher_b_3860804.

183 it was the academic major students chose: Anthony P. Carnevale et al., "Major Matters Most: The Economic Value of Bachelor's Degrees from the University of Texas System," The University of Texas System, 2017, https://files.eric.ed.gov/fulltext /ED590598.pdf.

184 eye-opening details: David Deming, "In the Salary Race, Engineers Sprint but English Majors Endure," *New York Times*, September 20, 2019, https://www.nytimes .com/2019/09/20/business/liberal-arts-stem-salaries.html.

Chapter 20: How the College of Wooster Puts It All Together

189 back to that Gallup research: Julie Ray and Stephanie Marken, "Life in College Matters for Life After College," Gallup, May 6, 2014, https://news.gallup.com /poll/168848/life-college-matters-life-college.aspx.

190 forty-third tip: Roberts, *The Thinking Student's Guide to College*, 91–92.

Chapter 21: Community College Will Save You Money, but What Might You Lose?

199 more than 700,000 students: Davis Jenkins and John Fink, "Tracking Transfer: New Measures of Institutional and State Effectiveness in Helping Community College Students Attain Bachelor's Degrees," Community College Resource Center, January 2016, https://ccrc.tc.columbia.edu/media/k2/attachments/tracking -transfer-institutional-state-effectiveness.pdf, 7.

199 only 18 percent: Ibid., 28.

200 earned degrees at the highest rates: Ibid., 1–2.

200 One study showed: Jennifer Ma and Sandy Baum, "Trends in Community Colleges: Enrollment, Prices, Student Debt, and Completion," College Board, April 2016, https://research.collegeboard.org/pdf/trends-community-colleges-research -brief.pdf, 1.

204 According to that research: Jennifer Glynn, "Persistence: The Success of Students Who Transfer from Community Colleges to Selective Four-Year Institutions," Jack Kent Cooke Foundation, January 2019, https://files.eric.ed.gov/fulltext/ED593989 .pdf.

204 29 percent: "California Community Colleges Facts and Figures," Foundation for California Community Colleges, https://foundationccc.org/About-Us/About-the -Colleges/Facts-and-Figures.

204 62 percent: Ben Terris, "Transfer Students Are Less Likely to Take Part in 'High Impact' Activities," *Chronicle of Higher Education*, November 8, 2009, https:// www.chronicle.com/article/transfer-students-are-less-likely-to-take-part-in-high -impact-activities/.

204 Another study documented: Barbara K. Townsend and Kristin B. Wilson, "The Academic and Social Integration of Persisting Community College Transfer Students," *Journal of College Student Retention: Research, Theory & Practice* 10, no. 4 (February 2009): 405–23.

205 Fink's research group wrote: Joshua Wyner et al., "The Transfer Playbook: Essential Practices for Two- and Four-Year Colleges," Community College Research Center, Teachers College, Columbia University, 2016, https://ccrc.tc.columbia.edu/media /k2/attachments/transfer-playbook-essential-practices.pdf.

Chapter 22: Honors Colleges and Programs Can Make Bigger Schools Smaller— if You Stick with the Program

208 15 percent: Unless otherwise noted, the statistics in this chapter are from the 2016 National Collegiate Honors Council's biannual census.

211 wrote a book chapter: Richard Badenhausen, "Honors Housing: Castle or Prison?," in *Housing Honors*, edited by Linda Frost, Lisa W. Kay, and Rachael Poe (Lincoln, NE: National Collegiate Honors Council, 2015), 183–191, https://files.eric.ed.gov /fulltext/ED566720.pdf.

211 wrote an article: Kevin Knudson, "'Honors' Should Mean a Challenge, Not an Upgrade to First Class," *Chronicle of Higher Education*, July 14, 2011, https://www .chronicle.com/article/honors-should-mean-a-challenge-not-an-upgrade-to-first -class/.

212 just 57 percent: Snyder, de Brey, and Dillow, *Digest of Education Statistics, 2017*, Chapter 3.

212 20 to 25 percent: Badenhausen, "Honors Housing: Castle or Prison?," 188.

Chapter 23: Attending College Abroad Is Often Cheaper, but You Won't Get What You Don't Pay For

214 Her book on the topic: Viemont, *College Beyond the States*.

Chapter 24: Athletic Scholarships for the Few (and Probably Not in Full or at Your First-Choice School)

221 Data that sprang loose: William L. Wang, "Filings Show Athletes with High Academic Scores Have 83 Percent Acceptance Rate," *Harvard Crimson*, June 30, 2018, https://www.thecrimson.com/article/2018/6/30/athlete-admissions/.

221 According to 2020 NCAA data: "NCAA Recruiting Facts," https://ncaaorg.s3 .amazonaws.com/compliance/recruiting/NCAA_RecruitingFactSheet.pdf.

222 a magazine-length story: Brad Wolverton, "The Myth of the Sports Scholarship," *Chronicle of Higher Education*, November 20, 2016, https://www.chronicle.com /article/the-myth-of-the-sports-scholarship/.

223 "Athletic recruiting is": Quoted in Edward B. Fiske, "Gaining Admission: Athletes Win Preference," *New York Times*, January 7, 2001, https://www.nytimes.com /2001/01/07/education/gaining-admission-athletes-win-preference.html

224 Gallup's survey data on the topic: Brandon Busteed and Julie Ray, "Former Student-Athletes Are Winners in Well-Being," Gallup, February 17, 2016, https:// news.gallup.com/poll/189206/former-student-athletes-winners.aspx.

Chapter 25: Gap Years: Great, Sometimes Pricey, Might Help You Get a Better Job Someday

225 I coauthored the first book: Hall and Lieber, *Taking Time Off*.

225 enrolled at the same rate: Claire Crawford and Jonathan Cribb, "Gap Year Takers: Uptake, Trends and Long Term Outcomes," Centre for Analysis of Youth Transitions (CAYT), November 30, 2012, https://assets.publishing.service.gov.uk/ government/uploads/system/uploads/attachment_data/file/219637/DFE-RR252 .pdf.

226 The effective minimum: Stacey Vanek Smith and Cardiff Garcia, "The Real Minimum Wage," NPR, May 16, 2019, https://www.npr.org/2019/05/16/723947780/ the-real-minimum-wage.

227 One Berkeley economist: Devin G. Pope, "Benefits of Bilingualism: Evidence from Mormon Missionaries," *Economics of Education Review*, 27, no. 2 (April 2008): 234–42.

228 conducted his own study: Bob Clagett's unpublished research is cited and explained in detail at https://www.gapyearassociation.org/data-benefits.php.

Chapter 26: Army, Navy, Air Force, Marines, Coast Guard: Decent Money, Big Responsibility

230 "It depends on the Army branch": "Army ROTC FAQ," U.S. Army, April 20, 2020, https://www.goarmy.com/rotc/high-school-students/faq.html.

231 Students also get a housing allowance: "Undergraduate and Graduate Degrees," U.S. Department of Veterans Affairs, April 30, 2020, https://www.va.gov/education /about-gi-bill-benefits/how-to-use-benefits/undergraduate-graduate-programs/.

231 about $25,000 per year: "Education and Training," U.S. Department of Veterans Affairs, https://www.benefits.va.gov/gibill/resources/benefits_resources/rate _tables.asp#ch33_TUITION.

231 Yellow Ribbon Program: "Yellow Ribbon Program," U.S. Department of Veterans Affairs, August 19, 2020, https://www.va.gov/education/about-gi-bill-benefits/post-9-11/yellow-ribbon-program/.

231 is not considered income: "Tax Exclusion for Veterans Education Benefits," IRS, April 30, 2020, https://www.irs.gov/individuals/tax-exclusion-for-veterans-education-benefits.

231 pay starts: "Monthly Rates of Basic Pay," Defense Finance and Accounting Service, January 1, 2020, https://www.dfas.mil/militarymembers/payentitlements/Pay-Tables/Basic-Pay/EM.html.

232 education benefits may be available: "What Is the College Fund ('Kicker') and Am I Eligible?," U.S. Department of Veterans Affairs, September 18, 2002, https://gibill.custhelp.va.gov/app/answers/detail/a_id/97/session/L3RpbWUvMTU3Mzc2MTAxNi9zaWQvZ1U4X01UdG8%3D.

232 People who want to serve: "Marine Corps," NROTC, https://www.nrotc.navy.mil/marine.html.

232 precommissioning program: "College Student Pre-Commissioning Initiative (Scholarship Program)," United States Coast Guard, https://www.gocoastguard.com/active-duty-careers/officer-opportunities/programs/college-student-pre-commissioning-initiative.

232 may pay some or all: "Army ROTC: College Scholarship FAQ," U.S. Army, April 28, 2020, https://www.goarmy.com/rotc/college-students/faq.html.

Chapter 27: Skipping College Is Probably Not a Great Idea

233 It noted that: Jaison R. Abel and Richard Deitz, "Despite Rising Costs, College Is Still a Good Investment," Federal Reserve Bank of New York, June 5, 2019, https://libertystreeteconomics.newyorkfed.org/2019/06/despite-rising-costs-college-is-still-a-good-investment.html.

234 Other data: Jaison R. Abel and Richard Deitz, "Staying in College Longer than Four Years Costs More than You Might Think," Federal Reserve Bank of New York, September 3, 2014, https://libertystreeteconomics.newyorkfed.org/2014/09/staying-in-college-longer-than-four-years-costs-more-than-you-might-think.html.

234 crunched some numbers: Douglas Webber, "Is College Worth It? Going Beyond Averages," Third Way, September 18, 2018, https://www.thirdway.org/report/is-college-worth-it-going-beyond-averages.

235 A full 25 percent: Jaison R. Abel and Richard Deitz, "College May Not Pay Off for Everyone," Federal Reserve Bank of New York, September 4, 2014, https://libertystreeteconomics.newyorkfed.org/2014/09/college-may-not-pay-off-for-everyone.html.

235 But two economists: Timothy J. Bartik and Brad J. Hershbein, "Degrees of Poverty: The Relationship Between Family Income Background and the Returns to Education," W. E. Upjohn Institute for Employment Research, March 1, 2018, https://research.upjohn.org/cgi/viewcontent.cgi?article=1302&context=up_workingpapers.

236 What St. Louis Fed researchers found: William Emmons, Ana Hernández Kent,
      and Lowell Ricketts, "Is College Still Worth It? It's Complicated," Federal Reserve
      Bank of St. Louis, February 7, 2019.

236 In 2018: Sean R. Gallagher, "Educational Credentials Come of Age: A Survey on
      the Use and Value of Educational Credentials in Hiring," Northeastern University
      Center for the Future of Higher Education and Talent Strategy, December 2018,
      https://www.northeastern.edu/cfhets/wp-content/uploads/2018/12/Educational
      _Credentials_Come_of_Age_2018.pdf.

238 Paul Tough did a good job: Paul Tough, "Welding Won't Make You Rich," *Atlan-
      tic*, September 13, 2019, https://www.theatlantic.com/education/archive/2019/09
      /welding-doesnt-pay-as-well-as-republicans-think/597733/.

239 In his book on adjunct professors: Childress, *The Adjunct Underclass*, 48.

Chapter 28: How to Make the Big Financial Plan

245 To do that: Zaloom, *Indebted*, 48.

246 The most calming formula for planning: Ron Lieber, "18 Years in the Making,"
      New York Times, April 14, 2009, https://www.nytimes.com/2009/04/19/education
      /edlife/lieber-saving-t.html.

246 In his book: McKinley, *Make Your Kid a Millionaire*, 27.

247 "Most people with kids": Ron Lieber, "How to Pay for College with Less
      Stress," *New York Times*, September 23, 2016, https://www.nytimes.com
      /2016/09/24/your-money/paying-for-college/how-to-pay-for-college-with
      -less-stress.html.

249 "In most otherwise healthy families": Lieber, "18 Years in the Making."

250 In Zaloom's anthropological study: Zaloom: *Indebted*, 66–69.

Chapter 29: How to Have the College Money Talk with Your Child

252 These studies merely show correlation: Jessica Martin, "Kids with Savings Accounts
      in Their Names Six Times More Likely to Attend College," Washington University
      in St. Louis, April 25, 2011, https://source.wustl.edu/tag/tuition-savings/.

254 "nested silences": Zaloom: *Indebted*, 147.

Chapter 31: How to Shop for College (and Where to Find the Juicy Merit Aid Data)

283 a Gallup economist: Jonathan Rothwell, "Assessing the Validity of Consumer
      Ratings for Higher Education: Evidence from a New Survey," *Journal of Consumer
      Affairs* 53, no. 1 (Spring 2019): 167–200.

Chapter 33: How to Appeal Your Financial Aid Award

295 I called up: Ron Lieber, "Appealing to a College for More Financial Aid," *New York
      Times*, April 4, 2014, https://www.nytimes.com/2014/04/05/your-money/paying
      -for-college/for-many-families-college-financial-aid-packages-are-worth-an-appeal
      .html. Change per source cited.

296 "Want to attend Cornell": "Cornell's Committent to Access and Affordability," Cornell University, https://finaid.cornell.edu/cost-attend/cornell%E2%80%99s -commitment-access-and-affordability.

296 Among the 455 colleges: Stephen Burd et al., "Decoding the Cost of College: The Case for Transparent Financial Aid Award Letters," New America and uAspire, June 5, 2018, https://d1y8sb8igg2f8e.cloudfront.net/documents/Decoding_the _Cost_of_College_Final_6218.pdf.

298 sniffing out cheaters: Kantrowitz, *How to Appeal for More Financial Aid*, 65.

298 "You know how there was": Stephen Burd, "Merit Aid Madness," *Washington Monthly*, September–October, 2013, https://washingtonmonthly.com/magazine /septoct-2013/merit-aid-madness/.

301 "Colleges have to deal": Lieber, "Appealing to a College for More Financial Aid."

Chapter 34: All the Student Loan Basics in One Tidy Place

306 One study: Judy T. Lin et al., "The State of U.S. Financial Capability" The 2018 National Financial Capability Study," FINRA Investor Education Foundation, June 2019, 28.

308 Gallup research from 2015: Sean Seymour, "Gallup-Purdue Index 2015 Report Now Available," Gallup, September 29, 2015, https://news.gallup.com/opinion /gallup/185942/gallup-purdue-index-2015-report-available.aspx.

308 Consider the study: Ruffalo Noel Levitz, "2019 Discounting Report for Four-Year Private and Public Institutions," 9.

309 According to a 2019 study: Sandy Baum, Kristin Blagg, and Rachel Fishman, "Re-shaping Parent PLUS Loans," Urban Institute, April 2019, https://www.urban .org/sites/default/files/publication/100106/reshaping_parent_plus_loans.pdf, 2, 6, 7, 8.

310 fell by 36 percent: Nick Anderson, "Tighter Federal Lending Standards Yield Turmoil for Historically Black Colleges," *Washington Post*, June 22, 2013, https:// www.washingtonpost.com/local/education/tighter-federal-lending-standards -yield-turmoil-for-historically-black-colleges/2013/06/22/6ade4acc-d9a5-11e2 -a9f2-42ee3912ae0e_story.html.

310 as I was writing a column: Ron Lieber, "Why It Makes Good Sense to Save for College Now," *New York Times*, October 23, 2015, https://www.nytimes.com/2015 /10/24/your-money/why-it-makes-good-sense-to-save-for-college-now.html.

311 25 percent of people: Baum, Blagg and Fishman, "Reshaping Parent PLUS Loans," 9.

BIBLIOGRAPHY

Akers, Beth, and Matthew M. Chingos. *Game of Loans: The Rhetoric and Reality of Student Debt.* Princeton, NJ: Princeton University Press, 2016.

Alumni Factor. *The Alumni Factor: A Revolution in College Rankings.* Avondale Estates, GA: Alumni Factor, 2013.

Anders, George. *You Can Do Anything: The Surprising Power of a "Useless" Liberal Arts Education.* New York: Back Bay Books, 2019.

Archibald, Robert B., and David H. Feldman. *Why Does College Cost So Much?* New York: Oxford University Press, 2011.

Arum, Richard, and Josipa Roksa. *Academically Adrift: Limited Learning on College Campuses.* Chicago: University of Chicago Press, 2011.

———. *Aspiring Adults Adrift: Tentative Transitions of College Graduates.* Chicago: University of Chicago Press, 2014.

Belasco, Andrew, Dave Bergman, and Michael Trivette. *Colleges Worth Your Money: A Guide to What America's Top Colleges Can Do for You.* Lanham, MD: Rowman & Littlefield, 2020.

Berlinerblau, Jacques. *Campus Confidential: How College Works, or Doesn't, for Professors, Parents, and Students.* Brooklyn, NY: Melville House, 2017.

Bissonnette, Zac. *Debt-Free U: How I Paid for an Outstanding College Education Without Loans, Scholarships or Mooching Off My Parents.* New York: Portfolio, 2010.

Blumenstyk, Goldie. *American Higher Education in Crisis? What Everyone Needs to Know.* New York: Oxford University Press, 2015.

Bruni, Frank. *Where You Go Is Not Who You'll Be: An Antidote to the College Admissions Mania.* New York: Grand Central Publishing, 2015.

Cappelli, Peter. *Will College Pay Off? A Guide to the Most Important Financial Decision You'll Ever Make.* New York: Public Affairs, 2015.

Carey, Kevin. *The End of College: Creating the Future of Learning and the University of Everywhere.* New York: Riverhead Books, 2015.

Chambliss, Daniel F., and Christopher G. Takacs. *How College Works.* Cambridge, MA: Harvard University Press, 2014.

Childress, Herb. *The Adjunct Underclass: How America's Colleges Betrayed Their Faculty, Their Students, and Their Mission.* Chicago: University of Chicago Press, 2019.

Craig, Ryan. *College Disrupted: The Great Unbundling of Higher Education.* New York: Palgrave Macmillan, 2015.

Damon, William. *Greater Expectations: Overcoming the Culture of Indulgence in Our Homes and Schools*. New York: Free Press, 1996.

Deresiewicz, William. *Excellent Sheep: The Miseducation of the American Elite and the Way to a Meaningful Life*. New York: Free Press, 2014.

Duffy, Elizabeth A., and Idana Goldberg. *Crafting a Class: College Admissions and Financial Aid, 1955–1994*. Princeton, NJ: Princeton University Press, 1998.

Ehrenreich, Barbara. *Fear of Falling: The Inner Life of the Middle Class*. New York: HarperPerennial, 1990.

Epstein, Joseph. *Snobbery: The American Version*. New York: Mariner Books, 2002.

Ferguson, Andrew. *Crazy U: One Dad's Adventures in Getting His Kid into College*. New York: Simon & Schuster, 2011.

Fussell, Paul. *Class: A Guide Through the American Status System*. New York: Touchstone, 1992.

Gobel, Reyna. *CliffsNotes Parents' Guide to Paying for College and Repaying Student Loans*. New York: Houghton Mifflin Harcourt, 2016.

Goldrick-Rab, Sara. *Paying the Price: College Costs, Financial Aid, and the Betrayal of the American Dream*. Chicago: University of Chicago Press, 2016.

Grawe, Nathan D. *Demographics and the Demand for Higher Education*. Baltimore: Johns Hopkins University Press, 2018.

Hall, Colin, and Ron Lieber. *Taking Time Off: Inspiring Stories of Students Who Enjoyed Successful Breaks From College and How You Can Plan Your Own*. New York: Noonday Press, 1996.

Hibbs, B. Janet, and Anthony Rostain. *The Stressed Years of Their Lives: Helping Your Kid Survive and Thrive During Their College Years*. New York: St. Martin's Press, 2019.

Hoxby, Caroline (editor). *College Choices: The Economics of Where to Go, When to Go, and How to Pay for It*. Chicago: University of Chicago Press, 2004.

Kantrowitz, Mark. *How to Appeal for More Financial Aid: The Secrets to Negotiating a Better Financial Aid Offer . . . and Getting More Financial Aid in the First Place!* Skokie, IL: Cerebly, 2019.

Kelchen, Robert. *Higher Education Accountability*. Baltimore: Johns Hopkins University Press, 2018.

Klinenberg, Eric. *Palaces for the People: How Social Infrastructure Can Help Fight Inequality, Polarization, and the Decline of Civic Life*. New York: Crown, 2018.

Lieber, Ron. *The Opposite of Spoiled: Raising Kids Who Are Grounded, Generous, and Smart About Money*. New York: Harper, 2015.

Maguire, John, and Lawrence Butler. *EM = C Squared: A New Formula for Enrollment Management*. Bloomington, IN: Trafford Publishing, 2008.

Martin, Robert E. *The College Cost Disease: Higher Cost and Lower Quality.* Northampton, MA: Edward Elgar, 2011.

McCabe, Janice M. *Connecting in College: How Friendship Networks Matter for Academic and Social Success.* Chicago: University of Chicago Press, 2016.

McGee, Jon. *Breakpoint: The Changing Marketplace for Higher Education.* Baltimore: Johns Hopkins University Press, 2015.

———. *Dear Parents: A Field Guide for College Preparation.* Baltimore: Johns Hopkins University Press, 2018.

McKinley, Kevin. *Make Your Kid a Millionaire: 11 Easy Ways Anyone Can Secure a Child's Financial Future.* New York: Fireside, 2002.

Muller, Jerry Z. *The Tyranny of Metrics.* Princeton, NJ: Princeton University Press, 2018.

O'Shaughnessy, Lynn. *The College Solution: A Guide for Everyone Looking for the Right School at the Right Price.* Upper Saddle River, NJ: Pearson, 2012.

Porter, Eduardo. *The Price of Everything: Finding Method in the Madness of What Things Cost.* New York: Portfolio, 2012.

Quart, Alissa. *Squeezed: Why Our Families Can't Afford America.* New York: Ecco, 2018.

Richards, Carl, *The Behavior Gap: Simple Ways to Stop Doing Dumb Things with Money.* New York: Portfolio, 2012.

Rivera, Lauren A. *Pedigree: How Elite Students Get Elite Jobs.* Princeton, NJ: Princeton University Press, 2015.

Roberts, Andrew. *The Thinking Students Guide to College: 75 Tips for Getting a Better Education.* Chicago: University of Chicago Press, 2010.

Schlesinger, Jill. *The Dumb Things Smart People Do with Their Money: Thirteen Ways to Right Your Financial Wrongs.* New York: Ballantine, 2019.

Selingo, Jeffrey J. *There Is Life After College: What Parents and Students Should Know About Navigating School to Prepare for the Jobs of Tomorrow.* New York: William Morrow, 2016.

Sidanius, James, Shana Levin, Colette Van Laar, and David O. Sears. *The Diversity Challenge: Social Identity and Intergroup Relations on the College Campus.* New York: Russell Sage Foundation, 2008.

Smith, Daryl G. *Diversity Works: The Emerging Picture of How Students Benefit.* Washington, D.C.: Association of American Colleges and Universities, 1997.

Snyder, Thomas D., Cristobal de Brey, and Sally A. Dillow. *Digest of Education Statistics, 2017.* Washington, D.C.: National Center for Education Statistics, January 2019.

Stack, Carol, and Ruth Vedick. *Financial Aid Handbook: Getting the Education You Want for the Price You Can Afford.* Franklin Lakes, NJ: Career Press, 2011.

Steinberg, Jacques. *The Gatekeepers: Inside the Admissions Process of a Premier College*. New York: Penguin Books, 2003.

Stross, Randall. *A Practical Education: Why Liberal Arts Majors Make Great Employees*. Stanford, CA: Redwood Press, 2017.

Tough, Paul. *The Years That Matter Most: How College Makes or Breaks Us*. New York: Houghton Mifflin Harcourt, 2019.

Zaloom, Caitlin. *Indebted: How Families Make College Work at Any Cost*. Princeton, NJ: Princeton University Press, 2019.

INDEX

Abboud, Araam, 146–147, 193

ABLE accounts, 268

Academically Adrift (Arum and Roksa), 110, 111, 112

ACCEPT (Admissions Community Cultivating Equity & Peace Today), 144

accreditation, 63

Active Minds, 120

adjunct professors, 99, 100–102, 107, 153, 239

Adjunct Underclass, The (Childress), 104, 239

administrative bloat, 19–20

admission scandal, 93

admissions. *See also* financial aid
    evolution of, 37–38
    legacy, 71
    merit aid and, 37–40
    mistrust of process for, 93
    need-blind, 275
    race and, 221
    tightening standards for, 71
    transfer, 199–206

advisor fees, 262

Allen, Jeff, 254

Alumni Factor, 283–284

alumni giving, 155

alumni networks, 155

alumni support for troubled colleges, 65–66

amenities, 18–19, 160–167

American Airlines, 43

American Association of University Professors (AAUP), 99, 101

American Institute of Certified Educational Planners (AICEP), 291

AmeriCorps, 227

Amherst College, 57, 116, 143, 161, 179

Amsterdam University College, 219–220

Anderson, David R., 38–39, 144, 146, 173–174

Anglo-American University, 218

annual discounting study, 16, 24–25, 47

application fee waivers, 43

architecture, 161–162

Arizona State University, 66, 159

Armstrong, Elizabeth A., 128–129

articulation agreements, 201

Arum, Richard, 110, 111, 112, 114, 132

Aspiring Adults Adrift (Arum and Roksa), 132

assets
    financial aid determination and, 26
    graduation rates and, 252

Association for University and College Counseling Center Directors Annual Survey, 118–119

Association of American Medical Colleges, 179

athletic scholarships, 221–224, 256

Augustana College, 150

baby bust, 58–59

Bad with Money with Gaby Dunn (podcast), 55

Badenhausen, Richard, 209–210, 211, 212

Bain, 90

Baker, Kathleen, 117
Barrett, the Honors College at
    Arizona State University, 209
Bates College, 169–171
bed sizes, 165
Bentley University, 105–106
Berlant, Lauren, 78
Berlinerblau, Jacques, 98, 107–108,
    112, 153
"better off," data regarding, 72–74
Beyond the States, 214
"big fish in a little pond" effect,
    130–131
BigFuture website, 245
Bigham, Marie, 144–145, 146
Bischoff, Rick, 29, 50
Bob Jones University, 133
Boeckenstedt, Jon, 27
Bok, Derek, 98
Bolton, Sarah R., 189–191, 192, 195
Bontrager, Bob, 41
Boston University, 46
Bowdoin, 61, 122, 164, 284
*Breakpoint: The Changing
    Marketplace for Higher
    Education* (McGee), 41, 66
Bribitzer-Stull, Matthew, 210
Brigham Young University, 132, 177,
    178
brokerage accounts, 26, 269–271
Brown, Dorothy A., 143
Bruni, Frank, 91, 92
Busteed, Brandon, 103, 104–105,
    106, 162
Butler University, 106

California State University, 151
California State University, Chico,
    151
Calvin University, 178
Campbell, Mary Schmidt, 6
Campus Confidential (Berlinerblau),
    153

campus visits, preparing for, 274–279,
    283–284
"'Career Services' Must Die" (Chan),
    168–169
careers/jobs
    counseling offices for, 168–176
    impact of selective colleges on
        prospects for, 85–86, 88–94
    salary levels after graduation,
        181–186, 233–235, 279–280
Carey, Kevin, 64–66, 67, 160, 167
Carleton, 177–178
Carnegie Mellon, 53
Case, Joe Paul, 9
Case Western Reserve University, 39,
    49–50
Center for Collegiate Mental Health
    at Penn State University, 118
Centre College in Kentucky, 282
certified financial planners (CFPs),
    289–290
Chambliss, Daniel F., 108, 313
Chan, Andy, 168–169, 172
Chany, Kalman A., 25
checking accounts, EFC calculations
    and, 26
Chetty, Raj, 84, 142
children
    of faculty, 156–157, 194–195
    savings accounts for, 252
    talking about money to, 252–259
    teaching about money, 134–135
children, talking about college money
    with, 252–259
Childress, Herb, 104, 107, 239
Chivas Regal effect, 51–52
Christensen, Clayton M., 58
Chronicle of Higher Education, 280
CLA (Collegiate Learning
    Assessment), 111, 112–114
Clagett, Bob, 227–228
Claremont Colleges consortium, 120,
    178

Clark, Kim, 295

clash of ideas, 115

Class: A Guide Through the American Status System (Fussell), 86

class size
 impact of, 150–153
 at large schools, 155–156
 preferences regarding, 157–159
 at women's colleges, 137

Clemson University, 155, 285

climbing walls, 162–163

clinical load index, 119

Colby College, 143

Coleman, David, 108–109

College Beyond the States (Viemont), 214

College Board
 on price increases, 17
 SAT and, 108
 on women's colleges, 137

College Financial Lady, The (blog; Garcia), 23

College Insights, 279

college newspapers, 280, 284

College of Saint Benedict, 66–67

College of the Atlantic, 185

College of the Holy Cross, 46

College of Wooster, 146–147, 187–195, 276

College Raptor, 279

college savings calculator, 245

College Scorecard, 181–184, 279–280

college wage premium, 233

Colleges Worth Your Money (Belasco, Bergman, and Trivette), 192

Collegiate Learning Assessment (CLA), 111, 112–114

Collins, Billy, 193

Colorado College, 122, 143, 225–226

Columbia University, 61, 282

common data set (CDS), 49, 141–142, 182, 277–278

Community College Research Center, 199, 200

community colleges, 199–206

Compton, Darlene, 122–123

Congress, 91, 138

Connecticut College, 39

Connecting in College (McCabe), 127

consultants, 44–45, 47–48, 53

consumption amenities, 160–167

Cornell University, 151, 178, 179, 294–295

coronavirus pandemic, 5–7, 60–63, 65, 153

cosigning loans, 303, 306–307

cost, price versus, 15. *See also* financial aid; tuition costs

Council of Independent Colleges, 154

Council on Undergraduate Research, 194

Crafting a Class: College Admissions and Financial Aid: 1955–1994 (Duffy and Goldberg), 37

credential inflation, 237

credit card rewards, 273

Cruel Optimism (Berlant), 78

Crush, The (podcast; Sweeney), 42

CSS Profile form, 29–30, 33, 35, 275

curricular choice, 257

Cuseo, Vince, 12, 277

Dale, Stacy, 83

Dale-Krueger research, 83

Daniels, Mitch, Jr., 102–103, 114–115

Darcy-Mahoney, Ashley, 255–256

Dartmouth College, 108, 127, 294

de Aguiar, Molly, 217, 219–220

Deardurff, Mindy, 174–175

Decatur, Sean M., 54

deferment on loans, 304

Delahunty, Jennifer, 297

Delta Cost Project, 19–20

Deming, David, 184

Demographics and the Demand for Higher Education (Grawe), 59
demonstrated interest, 53
Demos (think tank), 18, 20
Denison University, 39–40, 108, 122, 122–123, 172–173, 223
Deresiewicz, William, 98, 104
dining halls, 163–165
direct loans, 304–305
Direct PLUS Loan program, 247, 304, 305, 309–311
disabilities, accounts for, 268
Discounting Report for Four-Year Private and Public Institutions, 142
discounts. *See* financial aid; merit aid; need-based aid
disengagement compact, 112
diversity
    administration needs and, 19–20
    benefits of, 140–141
    honors colleges and programs and, 212
    income and, 141–144
    race and, 144–145
    religious, 146–147
    roommates and, 128
    self-perpetuating cycles and, 148
divorce, financial aid determination and, 26
dorms, 129, 130, 133–134, 161–162, 165, 211–212. *See also* roommates
double beds, 165
downward mobility, fear of, 72
Drew University, 53
Duke University, 127, 128
Dunn, Gaby, 57
dysfunctionality narrative, 18

early action, 286
Early Aid Estimator, 192

early decision, size of discounts and, 54
Edmit, 280, 298
"Educational Credentials Come of Age" (Gallagher), 236–237
elitism, snobbery and, 85–94
Ellis, Zakiya Smith, 56
Emory University, 60, 143, 283
End of College, The (Carey), 65, 68
enrollment management, 44
Epstein, Joseph, 86, 94
equivalency sports, 222
Excellent Sheep (Deresiewicz), 104
expected family contribution (EFC), 25–33, 35, 263

faculty and teaching staff
    adjunct professors as, 99, 100–102, 107, 153, 239
    children of, 156–157, 194–195
    experienced, 97–109
    graduate students as, 99, 101–102
    part-time, 100–102, 107
    ratio of to administrators, 20
    salaries and benefits of, 21–22
    student-faculty ratio and, 100, 153, 155–156
    teaching quality and, 97–109
    tenure track positions for, 99–102
    at women's colleges, 137
"Fading American Dream, The," 73
FAFSA (Free Application for Federal Student Aid), 24–27, 29, 30–31, 34, 36, 46, 275
Faith Baptist Bible College and Theological Seminary, 132
Falik, Abby, 229
family contribution, expected, 23–34, 264
Family Educational Rights and Privacy Act (FERPA; 1974), 123–124
fear, 71–75

Federal Reserve Bank of St. Louis, 235–236
fees, waivers for application, 44
Fidelity Rewards Visa Signature Card, 273
financial aid. *See also* merit aid; need-based aid
  appealing award of, 294–302
  application process for, 2
  award letters for, 35–36
  divorce and, 26
  529 plans and, 263–265
  gap years and, 226
  grades and, 254–257
  income and, 26
  optimization of, 44
  Roth IRAs and, 269
  test scores and, 278
  for veterans, 231
  at Wooster, 191–192
Financial Industry Regulatory Authority (FINRA), 306
financial plan, 243–251
financial planners, 289–292
FinancialAidLetter.com, 296
Fink, John, 200, 202, 203, 205–206
first destinations, 174
529 plans, 27, 215–216, 260–273
Florida State, 179
fly-in weekends, 146
food services, 163–165
forbearance for loans, 305
Forbes, 282
for-profit education, 64
Fortune 500 CEOs, 91
457 plan, 260–261
401(k), 260–261, 267
403(b), 260–261
Fox, Deborah, 301
Franklin & Marshall, 40
fraternities, 129–130, 134, 155
Freakonomics podcast, 115
Friedhoff, Scott, 188

Frye, Lisa, 201–202
full-tuition scholarships, 286–287
Fussell, Paul, 86

Gallagher, Sean, 236–237
Gallup-Purdue Index Report, 103–106
gap years, 225–229
gapping, 275, 297, 308–309
Garcia, Ann, 23–24, 31–33, 311
Garrett Planning Network, 291
gender
  class size and, 151–152
  gap years and, 226
  honors colleges and programs and, 212
  impact of selective colleges and, 83–84
  income potential and, 73
  post-college earnings and, 235
  salary levels after graduation and, 184
  STEM courses and, 151–152
  women's colleges and, 136–139
genius grants, 92
George Washington University, 60–61, 174, 255–256
Georgetown University Center on Education and the Workforce, 183
Georgia Tech, 155, 178
GI Bill benefits, 216, 231
Ginsburg, Ruth Bader, 145
Gladwell, Malcolm, 163–164
Global Citizen Year, 227, 229
global commerce program, 173
goals of college attendance, 5
Goddard College, 185
Goldberg, Maureen McRae, 206, 258–259, 300–301, 302
grades, merit aid and, 254–257
graduate schools, improving odds regarding, 177–180

graduate students, instruction from, 99, 101–102

graduation rates, 181, 252

Grafton, Anthony, 98

Granello, Paul, 121, 122

Grawe, Nathan D., 59–60

Greek system, 128–130, 134, 155

Green Mountain College, 66

Guilford College, 40

Guillen, Priscila, 170–172

guilt, 76–84

Gutow, Jonathan, 194

Hamilton, Laura T., 129

Hamilton College, 40, 108, 113, 130

Hampshire College, 66–67

Handshake, 171

Hanycz, Colleen M., 57

Harbeck, Stephen, 201–202

Harding University, 133

Harrington, Katharine, 30, 55, 277

Harvard University, 178, 221

Harvey Mudd College, 120, 124, 133, 178

Hatch, Mark, 225–226

head-count sports, 222

health care, costs of, 20, 79

Health Insurance Portability and Accountability Act (HIPAA; 1996), 123–124

Herman, Tom, 135

High Point University, 165–166, 285

"high-contact dorms," 133

Higher Education Consultants Association (HECA), 292

home equity
   CSS Profile form and, 31
   excluded from EFC calculations, 27

honors colleges and programs, 207–213

honors contracts, 209, 210

honors housing, 211–212

honors living communities, 211–212

hope, 313–317

housing costs, 79

How College Works (Chambliss and Takacs), 108, 133, 314

How to Appeal for More College Financial Aid (Kantrowitz), 298

How to Raise an Adult (Lythcott-Haims), 145

Husky Rock, 162

IDEA Center, 150–151

income
   diversity and, 141–144
   effect on price of, 17
   financial aid determination and, 25–26
   inequality of, 60, 235
   mobility and, 72–74

income-driven payment programs, 305, 307

incubators, 91

Indebted: How Families Make College Work at Any Cost (Zaloom), 29, 77, 244–245, 253–254

independent college counselors, 288–289, 292–293

Independent Educational Consultants Association (IECA), 292

Independent Study (IS), 188–190, 192–193

Indiana University, 129

individual retirement account (IRA), 260–261

inequity in merit aid process, 46–48

Innovator's Dilemma, The (Christensen), 59

Inside Higher Ed, 281

instructors, experienced, 97–109

internships, 175, 204, 208, 218

investment 529 plans, 262, 265–267
"Is College Worth It? Going Beyond
    Averages" (Webber), 234–235
Itzkowitz, Michael, 184–185

Jack Kent Cooke Foundation, 204
James Madison University (JMU), 87
jobs/careers
    counseling offices for, 168–176
    impact of selective colleges on
        prospects for, 85–86, 88–94
    salary levels after graduation,
        181–186, 233–235, 281

Kantrowitz, Mark, 246, 247–248,
    298, 299, 301
Kelchen, Robert, 7, 164
Kent, Jennie, 215, 217
Kenyon College, 39, 56
Kerr, Clark, 165
Kleiner Perkins, 91
Knudson, Kevin, 211
Krueger, Alan, 83
K-shaped recovery, 63
Kuh, George D., 112
Kutztown University, 201–202
Kyle, Michael, 57

La Salle University, 56–57
Lafayette College, 178
lasagna test, 108
laundry facilities, 162
law school, 179
Law School Admissions Council, 179
lazy rivers, 18, 163
learning, quality of, 110–115. See also
    faculty and teaching staff
legacy admissions, 71
leisure pools, 163
Leonhardt, David, 142
loan defaults, 306
loan delinquencies, 305–306

loans
    cosigning, 304, 307–308
    deferment on, 305
    direct, 304–305
    Direct PLUS Loan program for,
        247, 304, 305, 308–312
    forbearance for, 305
    parent, 304, 308–309
    private, 304, 307
    student, 76–77, 246, 247–248,
        296–297, 303–312
    subsidized student, 304–305
    unsubsidized student, 304–305
Louisiana State University, 163
Loyola University, 286
Lucido, Jerome A., 48
Lythcott-Haims, Julie, 145

Macalester College, 124, 174–175
MacArthur Foundation, 92
MacKenzie, Lauren, 211–212
Mahoney, Kevin, 248, 250, 256
Make Your Kid a Millionaire
    (McKinley), 246–247
Marlboro College, 185
marriage prospects, 131–133
Martin Luther College, 133
Massa, Bob, 257
Maurer, Tim, 9
McCabe, Janice M., 127
McCartney, Kathleen, 40, 136,
    139
McClure, Kevin, 166
McGee, John, 41, 66–67
McGill University, 215
McKinley, Kevin, 246–248,
    249–250, 257–258
McKinsey, 90
medical school, 179–180
medical services, cost of, 21, 79
mental health, 19, 116–125
mentors, 102–109, 139, 189, 191, 205

merit aid/discounts. *See also* financial
        aid; need-based aid
    appealing award of, 294–295,
        301–302
    athletes and, 223
    average rate of, 16–17
    to cover demonstrated financial
        need, 49
    eagerness and, 53–54
    early decision and, 54
    expansion of, 39–42
    finding data on, 274–286
    grades and, 254–257
    inequity of, 46–48
    list prices and, 52–53
    mainstreaming of, 35–42
    need-based aid in lieu of, 55–56
    opaqueness of process for, 50–52
    origins of, 38–39
    prevalence of, 187
    at private colleges and universities,
        16–17
    at public universities, 17, 40–41
    rates of, 16
    reasons for, 15–16
    system of, 42–56
MeritMore, 279
middle class, economic precariousness
    of, 77–78
Middlebury College, 132, 227–228
Mihalick, Jennifer, 194–195
military, 230–232
mobility
    fear of downward, 72
    impact of selective colleges and,
        84
    income, 72–74
    political leanings and, 74
    relative versus absolute, 73
    upward, 71–72
money. *See also* financial aid; merit
        aid; need-based aid; tuition costs

    talking to children about, 252–259
    teaching kids about, 135
Money magazine, 282
Morehouse College, 179
Morningstar, 267
Morse, Bob, 281
mortgages
    reverse, 244
    tuition costs compared to, 2
Mount Holyoke College, 40, 53
Mydland, Anabel, 149, 157–158
"Myth of Sports Scholarship, The"
        (Wolverton), 222

National Association of College and
        University Business Officers
        (NACUBO), 16–17, 48
National College Advocacy Group
        (NCAG), 292
National Collegiate Honors Council,
        210, 211, 212, 213
National Hispanic Recognition
        Program, 24
National Science Foundation, 177
National Survey of Student
        Engagement study, 138
NCAA, scholarship rules and,
        223–224
need-based aid. *See also* financial aid;
        merit aid
    appealing award of, 294–295,
        298–301
    description of, 15
    FAFSA and, 25
    in lieu of merit aid, 55–56
    merit aid for, 49
    rates of, 16
need-blind admissions, 275
nested silences, 254
net price calculators, 31–32, 49
        276–277
New America, 55, 296

"New Depression in Higher Education, The," 58

New School's Eugene Lang College of Liberal Arts, 295

New York Times, 281

New York University, 60–61, 283

NOLS (National Outdoor Leadership School), 227

nonacademic construction, costs of, 18

Northeastern University, 60–61, 62, 282, 283

Northwestern University, 102, 105, 155

Obama, Barack, 181, 310

Oberlin College, 40, 116

Occidental College, 295

Oglethorpe University, 276

Ohio State University, 189

Ohio Wesleyan University, 38

O'Malley, Martin, 310–311

online learning, 6–7, 61–64, 66

Organisation for Economic Co-operation and Development, 17–18

Orzel, Chad, 152

Osborne, Peter, 171

Outward Bound, 227

pandemic, 5–7, 61–64, 66, 153

parent loans, 304, 308–309

parents (student's grandparents) help from, 79, 248–250, 272

part-time faculty, 100–102, 107

party pathway, 128–130

Paying for College 101 Facebook group, 280, 286, 287

Paying for College (Chany), 25

Paying for the Party: How College Maintains Inequality (Armstrong and Hamilton), 129, 130

Pedigree: How Elite Students Get Elite Jobs (Rivera), 89–90

peer relationships, 126–135

Pell Grants, 25, 141–142, 143–144, 164, 182, 201

Pennsylvania State University, 177, 286

Perrault, Lara Mordenti, 286–287

persistence data, 154, 181–182

Pew Research Center, 72

PhD programs, 177–178

PLUS Loans, 246, 247, 295–296, 307–311

political leaning, mobility expectations and, 74

Pomona College, 116, 178, 179

Porter, Dusty, 121, 124

prepaid 529 plans, 261–262

price. *See also* financial aid; tuition costs

    Chivas Regal effect and, 52–53

    cost versus, 15

    effect of income on, 17

Princeton Review, 283

Princeton University, 62, 131–132, 189, 283

Private College 529 plan, 263

private colleges and universities, discounts at, 16–17

private loans, 304, 307

professional pathway, 129

provisioning, 250

PSAT information, 44

public universities

    decline in state appropriations for, 20

    discounts at, 17, 40–41

Purdue University, 102–103, 178, 209, 211–212

purpose gap, 170

Quart, Alissa, 77–78

race
    CLA scores and, 111
    community colleges and, 200
    diversity and, 144–145
    Harvard's admissions policies and,
      221
    honors colleges and programs and,
      212
    impact of selective colleges and,
      83, 94
    income potential and, 73
    mental health and, 120
    post-college earnings and, 235
    roommates and, 127–128
    at women's colleges, 138–139
rankings, 280–283
relative versus absolute mobility, 73
religious diversity, 146–147
Repella, Michael, 209, 211
research, prioritized over teaching,
    98–99
Reserve Officers Training Corps
    (ROTC), 232
residence halls, 128, 130, 133–134,
    161–162, 165, 211–212. *See also*
    roommates
retention data, 154, 181–182,
    212–213, 277
retirement accounts, 26, 244,
    260–261, 269
reverse mortgages, 244
Rhodes, Dawn, 41
Rice University, 53
Richards, Carl, 9, 75, 245
Richards, Kelly, 256–257
Rivera, Lauren A., 89–90
Roberts, Andrew, 99, 190
Rochester Institute of Technology,
    181
Roksa, Josipa, 110, 111, 112, 114, 132
roommates, 126–128. *See also* dorms
Rose-Hulman Institute of
    Technology, 132, 223

Rosenberg, Brian, 19, 56, 124, 125, 156
Roth IRAs, 269
Royo-Schottland, Marguerite,
    80–82, 83
Ruffalo Noel Levitz, 16–17, 24–25,
    45, 142, 308
Rutgers University, 219

Saint John's University, 66–67
salaries and benefits, as percentage of
    tuition costs, 21–22
salary levels after graduation,
    181–186, 233–235, 279–280
Salisbury, Mark, 150
Sarah Lawrence College, 295
SAT, 109
Savingforcollege.com, 267
savings
    children's accounts for, 252
    EFC calculations and, 26
    interest on, 246, 265–266
    plan for, 246–248
savings bonds, 268–269
Schapiro, Morton, 105
ScholarshipStats.com, 222
science, at women's colleges, 138
Seattle University, 117
seekUT, 186
sexual intercourse, 165
Shaiko, Ronald G., 147
shopping for college, 274–286
Singer, Rick, 93
single-session approach, 122
size of schools, 149–159
skipping college, 233–239
SMART Lab, 121–122
Smith, Philip, 223
Smith College, 40, 116, 136, 139, 178
Smucker, Jeremy, 193
Sneed, Greg, 172
snobbery and elitism, 85–94
Snobbery: The American Version
    (Epstein), 86

sororities, 128–130, 134, 155
Southern New Hampshire University, 66
Spelman College, 179
Spencer, Clayton, 169–170
sports general managers, 92
Squeezed: Why Our Families Can't Afford America (Quart), 77–78
St. John's College, 52
St. Olaf College, 169, 173–174, 178
Standifird, Stephen, 106
Stanford University, 57
Stange, Kevin, 152–153
Starr, G. Gabrielle, 117–118, 123, 156
startup schools, potential for, 63–64
STEM courses, 154, 184
strategic plans, 275
Student Aid Index (SAI), 25, 27, 30–31, 263
student loans, 76–77, 246, 247–248, 295–296, 302–311
student-faculty ratio, 100, 153, 155–156
studying, hours spent, 111–112
studying abroad, 214–220
"Subsidies, Hierarchy and Peers: The Awkward Economics of Higher Education," 5
subsidized student loans, 304–305
success, description of, 312–313
suicide attempts, 120, 122, 124
"summer melt" period, 44
Survey of Earned Doctorates, 177
Swarthmore College, 178
Sweeney, Davin, 42
Sweet Briar College, 65–66
Swierczewski family, 87–88
SwiftStudent, 297
Symposium, 192–193

Takacs, Christopher G., 108, 133, 313
target-date funds, 266

taxes
    expected family contribution (EFC) an, 25
    529 plans and, 215–216, 261, 262–263, 267–271, 273
    GI Bill benefits and, 231
    retirement accounts and, 260–261
teaching, quality of, 97–109
tenure track positions, 99–100
test scores, 278
Thinking Student's Guide to College, The (Roberts), 190
Third Way, 184–185, 234–235
Thompson, Roger, 40
threshold earnings data, 184
tips system, 223
Tough, Paul, 238
transfer admissions, 199–206
"Transfer Playbook, The," 205
Treadgold, Steve, 135
Trinity College, 143
Tufts University, 59–60, 179, 282
tuition costs
    allotment of to operational costs, 18
    compared to mortgage, 2
    increases in, 1
    lowering of, 55–56
    negotiation over, 2
    percent of needed for salaries and benefits, 21–22
Tuition Tracker, 279
TuitionFit, 150, 279
Tulane University, 59–60, 120–121, 282, 286

uAspire, 295
UC Berkeley Center for Labor Research and Education, 100–101
UGMAs (Uniform Gifts to Minors Act), 271–272
Umbricht, Mark, 152–153

Unigo, 158
United States Air Force Academy, 132
United States Coast Guard Academy, 132
United States Military Academy, 132
University of Alabama, 40, 285
University of Amsterdam, 219–220
University of California at Berkeley, 100–101, 162, 177, 178, 179
University of California, Los Angeles (UCLA), 177, 179
University of California San Diego, 179
University of California system, 204
University of Cambridge, 215
University of Chicago, 282
University of Delaware, 285
"university of everywhere," 64–65
University of Florida, 178, 179, 211
University of Georgia, 285
University of Illinois, 178
University of Maryland, Baltimore County, 283, 285
University of Michigan, 177, 179
University of Minnesota, 116, 151, 208–209, 210
University of Missouri, 163
University of North Carolina, 61, 87, 155, 228, 285
University of Notre Dame, 150, 155
University of Oregon, 255
University of Oxford, 215
University of Pennsylvania, 122, 164–165
University of Puget Sound, 151
University of Southern California, 53–54, 59–60, 155, 161, 211
University of Southern California's Center for Enrollment Research, Policy and Practice, 47
University of St. Andrews, 215

University of Texas, 179, 183, 186, 255
University of Toronto, 215
University of Vermont, 116, 282
University of Washington, 162
unsubsidized student loans, 303–304
Upromise, 272
upward mobility, expectations regarding, 71–72
Urban Institute, 308, 310
U.S. Bureau of Labor Statistics, 238
U.S. Department of Education, 110–111, 181, 279–280, 309
U.S. Government Accountability Office, 201
U.S. News & World Report ranking, 85, 149–150, 280–281
U.S. Senate, 91
USC Village, 161, 211
UTMAs (Uniform Transfers to Minors Act), 271–272

value, determining, 4
Vanguard, 245
Vassar College, 164
Viemont, Jennifer, 214, 217, 218
vocational pathway, 129

Wabash College, 276
Wai, Jonathan, 92
waivers for application fees, 43
Walker, Justine, 193–194
Wall Street Journal, 19, 280, 281–282
Washington and Lee University, 143
Washington Monthly, 281
Washington University, 142–143
watch lists, 124
W.E. Upjohn Institute for Employment Research, 235
wealth measurements, 235–236
Webber, Douglas, 234–235

Weinberg, Adam S., 173
Wellesley College, 178, 179
Wellman, Jane, 18–19
Wesleyan University, 179
Wheaton College, 39, 283
Where You Go Is Not Who You'll Be
    (Bruni), 91
Whitman College, 276
Why Does College Cost So Much?
    (Archibald and Feldman),
    18
Williams College, 189, 223
Wolverton, Brad, 222
women's colleges, 136–139
Wooden, John, 312

Wooster. *See* College of Wooster
work-study jobs, 295–296

XY Planning Network, 290

Y Combinator, 91
Yale University, 178, 282
Years that Matter Most, The (Tough),
    238
Yellow Ribbon Program, 231
yield management, 43

Zaloom, Caitlin, 28, 29, 77, 244–245,
    250, 253–254
Zimmerman, Jonathan, 6

ABOUT THE AUTHOR

RON LIEBER is the author of *The Opposite of Spoiled* and is the Your Money columnist for the *New York Times*. Three of his books have been *New York Times* bestsellers, and he is a three-time winner of the Gerald Loeb Award, business journalism's highest honor. He lives in Brooklyn with his wife, *New York Times* reporter Jodi Kantor, and their two daughters

Ron speaks frequently to schools, community forums, and other groups about college, parenting, money, and values. To book him for a talk—or learn about his interactive course on merit aid and how to get more of it—please visit www.ronlieber.com.

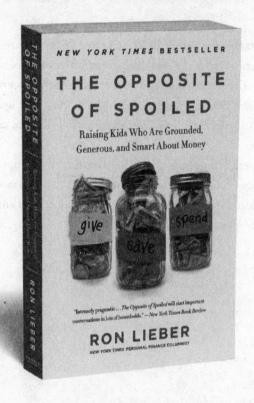